STEPHANIE —
CONGRATS ON WINNING.
HOPE YOU ENJOY MY BOOK — AND LAUGH!

LIFE SUCKS

LIFE SUCKS

MEMORIES AND INTROSPECTIONS DURING THE GREAT COVID LOCKDOWN

PS Conway

Boston
2025

Published in the United States of America by Fictional Café Press
Copyright © 2025 PS Conway
All rights reserved. This book or any portions within may not be reproduced or used without the express written permission of the publisher or the author.

ISBN (print): 979-8-9874421-5-9
ISBN (ePub): 979-8-9874421-6-6
Library of Congress Control Number: 2025902207

Cover Design and Fleuron: Yucen Yao, https://yucenyao.com/

Interior Design: Sophie Hanks, https://sophiehanks.com/

Fictional Café Press is the book publishing division of The Fictional Café, an online 'zine. https://www.fictionalcafe.com

The Author would like to thank and recognize the following mentions of other works which influenced his writing:

"The world was moving she was right there with it and she was..."

"And She Was" by Talking Heads. Words and music by David Byrne. Copyright © 1985 Sire Records. Copyright Renewed. All Rights Reserved. Used by Permission. Reprinted by permission of Hal Leonard Corporation.

"One can choose to go back toward safety or forward toward growth. Growth must be chosen again and again; fear must be overcome again and again."

The Psychology of Science: A Reconnaissance by Abraham Maslow. Copyright © 1966 Harper & Row, Publishers, Inc. All Rights Reserved. Reprinted by Permission of HarperCollins Publishers.

"A horcrux is "the word used for an object in which a person has concealed part of their soul..."

Harry Potter and the Half-Blood Prince by J.K. Rowling. Copyright © 2005 by J.K. Rowling. All Rights Reserved. Reprinted by permission of Bloomsbury Publishing.

"It is your attitude, more than your aptitude, that will determine your altitude."

See You at the Top by Zig Ziglar. Copyright © 1987 by Zig Ziglar. All Rights Reserved. Reprinted by permission of Pelican Publishing Company.

"*Rage against the dying of the light.*"

Dylan Thomas, *In Country Sleep, and Other Poems*. Copyright © 1952 University of Michigan; entered the public domain in the United States in 2024.

(Brian, as he hangs on the cross, sings,) "Always look on the bright side of life. Life's a piece of shit when you look at it."

Monty Python's Life of Brian. Copyright © 1979 HandMade Films and Python (Monty) Pictures. All Rights Reserved. Reprinted by permission of Python (Monty) Pictures Ltd.

"It is a tale
Told by an idiot, full of sound and fury,
Signifying nothing."
-Macbeth, Act V, Scene V, Lines 19-28
Macbeth by William Shakespeare, edited by Dr. Barbara A. Mowat and Paul Werstine, Ph.D. Copyright © 2003 by Simon & Schuster. All Rights Reserved. Reprinted with permission of Simon & Schuster.

"I don't know if we each have a destiny, or if we're all just floatin' around accidental-like on a breeze. But I, I think maybe it's both."
—"Mama always said life was like a box of chocolates. You never know what you're gonna get."
—"That's all I have to say about that."
Forrest Gump (for all three quotes above). Film Copyright © 1994 Paramount Pictures. Novel Copyright © Winston Groom, Jr.,1986.

"Two things are infinite: the universe and human stupidity; and I'm not sure about the universe."
Attributed to Albert Einstein, a deceased public figure. Considered to be in the public domain because there is no known claim to copyright.

"This is the end / My only friend, the end."

"The End" by The Doors. Words and Music by Jim Morrison, John Densmore, Robby Krieger, and Ray Manzarek. Copyright © 1967 by Elektra Music Group. Copyright renewed by Primary Wave Music. All Rights Reserved. Reprinted by permission of Doors Music Company.

"These are the times of dreamy quietude, when beholding the tranquil beauty and brilliancy of the ocean's skin, one forgets the tiger heart that pants beneath it; and would not willingly remember, that this velvet paw but conceals a remorseless fang."

Moby Dick by Herman Melville, Quoted from the original, now in the public domain.

"The house smelled musty and damp, and a little sweet, as if it were haunted by the ghosts of long-dead cookies."

American Gods by Neil Gaiman. Copyright © 2001 by Neil Gaiman. All Rights Reserved. Reprinted by permission of William Morrow, an imprint of HarperCollins Publishers, and Headline Publishing Group, a division of Hachette Book Group.

"Man is fond of counting his troubles, but he does not count his joys. If he counted them up as he ought to, he would see that every lot has enough happiness provided for it."
Notes from the Underground by Fyodor Dostoyevsky. Quoted from the original, now in the public domain.

Sancho Panza to Don Quixote: "Let your worship keep count of the goats the fisherman is taking across, for if one escapes the memory there will be an end of the story, and it will be impossible to tell another word of it."
The complete text of *The Ingenious Gentleman Don Quixote of La Mancha* by Miguel de Cervantes is in the public domain.

"Gratitude is a quality similar to electricity; it must be produced and discharged and used up in order to exist at all."
Attributed to William Faulkner, a deceased public figure. Considered to be in the public domain because there is no known claim to copyright.

Additional quotations, if any, fall under the "fair use" clause of the Copyright Disclaimer under Section 107 of the Copyright Act of 1976. Any copyright holder who believes their rights have been overlooked is asked to contact the author.

Publisher's Foreword

PS Conway (who may or may not be a real living person) has asked me to comment on this book you are about to read. I've worked in publishing all my adult life, with hundreds of authors and their books, and wish to be clear: I've never read anything quite like this, in either fiction or nonfiction.

One thing an editor learns in this business is that the book—its art, if you will—mirrors the mind, the nervous system, indeed even the soul, of its creator.

So what will you take away from the experience of reading *Life Sucks?* Will you come to some kind of sense about the mind of its purported author? (Hint: It wasn't written by an AI.) Will you, as many of us readers do, seek *likes*—those transitive verbs which identify *some thing* or other—thought to be similar to the *thing* under discussion? For example, how many exotic or unfamiliar foods are said to taste *like* chicken? Or consider how today's youth jabbers *like* about this or that as if it were a comma or a glottal stop. Is the quest for finding and linking acceptable similitudes distracting us from our quest for meaning in life?

I don't know. Maybe. Probably. If so, then abandon your journey now because *Life Sucks* just isn't *like* anything you or I have ever read. And I've read a lot. For example, David Foster Wallace's *Infinite Jest* is *waaay* overrated as *like* satirical or ironic, while nonfiction works *like* H.L. Mencken's *Prejudices* ("Those who can, do. Those who can't, teach. Those who can't teach, teach education.") are spot on. Finding *likes* for Conway's book may be tough for you, too. Withhold your opinion until you've finished it and then, *like,* try to write a summary or review of *Life Sucks*. Does it taste like chicken? I double-dog-dare you.

Wait! Be honest for a moment: why on earth would a reader *like you* be interested in what some total stranger did or thought about during COVID lockdown? Well, to paraphrase Nike, just read it to find out. Then ask yourself, does the book not give you a deep glimpse into this author's view of life, his thoughts, habits, palsies, fantasies, weaknesses, and (although infrequently his apparently elusive) strengths? *His likes and dislikes?* Do the people of America *like* need to read this book? I asked that question myself which, I must add, perhaps in my own defense (but only perhaps), is why I decided to publish it. So get straight with yourself: Did this book not change your viewpoint on life?

I'll double-dog-dare you a second time to explain what this book is *like* for purposes of categorizing and placing it on the proper bookshelf at Barnes & Noble. Think about that. It's important. As a publisher who prefers offbeat books—satirical, dystopian, experimental, ribald, ironic, unconventional, stream-of-consciousness, whether fiction or nonfiction but always thought-provoking—I'm still on the lookout for the author who's writing the progeny of the *Fear and Loathing* saga.

Until then, we'll have to ask ourselves, individually and as a society, does *Life Sucks* by PS Conway deliver on its promise?

If you were ever to meet PS Conway in an Irish pub, you would, *like,* never in a million years deduce he is the author of this book. But sit down at his table. Say hello. Have a black and tan with him. I promise you a revelatory conversation about why he like, *likes* William Faulkner so much.

If you are still reading my drivel at this point, you're probably asking yourself if I'm ever going to explain what this book is about. After all, isn't that the purported reason for including my two cents? Well, sorry about that, but it's quite beyond me. And for good reason, because the prevailing opinion in publishing circles is that nobody cares a whit about my opining. Fair enough, at least up to a point. Upon reading a very fine novel recently, I noted a publisher's introduction in the front matter. Below those two words, some junior editor had slipped in a message (in italics) suggesting the reader peruse it after—not before—reading the novel. I considered that good advice and encourage you to do the same.

Jack B. Rochester

Introduction

Hello, friends. It's been a while. Did you miss me? That is, of course, me taking into consideration that many of you are new to my erudite genius. You lucky bastards. You're in for a treat.

What you do need to know upfront, dear reader, is that I started an epic comedy website entitled "Life Sucks Laugh Here" in January 2020, near the beginning of COVID lockdown. I posted shticks most weeks throughout the remainder of the year. That is, until a new employer told me my writing was too "controversial" and "crass" for the "image" of their bullshit failing start-up company.

After the 2020 U.S. presidential election, I took down the site. Turns out, my family liked food, clothing, and a college education for the kids too much. Despite the time, energy and psychic despair I put into those words, I did not make a nickel on any of it. Cuz I'm a giver.

During those 40+ weeks, thousands of dedicated readers would tune into my delicious Sunday essays like Jim Jones' disciples showing up for grape Kool-Aid. The COVID lockdown had us trapped inside craving any distraction possible. Like Rolaids, my rants spelled R.E.L.I.E.F. for many.

Under the first regime of Donald Trump, herein "Cheeto Christ," over 1,100,000 Americans lost their lives to COVID. We were forced to shelter-in-place and consume a relentless litany of conspiracy theories, fake truths, and other such *navacancha*. All generously fed into our gaping beaks, baby-bird style, by the government, cable news, and the interwebs.

My vision for the website was simple: distraction. Laughter was a given. The general idea was to create a type of "Literary Comedic Nihilism." You'd learn a little, laugh a lot, and then forget about it all . . . because it never really mattered anyway.

I created a character, PS Conway. A pseudo-me. An amalgamation of Me, a Not-Me, and an alpha asshole who was christened Pygmalion Shitake a.k.a. Pig Shit a.k.a. PS (Conway). This is where the nihilism comes into play. Some readers took what they read at face value. This created a perception that this character was me speaking my opinions. The real PS. Not the character PS. Geez. When I put it that way, how could there have ever been any confusion?

Ugly consequences followed. Some real-world friends became collateral damage. I had switched tribes on them, or so they thought. And we still have not spoken to this day. That's why I am so comforted by the immortal words of the greatest band of all time, Toad the Wet Sprocket, in their song "Little Buddha," "Life is suffering. Tee-hee, Ha-ha."

Since the 2020 essay series, *Life Sucks Laugh Here*, the words have continued to flow. I have redirected my genres. Humor has since transformed into poetry. And I have been successfully publishing my lyrical words for a smaller, more focused community of readers.

Honestly, I probably would have stayed in my artsy lane, were it not for a consequential 2024 U.S. presidential election, a re-read of my 2020 essays, and a profound sense of déjà vu. Time (and human stupidity) have such a wonderfully ironic sense of repeating the same failing behaviors expecting a different result. Or, at least, so said Einstein.

My invisible friends, let us now enter this wee time capsule. Perhaps you'll laugh. Perhaps you'll intuit a cautionary tale. Perhaps you'll be irretrievably scarred and offended by all the dark humor.

Here are a few tips to prepare you for this exploration of learning, laughter, and life:

1. Read this book of assembled essays like chapters in a normal book. There are a lot of callbacks as you progress that won't make a lot of sense if you do not.
2. Read more literature and philosophy. Seriously. Learn to think more critically and form your own opinions. Those timid herds of Sames will always be there, lowing in the fields of conformity, awaiting your return if independent thought becomes too daunting.
3. Read my poetry book *Echoes Lost in Stars*. Available now globally in all Amazon markets. It's like looking in the face of god and beholding beauty through her eyes.
4. If you have a delicate constitution, deeply held religious or political beliefs, a mind that cannot comprehend satirical writings, or are offended by well-placed profanity, then kindly piss off. Walk away now. My witty brilliance will never be for you. The goal is to truly make you smile, giggle, and laugh. Forget about all the bullshit in your life for a few minutes. My grandmother had an Irish phrase for life's BS . . . *navacancha*. Instead of cussing, she was known for saying, "That's a bunch of *navacancha*." Turns out, it was a completely made-up word, and a delicious example of irony when a word for "complete BS" actually was complete BS. Ha!

5. Last Warning: remember, this is satire. Keep your ingrained biases in check. In the immortal words of Sergeant Hulka in *Stripes*, "Lighten up, Francis." If you laugh hard enough, and perhaps pee just a little, then perhaps you will remember me fondly, tell your friends to read this book, and re-read it yourself a second or third time. If you remember me too fondly, then you have a serious pee fetish, and this material is likely a little too intense for you ... sorry.

Enjoy, and namaste.
PS Conway

Table of Contents

Publisher's Foreword vii
Introduction xi

LIFE SUCKS 1
Quit Clowning Around 3
Useless Pets 7
In Vino Veritas 15
Jeux Sans Frontières 21
Nature Abhors a Vacuum 29
Dark Shorts 1: Ol' Scruff 35
What Doesn't Kill You Gives You Colitis 37
Erin Go Bragh 43
But Who is Man that is Not Angry? 51
Surviving Elephant's Foot 59
Finding Jesus in the Easter Bunny 67
Dark Shorts 2: Dingle Sneem 73
Manscaping with Occam's Razor 75
Back Toward Safety, Forward Toward Growth 81
Bridge Street Run: A Tradition of Oswego Debauchery 89
Weight a Moment. Am I Dying? 97
Colonoscopies: Show Your Inner Beauty 105
Grandma Healy's Hooley 111
Dark Shorts 3: Rosebud 119

Are You There, God? It's Me, PS	121
Moby's Dick	129
Manopause: A Treatise on Aging & Severus Snape	137
Your Pain. My Pleasure. Thanks, Schadenfreude.	145
A Tale Told by an Idiot	153
Dark Shorts 4: Digbert & Egbert go to MARS	161
Stupidity: The Buck Stops with Everybody	163
Reflections from a Midsummer's Walk with Hairy Kerry	171
Sneak Peek: 10 Reasons I'm Better Than You	181
Consumerism: Peace Instead of Another Television Set?	191
The Mandela Effect: Play It Again, Sam	199
Dark Shorts 5: Father Pat McGroin	209
Psilocybin: What A Long Strange Trip It's Been	211
My Favorite Positions: PS Conway for President	221
Labor Day: A Reflection on Love, Labor, & Loss	229
Are You Ready for Some Football?	241
Reality TV: I Am Not What I Am	249
Dark Shorts 6: Bingo and Gomorrah	261
What a Coincidence!	263
Stop Telling Me What I Should Think!	271
The Ocean: Velvet Paw. Remorseless Fang.	281
Halloween: Ghosts of Long-Dead Cookies	293
Dark Shorts 7: Above the Clouds	303
Counting Troubles, Counting Joys	305
Gratitude: A Quality Similar to Electricity	313
Epilogue	321
Wait! There's More!	323
About the Author	325
About the Publisher	327

LIFE SUCKS

Quit Clowning Around

Clowns. Brrrrrrr... they give me the heebie-jeebies.

Even the sweetest-looking clowns seem to be hiding something under their painted faces. It's in the eyes. There is always a disconnect between the happy smile paint and their sad eyes, or vice versa. Forces you to question their intentions and motivations. They're not hiding a squirting bouquet of carnations behind their back. Oh no. Nothing so innocent and whimsical. More like hiding a dead puppy behind their back. Something far crueler and sinister. History is rife with examples of this scary clown trope.

This image began most likely with Charles Dickens. History remembers Dickens for his "light comedies" and ability to capture the brighter side of life. Or was that his lesser-known half-brother, U. Little?

Dickens' 1836 work, *The Pickwick Papers*, paints the enduring image of a self-destructive clown. So widely circulated in its time, that image made it impossible for many in society to separate the act from the actor. They were left questioning if the person who uses humor and makeup as a mask is hiding something far more insidious.

In the closing moments of the famous 1892 opera *Pagliacci*, the scorned clown husband, Canio (dressed as the clown, Pagliaccio) brutally stabs his unfaithful wife and her lover to death. Canio, standing over the lifeless bodies, delivers the infamous line, "La commedia è finita!" ("The comedy is over!")

This prolific historical scary clown imagery created widespread disordered thinking that had not existed prior. As time passed, clown books and movies proliferated, leading to true mental health challenges and real phobias.

I, in fact, have a resulting affliction known clinically as coulrophobia. A morbid fear of clowns. It has been with me since my teens, best I can recollect. This is not to be confused with coulrophilia, which describes a strong sexual attraction to clowns (he said with a full body shudder).

Now I like a good shag as much as the next person, but there are a lot of complications in having sexual relations with clowns.

- **First**, there is the practical consideration; and that is cleaning all the makeup off your *bait-n-tackle*. What a mess. And the dry-cleaning bill? Yikes. God forbid you met in a hotel bar. What kind of housekeeping surprises await you at check-out? Hint: hazmat suits and oxygen tanks.
- **Second** complication is that most clowns are gingers, and we all know what that means ... cray-cray. The kind of crazy that leaves you alone in bed the next morning with a severed pinkie on your nightstand, and a note on the back of the CVS condom receipt, written in blood, that reads, "Call me, bitch."
- **Third** complication is the sheer exhaustion from having your clown partner consume part of your soul while you

sleep. Picture a Harry Potter Dementor in pasty face-paint, skulking on the side of your bed, but with a Krazy Straw stuck in your ear, manically slurping your eternal essence into their smiling maw. Milkshake, anyone? I promise, that will not *"bring the boys to the yard."*
- **Fourth** complication, and maybe the trickiest, is your inability to properly integrate into Big Top culture. What if you develop real feelings for Bobo after a few fetish baths in your psychic tub of coulrophilia? What does that look like when you go to meet their circus family? You, with no white face makeup. An interloper into a closed community of outcasts and misfits. Eating "crick shrimp" in the cookhouse while your "intimates" are line-drying near a cage of mangy, sexually abused elephants. An almost impossible slog.

But I digress. I have a morbid fear of clowns called coulrophobia. For that I blame show business, and perhaps my childhood parish priest. Don't ask. But mostly show biz.

Just as Steven Spielberg permanently ruined the ocean for me with *Jaws*, so too did Stephen King ruin clowns for me with *It*. Although that sneaky shmuck Spielberg, in recent revelations, secretly came clean that he in fact directed *Poltergeist*. And who can forget the scene with the clown doll dragging the kid under the bed? Hell no, no, no. You're terrible humans, Steven and Stephen.

But *It*... OMG, how scary? Pennywise the Dancing Clown, creature from the macroverse void. That repulsive character who eats his victim's anxiety like food by embodying their greatest fears and who has a distinct preference for children since their fears are so easy to interpret in physical form? Is there any wonder why this fear exists? Is it so irrational after all? Simple answer is actually ... yes.

Pennywise was a monster from outer space who hitchhiked to earth and squatted in the sewers. The clown was his disguise ... and, can we be honest? A lazy metaphor from King. So, can I really be a coulrophobe if what scared me originally was in fact not a clown, but instead a monster? Monsters are way scarier than clowns.

Holy shit. Then I am actually a teraphobe. I fear monsters. I am not afraid of clowns after all. Wow. That was therapeutic. Good to know I am now properly labeled. Am I cured?

Useless Pets

While visiting China in 2007, I realized what a Western concept it was to view animals as pets.

My brother and I owned a business at the time manufacturing biometric deadbolt door locks that could open by using your fingerprint instead of a key. The products were developed and engineered in the US, and then manufactured and assembled by our partner in China. I am sure I will have a future book about the fun misadventures we had with our business.

We were taking a tour of the rural finish factory in China where they applied the color finish (bronze, satin nickel, etc.) to the bare metal locks. It was extremely important to our investors that we ensure our partner was performing to the quality, ethical, and environmental standards we had been guaranteed. Aside from a glowing silver stream of benzene running behind the assembly lines of underfed, tumorous children, I was proud to report everything appeared copacetic.

Charlie Chan—yes, I realize that sounds like a fake name – and his brother owned the partner manufacturing company in China. Charlie was schooled at Oxford. His English was quite passable, especially compared to my Mandarin. I knew "ni hao" (hello) from watching *Ni Hao, Kai-Lan* on Nickelodeon when the girls were younger. And I learned "pijiu" (beer) and "ganbei" (cheers) the night before the factory tour when Charlie, who weighed 130 pounds soaking wet, kept us intoxicated in a club until 3 a.m.... while drinking us under the table.

Driving back to their corporate office in Xiamen City after the factory tour, Charlie cranked up Norah Jones' song, *Don't Know Why*. Side note, did anybody but me ever wonder if she is singing about not having an orgasm with this song? Seriously. Read the lyrics. Is she teasing us with a double entendre? Naughty Norah!

Perhaps it was the hangover. Perhaps it was listening to him belt along with Norah Jones from his aching soul. Perhaps our wits were dulled from the benzene exposure. But we were mesmerized. Our minds were as permeable as a cell membrane during facilitated diffusion.

When Charlie tearfully finished, he began to randomly pontificate about the Chinese concept of pets. He recited a long litany of animals that could never be pets, because they were food. His view was that Westerners were wasteful with both their money and sentimentality when it comes to animals. Not that pets were a completely foreign concept to him. Aside from cats and dogs, which could still be food in a pinch, Charlie was adamant that animals were basically food.

With that as context, it got me thinking last week while I was exercising, bored senseless on the treadmill. As my mind floated in fantasies of jelly-filled doughnuts, I started to consider his point of view more seriously. We Westerners are too damn soft. Charlie was right. We should take a stand ... we do have far too many useless pets.

Cats and Dogs

Let's start with the elephant in the room: cats and dogs. I love dogs. They are mindless love machines who want nothing more than to be loved in return. Cats are nasty, selfish creatures. Cat owners exist at the cat's fickle tolerance to be fed, watered, and conditionally loved back. Plus, I am severely allergic to cats, so maybe that slightly skews my kitty contempt.

But cats and dogs, in this current context, must be off-limits. The topic is simply too polarizing. Opinions, as I may have already demonstrated, are strong and ubiquitous. Emotional attachment negates our logical ability to view these animals as food. They are our friends and our family, irrespective of which pet you prefer. Still, I would challenge any of you that roasted cat on a stick will taste damned good after the Zombie Apocalypse occurs.

Absent a cataclysm, for now, I will defer to the more obvious pet choices as either food, useless, or both.

Rabbits

Food. Never a pet. Totally useless. One solid reading of *Watership Down* will make it clear what the rabbit god, Frith, had in mind when he created the rabbits and told El-ahrairah, *"When they catch you, they will kill you."* Even their god told them they were food. Enough said?

If we are being morally honest with each other, was I really the only person who stood up and clapped when Glenn Close boiled the family rabbit in *Fatal Attraction*? Hell hath no fury, they say. Can't recall ever seeing such singularly unstable dedication to obsessive love . . . or me being as secretly turned on by some fresh hasenpfeffer. I named it Hyzenthlay.

Predators

While clearly not food, whoever heard of eating a lion or tiger or bear (oh my!)? What in the conscious realm of right-minded fuckery would ever delude a person enough to think they can control what Nature has created as wild from the beginning of time? I am not sure what is more useless, the pet or the person.

I am always amazed when the media is surprised by a guy who lives with Grizzlies ultimately getting eaten by the bears. Or when the magician's cuddly pet tiger lashes out and kills him. How can this be anything but the natural resolution of an unnatural situation? I always fantasized that *Born Free* ended with Elsa mauling Joy to death in front of George, his screams of despair the last thing heard as the screen fades to black.

Gerbils

I cannot think of a more useless pet. Specifically, I think my argument is more toward all Rodentia, but the gerbil serves as a good order representative. So as not to confuse anyone with word choices, need we briefly revisit high school biology? Species > Genus > Family > Order > Class > Phylum > Kingdom > Domain. Class dismissed.

I had once heard of a creative use for gerbils, called gerbilling. While not for me, this involved inserting an expended toilet paper roll in the anus and allowing the Cadbury Commando gerbil to make his way up the tunnel into the Hershey Highway. Apparently, this exacts some extreme pleasure from the participant. Perhaps Norah Jones should investigate?

Because I care and want my readers to really laugh until they pee, I also wanted to share a cautionary tale about gerbilling (aka felching) before you start experimenting. Search YouTube for the hysterical radio broadcast called *Armageddon*.

Snakes

Speaking of Armageddon, can you think of any animal that evokes more deep-seated fear than a snake? Growing up Catholic, next to clowns and priests, snakes filled me with abject spiritual terror. Snakes were Satan, evil sneaky creatures of temptation that were more predator than prey. So why the unholy HELL would anyone keep a snake as a pet? Completely useless.

Am I the only person who wishes that when you watch people holding giant pythons around their neck, the snake suffocates them and eats them? It would teach them, indeed all of us, a valuable lesson about why a snake is not a pet. Was anyone but me rooting for Kaa in *The Jungle Book*? Mowgli needed to learn his lesson. Jungles are dangerous places for a man cub.

And snakes as food!?!? Wretch. Unless you are Dusty Dan, a starving prospector who has been lost in the desert for weeks after wandering away in a drunken stupor from his failed gold claim, could a snake ever truly be a food source for you?

Birds

Loud, smelly, useless. I will forever be convinced that there is a correlation between your IQ and your delight in hearing a bird repeat your words back to you. Sure, for their brain size, they have developed a modicum of intelligence. Show me a cockatiel that comprehends what it is actually saying, and I will eat my words (instead of the cockatiel). Not impressed. If I was looking for intelligence, I would buy a dolphin (maybe two). Maybe an elephant, too. They last a long time.

And then there is the simple answer that birds, first and foremost, are food. How many varieties of birds do we eat? Delicious. All of them. Small, caged birds might not have enough meat to be worth the effort, but the bigger caged birds still make my mouth water. I think of the Bugs Bunny cartoon in which the hobo claims to Bugs' penguin buddy, *"Penguins is practically chickens."*

Perhaps my favorite bird scene in the movies was when the hitman in *Dumb and Dumber* decapitates Petey the parakeet to send a message to Lloyd and Harry. Harry thinks the bird's head fell off from old age and duct tapes it back on. Lloyd sells it to a blind kid, who can't understand why Petey is so quiet. Brilliant. Who is dumber? Harry? Lloyd? The kid? Or us for owning birds as pets in the first place?

Fish

I love seafood. And nothing makes me angrier than to see food in some glass menagerie, stolen from its natural aquatic element, meat spoiling in turd water by the moment. Animal cruelty aside, I want the small worthless fish that people turn into pets returned to the stream, lake, or ocean, so the larger fish can eat them, and we can eat the larger fish. Circle of life.

True story: My daughter won one of those useless beta fish at her elementary school Family Fun Night. And oh, what fun we had. She cleverly named it Beta. Beta raced around its tiny glass prison, swimming in its own filth for a few days. Novelty expired; my daughter acted like most kids with the newfound responsibility of having their own pets. She soon ignored it.

My conscientious wife, not wanting to let her baby down, scooped Beta into a strainer near the kitchen sink while she freshened the water and cleaned its grimy bastille. Beta, in likely the only useful act of control and defiance it ever performed in its useless life, leaped from the strainer, and fell into the garbage disposal. Looking around to confirm no witnesses, my wife, in her never-ending capacity for compassion, fired up the disposal and bid adieu to little Beta. Truly a mercy. And Beta was never missed.

Conclusion: The Inevitability of Cannibalism

Tying a bow around this conversation, Charlie Chan was correct. Cats and dogs are exempt (but mostly dogs). Every other animal should either be food for humans or allowed to live free to be eaten in its own natural setting.

Either way, doesn't this say something about the giant virus that humans have become? We consume everything we can. And what we cannot consume we control. We project our own human frailties on our furry, feathered, and scaly friends. Thanks to evolution, we have developed self-aware brains and opposable thumbs. We can rule this world as an apex predator with a conscience.

Unless the power grid utterly fails. Then we can still wink at each other knowing we are literally one power outage away from eating not only our cats and dogs, but maybe each other.

In Vino Veritas

Life's greatest truths are indeed revealed through wine.

Today, my fifty-something[th] birthday, I am sipping a gorgeous cabernet sauvignon while snow falls gently outside. Through the window, winter twilight descends as twinkling stars push the receding pink and purple clouds toward the dimming distant sunset. The room is quiet except for the occasional crackle of a lazy log sparking golden embers in the fire.

My dog is snuggled against my side in our worn leather chair. Warm and safe, lost in his own thoughts of chasing a squirrel, or humping a pillow, or digging a hole, or whatever other witless shit dogs think about.

Wine is sensuous. Rich cherries on the lips transition to dry smoky oak in the throat. Gentle heat fills your chest as your head thickens and swims in a viscous tranquility. The moment is transcendental. Your pulse slows; and thoughts wander into the universe in search of understanding and meaning. And then the dog farts. Loud.

The silence is rent asunder. Not a normal fart either—a nasty, greasy stank fart. What did he eat? And the blanket you were sharing is now damp. It wasn't wet before. What the hell? Did his anal glands express, too? Whether driven by guilt, or an instinctive fear of retribution, the dog immediately scuttles off the chair in search of safer quarter.

Startled, I flail, spraying the precious garnet elixir all over my great grandma's antique white couch. Painstakingly built by my great grandfather as a wedding gift to his Russian mail order bride, Oxana, "The Davenport" has survived the generations through meticulous, virtually sterile segregation and diligence. Now this curated artifact looks like crime-scene evidence following a heinous stabbing after years of unexpressed martial resentment.

As the wine permanently permeates the pristine, preserved fabric, destroying decades of assiduousness, I am certain my mother will disown me for ruining this beloved family heirloom. "Your sister would have never let this happen," Mom will inevitably say. Said more plainly, "You douche. You have destroyed our family. I disown you."

In the calm that follows the chaos, clarity prevails. I laugh. At first it is a nervous giggle into my hand as I stare at the carnage. This quickly devolves into me laughing from my toes at the sheer absurdity of it all – the misplaced hyper-sentimental nostalgia, the missed connection to something tantrically cosmic, the hilarity of a simple dog fart.

As of today, I have orbited the sun for many cycles. Throughout those innumerable days, I have collected insights into life that wine has helped elucidate. With that much time passed and wisdom amassed, I thought I would take precious celebration time away from my corporeal family and friends to share the ten most important lessons I have learned with you, my invisible friends.

- **Idioms are confusing.** "Less is more." Uh. Sure! On a cold winter night, take the blanket from Rabies Randy, a sleeping homeless guy under the highway overpass.

Let me know how that works out for you. Imagine how invested Rabies Randy is after the months spent creating that "blanket" from dozens of discarded paper bags, bound together with love by several more months of congealed rabies foam and saliva. Make sure to journal that experience for posterity's sake. If your hands are of no use, dictate it.

- **"Money can't buy you happiness" is total bullshit.** A luxury trip to an amazing exotic destination? Yeah. That sucks. Stay home and eat leftovers. Much more fulfilling. Better yet – stay home, eat leftovers, and watch someone else take that amazing trip on cable.
- **Safety is very important.** Ask Maslow. "There's safety in numbers" is a particularly true idiom when you are using those people as a human shield against an attacking horde of zombies. We are one mutated coronavirus away from that happening next time. Start formulating a plan now to expand your group of "friends."
- **"Your body is a temple" is a sacrilegious health mantra.** Does that imply that tattoos are graffiti? Has the temple therefore been desecrated? If I fart, does the temple lose some sort of spirit? Is that an exorcism? How would I know? When I eliminate waste, is that a daily restoration project? The lining of my digestive tract is like the ceiling of the Sistine Chapel? So much to consider, Michelangelo. A lot of colon pressure, too.
- **Take your time to understand every major world religion.** Don't commit to anything until you are 100 percent certain it is the one true religion. Clearly a large majority of people are wrong, and a small minority of

people are right. Use your brain, because anyone who truly believes in their "one true" religion will only use their heart. Taking that path will only lead to agonizing heartache when the aliens land and universally disappoint everyone with the actual truth.

- **Love your partner with every bit of your being—heart, mind, and body.** Be vulnerable and sensitive. Communicate openly and listen with the intent to understand and empathize. Hold their heart gently in the ethereal hands of your entwined souls. But, if that person is not currently in your life, go ahead and diddle every person you can. Hump them with reckless abandon and selfish gratuitousness. Lean into it and leave them with a lasting memory of your encounter and a lasting terror of ever riding a horse again. Stephen Stills knew what he was saying. *"If you can't be with the one you love, love the one you're with."*
- **Relentlessly control your children.** Over-parent the shit out of them until they bow to your will. Freedom is vastly overrated. Obedience is a lost art. Trust me; they will thank you later and pass this gift along to their children, their children's children, and so on. Subsequent generations later, their great-great-grandchildren's grandchildren will be born into a brave, new world where everyone is finally the same, conformity rules, creativity dies, and a few elite rulers will tell them the best direction to wipe their own asses. *Sieg heil and auf Wiedersehen, assholes.*
- **Formal college education—didactic learning—has a limited shelf life.** The college experience, though,

is priceless. Living independently, learning to speak to strangers, thinking critically, and strengthening reading and written communications are part of that experience. Doing keg stands, dealing with chlamydia, using recreational drugs, choosing the best bars, and getting fatter will round out that experience. Cannot tell you how many times those keg stands have been a cultural hit in the corporate boardroom.

- **"Fat is temporary, but ugly is forever."** You can lose weight any time, but what can you do about ugly? Not a lot. Better work on that personality, handsome. Or accept other equally viable options such as staying indoors permanently, wearing masks in public, getting lost on an uninhabited island, joining the World Association of Ugly People (Google it), or auditioning as the Unknown Comic on *The Gong Show* (younger audience, Google this reference). The world is your oyster. As an FYI, this slogan will also be the first chapter title in my upcoming tell-all, *Ten Reasons I Am Better Than You*.
- **Work is for suckers.** Money is a 20th-century medium that will soon be obsolete. Learn bartering and negotiating skills. Trading your broken record player for some turnips will be an invaluable skill when capitalism collapses. And who will be the real winner in that transaction? YOU. There will be no electricity to play the records with. But you can boil those turnips over a good old-fashioned flint-spawned fire anywhere, anytime.

I have consumed a lot of wine over a vast span of time on this Big Blue Marble to arrive at these truths about life. Sometimes when the ideas were not fully developed, I would drink some extra wine, and eventual clarity pervaded. Sometimes I rocked myself to sleep clutching an empty wine bottle, the abject enormity of it all filling me with awe.

The only thing I ask from my readers is to see them as absolute truths. These are not some quippy cute guidelines or suggestions that can be easily discarded. They are fact. If you are not abiding by these tenets, you ought to reexamine the very nature of your own existence.

Begin that process by drinking some wine in front of a winter twilight, the fire crackling as your essence begins to expand into the universe. Sans the dog. Keep that flatulent mutt caged in the basement with a muzzle. That way you can enjoy your astral evening.

"The world was moving she was right there with it and she was..." sang the Talking Heads.

Jeux Sans Frontières

Ah, the games of childhood. Did they screw you up, too?

From my earliest years, my parents—heck, even my grandparents—pushed games on us like a drug dealer pushes smack. Cards, dice, and board games were dealt like dime bags to occupy our time. This was before video games had fully hooked mainstream culture except for the most basic, but addictive, Atari *Asteroids* or *Space Invaders*. Bless their hearts, our families always had the best intentions.

Or did they? Did my parents have a greater insight into childhood that only now I can truly appreciate? Had they learned through age-formed wisdom that they needed to create distractions to contain the chaos brewing within children?

Having now raised my daughters into practicable adulthood, I can comment with certainty that children are inherently evil. There is no end to their feral cruelty, especially when running in packs. The pernicious will of the group transforms the will of even the best-reared child. Absent some form of imposed societal moral compass, there is no limit to their reckless, unhinged barbarism.

Little did my parents and grandparents know the unintended damage they caused by forcing these socially acceptable, misguidedly innocent games on us. The train was on the tracks toward derailment. These early games set the table and were just an appetizer for the deranged meals to come.

- **Pinochle**. My grandparents taught my sister and me to play this complex partner card game at a very young age. What did I learn? Mostly, I learned that my grandpa was a sore loser. He hated how good we were at pinochle. When my sister and I would beat my grandmother and him, he would slam the table, stand up and scream, "Goddamn it! You little shits are cheaters!" Grandpa had a delectable penchant for vulgarity around children. And he was not incorrect. My sister and I had developed an elaborate system of hand signals and eye movements to communicate our cards to each other. We almost always won. And grandpa never failed to disappoint in cultivating our developing cache of cusses.
- **Chess**. I know when you all think of me, you think, "This guy is so cool. Maybe the coolest person ever. I wish I could be like him." And I understand that thinking . . . today. But if you only knew me in my developing years, say, sixth or seventh grade? Nerd. When I got bored with being a self-described *mathlete*, I joined the chess club in search of a deeper hole to bury myself, far away from the prying eyes (and lips) of pretty pre-teen girls. What did I learn? I learned to keep nerdy things secret and act cool on the outside. Soon after quitting chess club, pining for social acceptance, I joined a wood shop class where I was subsequently beaten with a metal chair by a lesbian after blowing some wood dust in her face. Thought I was flirting. She just wanted to beat up a dork.

- **Operation.** I have always possessed a delicate constitution when it comes to being surprised by loud, sudden noises. Not sure what drew me to this godforsaken game. I did want to be a doctor while I was growing up, so I am sure my parents—secretly posing as Santa, by the way—brought me this gift to thoughtfully encourage my expanding intellectual curiosities. What did I learn? That wacky doctor's game gave me PTSD. God help anyone in my house to this day if they drop a metal pan on the hardwoods or some loud Snapchat blares from their phone. My startle reaction is embarrassingly dramatic. Having learned from my grandfather's tutelage, I leap from the chair, yelling in a borderline insane voice, "What the goddamn shit on a suck face ass nibbler?!" The expletives do not need to make sense. Sometimes the sheer random enthusiasm is half the fun.
- **Yahtzee.** This game is the marijuana of childhood games, a virtual gateway drug to the crack cocaine that is Las Vegas. What did I learn? Aside from developing an addictive adult affinity for craps, Yahtzee also taught me basic poker concepts: three of a kind, full house, etc. To exacerbate things, my grandfather had a secret society of seniors who all met at The Center, a recreation center in their retirement community, for afternoon games of low-stakes penny poker. He was working under the auspices of "painting" with my grandmother so he could sneak out with other elderly folks sporting *noms de guerre* like Shifty, Weasel, Schlepp, and Minx. He would regretfully bring me on occasion. They all thought I

was so darn adorable. Until I cleaned them out of every penny in their mason jars. My nicknames were endless – Shithead. Lil' Bastard. Satan's Spawn. Cheating Prick.

- **Twister.** Certain games should come with a warning label: *Not suitable for pubescent children between eleven and fifteen years old.* At least I would have had a heads up. While attempting a uniquely flexible Twister move, I got a boner from rubbing up against my pretty older cousin. What did I learn? Incest is generally looked down upon, particularly when playing a game. Erections really are an inappropriate response to family fun, regardless if you are thirteen years old with raging hormones. Also, getting punched in the nut sack by an offended cousin, falling to the floor in the fetal position, then running away crying in shame creates limitless fodder for future mockery.

With that initial psychological damage done, I quickly found myself bored. While establishing a baseline, these games only occupied an hour or two of our frenetic, Machiavellian energy. In cahoots with my brother, sister, and cousins, this led to the creation of our own, more childhood-relevant games. Games without so many rules and niceties. Games that fed the feral beast within. Games without frontiers.

- **Booger Baby.** My brother is the youngest sibling. My sister is four years older than him, and I am six years older. Our cousins were almost all older than me. As a child, my brother was on the receiving end of constant teasing, manipulation, and abuse by his elders. One such abuse was being the "Booger Baby." After a summer trip to the Baseball Hall of Fame in Cooperstown, we all received Louisville Sluggers for Christmas. My brother, likely three- or four-years-old at the time, had a penchant for picking his nose. The genesis of Booger Baby came to us when we noticed boogers on his Louisville Slugger. (Why they were there is irrelevant. They just were). What if we hid, while he hunted us with the "Booger Bat" and then beat us with it when he found us? Wouldn't that be fun? Made perfect sense, and my baby brother embraced his role with malevolent delight. In his little mind, this was his opportunity for revenge. It was terrifying. We would hide in the far reaches of our cousin's home, and he would count to twenty. Like Jack Torrance in *The Shining*, you could hear my brother shuffling down the hall, muttering *redrum* to himself, and then the distant screams for help when he found someone and started wailing on them. We never felt so alive from the adrenaline rush. Many of us are still in therapy today, thanks to our family volume discount.

- **Death in the Dark.** The same group of cousins came to our house every Christmas. We were very close with them growing up, but we hated this visit each year because they would ritualistically destroy our Christmas presents. While our parents drank to excess in the kitchen, we would be sequestered to the basement playroom, an unfinished dank room with no windows, bare concrete floor, and cheaply paneled walls. More of a dungeon than a playroom. And like inmates during a prison break, we would watch in horror as our cousins would smash our toys against the floor and walls, until the remaining detritus was unrecognizable. One year, a long strip of plastic Mattel racetrack jutted out of the debris field. And Death in the Dark was born. My brother—yes, Booger Baby—was handed the whip-like length of racetrack, the lights were turned off, plunging us into absolute blackness. One person would yell *Attack!* And then we would all quietly crawl into corners to hide. True to character, my little brother would slowly walk through the blackness, hunting, swinging the racetrack with a *whoosh whoosh*, sadistically giggling as his weapon found purchase. It hurt! And as we squealed in pain, he would laugh harder. The game always ended when someone got whipped across the face and started crying. Then we would all hug them, rock them, shush them, and whisper, "Don't tell. Don't tell."

- **Run for Your Life, summer and winter versions.** My cousins lived on a rural lake, and we spent a lot of time at their house growing up. They had the coolest stuff—dirt bikes, snowmobiles, BB guns, and so much more. The surrounding miles of woods, trails, and fields isolated their waterfront home, providing the perfect fodder for the scariest, most dangerous game of all – Run for Your Life. The summer version involved dirt bikes, and the winter version involved snowmobiles. Otherwise, the game was the same. Everyone received a Daisy Air Rifle and a pocket full of BBs. Coins were flipped for who got to start the game riding the two dirt bikes or two snowmobiles. Everyone else had to run for their life, defend themselves with their own BB gun, and had ten minutes to hide before the hunt began. The rules were not well defined from there.

Who was the hunter? Sometimes having the dirt bike or snowmobile was a disadvantage: you could be violently unseated and your vehicle commandeered. I have such vivid memories of being pursued in an open field by my cousin on a dirt bike, the BBs whistling over my head as I fled, the sound of the motor getting closer as my cousin attempted to either shoot me or run me down. Like John Wayne in *True Grit*, he steered the bike with one hand as the other hand fired the air rifle. I feigned injury, fake stumbled, and as he rode up on me, I leapt in the air and knocked him off the dirt bike. In this victorious moment, I gained my footing first, stood over him, and shot him in the face. As the blood spilled from the BB lodged in his forehead, I realized the game had run its course, *forever*, and I was going to get an ass-whooping beyond reckoning when we got back to the lake house.

While Booger Baby, Death in the Dark, and Run for Your Life stand out, we had a robust list of original masterpieces such as Surviving Elephant's Foot, Sled to Your Doom, One Went Over the Waterfall, Daddy or Danger, and When Autumn Comes.

I would be remiss to acknowledge that many of you may be reacting in disgust at the sadistic nature of our creations – these barbaric games. Where were your parents? Do you all have mental problems? Were you dropped as babies? Are your cousins in jail? How is Booger Baby today? Was he institutionalized? All reasonable questions.

And while I understand that instinctive, parental need to judge the behavior of seemingly psychotic children, suffice to say, my siblings, cousins, and I all survived the unfettered, animal drives of childhood and emerged as functional adults – raising families, holding jobs, and contributing to a better society... for the most part.

And isn't that really the larger point? Society. It tames us as adults. We trade some of our cherubic joy for safety and security. Society compels us to bury that childhood *id* that drives so many of our most base, natural instincts. By its very construct, society removes the danger that we innocently craved as children: because danger can be so much damn fun. And we grown-ups are left with a longing for that rapturous rush, realizing we will never quite feel that same way again.

Nature Abhors a Vacuum

Aristotle was wicked smart. But did he ever try selling vacuums door-to-door? Exactly.

When postulating on *horror vacui*, Aristotle was almost prescient. Thousands of years before major breakthroughs in physics, Aristotle believed all bodies moved to fill a void, once created. Objects made of earth moved toward earth, items made of air moved toward air, etc.

He wrote that empty spaces are usually filled, demonstrating a very rudimentary grasp of Einstein's theory of general relativity. Turns out, gravity is the only force preventing Earth's atmosphere from being sucked into the near vacuum of outer space. But is space a true vacuum?

With an ever-expanding understanding of quantum mechanics, physicists have not been able to physically demonstrate a true vacuum exists. By definition, a vacuum is nothing. And outer space is not nothing. The concept of nothing is theoretical only.

Space has quantum fields which are filled with appearing and disappearing pairs of virtual particles that leave their energy signature by impacting the energy in atoms. So, even a vacuum is not a true vacuum. Aristotle was correct, albeit without the factual depth of understanding why.

I like to know stuff. By knowing stuff, I can then think more broadly about fun things. In ruminating on those fun things, beyond the sheer science of Aristotle's theory, I will now share a childhood story that truly shows how nature abhors a vacuum.

Let's start with my uncle Colm's third and final wife, a stripper named Sky Cornflower. She was raised on a hemp farm in a commune of Northern Californian hippies. Her family were spiritual explorers, and from a young age, they used drugs – weed, mushrooms, ecstasy, and acid – to enhance their connection to the deepest secrets of the universe.

Clothes were optional material trappings, perhaps explaining her adult vocation. As were toilets. The children were often seen scampering naked around the compound, crapping on the ground and cleaning themselves later in a local lake, which was likely also their drinking water.

Knowing her non-traditional upbringing, as kids, we cleverly developed a nickname for Sky Cornflower: Mother Nature, shorthand was Nature. It was no surprise that, given her gypsy roots and crispy brain cells, Nature was not going to be constrained by marital norms like participating in cleaning her own house. The place was a dump, outdoors brought indoors. Hell, until she died, she could barely sleep indoors without a bong hit and a horse tranquilizer to quiet her down.

On one visit, my sister and I witnessed a pile of—dirt? Dust? Dog shit?—in a corner of their living room, with a dandelion growing from it. Ironically, there was an antiquated relic resembling a vacuum stored in the same corner, not feet away. When I pulled Uncle Colm's shirt and pointed at their indoor turd garden, he simply shrugged and said, "Nature abhors a vacuum." Unattributed at that time to Aristotle, and quite literal in translation, I thought my uncle was the funniest dude around.

Nature had a dog. At least I think it was a dog. It was seven pounds of shit-kicking sinew, bones, and tail. Purple mottled skin sprouted tufts of dry white hairs posing as fur. His head was an amalgam of thyroid bulging eyes, scraggly whiskers, patchy hair, and an irretractable, lolling red tongue, far too big for a pate so wee. His name was Red.

Red was a dick. An ill-tempered, misshapen little beast, he was bereft of all love or affection. Shivering constantly, Red was always twitching or nipping or yapping at invisible foes that tormented his malformed psyche. Cannot recount the number of times he would be nervously tottering through the house, fleeing invisible gremlins, looking over his shoulder and running headlong into furniture, the wall, or Nature. With a yip and a nip, he would be off again.

Even as kids, we always knew why he was really called Red ... his red rocket. With little to no provocation, his glistening sex lipstick would jut forth from its sheath like a tiny wet sword. As though riddled with shame, the moment his penis came out, he would halt what he was doing, drop his hips to a crooked sitting position, and start aggressively licking his choad with that massive, slobbering Gene Simmons tongue.

But the worst thing I have ever seen was the time Uncle Colm, clearly pissed off at Nature's domestic disinterest, fired up the presumed vacuum to clean up a massive spill of "charcuterie." Unsurprisingly, this redneck delicacy was comprised of cubed Velveeta cheese, pepperoni slices, and expired olives. Red lunged for the spilled snacks. We guessed it was his first meal in days.

The vacuum made a horrific, high-pitched sound. A sound that neglected creatures make when they cry out to god to end their suffering. Something snapped in Red. While mid-leap, his tattered ears shot skyward in abject terror, eyes bulging further from his head than anatomically possible, as his trouser mouse thrust like a fifth blood leg from its pouch.

Impossible to imagine, but Red, spindly purple legs aerodynamically splayed out to the side in the air, landed awkwardly and directly on his penis. Now, I am no veterinarian, nor could I be one after the mental trauma of witnessing this calamity, but poor Red's penis bent in a way that neither Nature nor nature could have conceivably intended.

I swear to this day the sound it made was like a plucked *boing* of a Jew's harp. Perhaps Red uttered the bizarre, cartoonish sound, that would make more sense. One can only hope.

Either way, Red tumbled across the floor like a nasty bowling ball, fur patches besot with squished cheese and olives. When he recovered from rolling, he began screeching and howling, attempting to mend his damaged tallywacker with his gargantuan tongue. Quickly displeased with that result, Red curled back into a ball and rolled away like a whimpering, gale-driven tumbleweed into parts unknown and unseen in Colm and Nature's house.

We all stared at each other in disbelief. Having faded into background noise, the vacuum once again filled the room, keening for a swift death. The moment Colm turned off the vacuum, the doorbell rang.

Nonplussed, Nature smoothed her shirt and walked over to the front door, as Colm returned the vacuum to its reliquary along the wall. Well past the *five-second rule*, I brushed some floor lint off a piece of pepperoni and nibbled in shock.

Nature opened the door to a cacophony of voices, clearly a choir of the damned coming to claim poor Red's lost soul on a dark Saturday afternoon:

"Good afternoon. Have you heard the good news of Jehovah and the path to enter God's Kingdom? Hello. My name is Elder Smith. And I would like to share with you the most amazing book. Hi, could I interest you in a free carpet cleaning today? No obligation to buy anything, we are doing market research, just looking for...."

It was like the set-up for a bad joke. A Jehovah's Witness, a Mormon, and a Kirby Salesman make a cold call together.... You fill in the punchline. Any unannounced knocker with any version of god to offer would have been a total non-starter for our little pagan, Nature. But the synchronicity of a vacuum cleaner salesman—and a handsome one at that!—arriving at their exact moment of need! Well, Nature said it best, "Cosmic! Come on in!"

Instinct is a funny thing with animals. Red, in a final attempt to show his programmed distemper in defense of the family home, rounded a corner from another room, still rolled into a ball, and made a beeline to the closing front door. His agonized whelps were now combined with aggressive snarls, spittle flying in all directions, doing his best impression of the Tasmanian devil from *Looney Toons*.

As the door began to close, Red rapidly rambled through the remaining gap in the doorway, directly into the unaware evangelists. Screams of terror and shock, followed by howling barks, the closing door sealed the rest of the noise from our wondering ears. Red was never seen again. A tattered Book of Mormon was all that remained on the front porch later that day.

Instinct is even funnier with hippy strippers. On cue, Nature shimmied off for an undiscovered part of the house, accompanied hand-in-hand with the Kirby salesman. We were kids, so we only knew the living room, dining room, and kitchen part of Colm and Nature's house. Colm looked at my dad and rolled his eyes. As Nature disappeared with her latest friend, we could hear her giggling softly, "Things are very dirty back here. I hope you can make them clean."

An hour later, Colm and Nature had a sparkling new Kirby vacuum – for FREE! Can you imagine?

Years later, as though an insider's joke at Nature's wake, I overheard Uncle Colm confide in my dad with a wry smile. The epitaph he had carved on Nature's gravestone read...

Nature Adored a Vacuum (Salesman)

Which brings us back to Aristotle. In the end, even with my family, his postulations still held true. Sky Cornflower, aka Nature, had a void that needed to be filled. Turns out, Uncle Colm had a micro-penis, and she loathed it. So, she cheated. The Kirby vacuum salesman was a more fully endowed partner in a series of trysts that inevitably gave her herpes, medical complications from which led to her eventual demise.

But a micro-penis is not a void. It is not nothing. Arguably it is not much, but hey, sometimes a winning personality carries the day, too. The vacuum was in Nature's heart, and that is what she detested. She was a lazy, shallow, vacuous person who filled that emptiness with anything that provided her with a few moments of fulfillment and contentment in her otherwise unhappy, cosmic existence. Thank the universe she and Colm never had kids. A dog was bad enough. R.I.P., Red.

Dark Shorts 1: Ol' Scruff

Jimmy and Timmy played a game of fetch in their rural backyard with their dog, Scruff. Although old and failing in health, Scruff loved to play fetch. They threw a tennis ball as hard and as far as they could. Scruff unfailingly retrieved it, tail wagging like a puppy. The game grew more fun, and the boys laughed as hard as Scruff's tail wagged. Jimmy, the older and stronger boy, loved showing Timmy how far he could throw. Timmy, the younger and sicklier boy, clapped with glee at his big brother's prowess. Jimmy threw the ball with all his might into the cornfield that bordered their property. Unfazed, Scruff crashed loudly into the corn after his quarry then burst forth exultantly in a spray of husks. Joy oozed out every pore as he ran the ball back for another toss, eyes twinkling with love for his boys. As Scruff approached, Farmer Jones shot Scruff through the head from his tractor, yelling, "I told you boys to keep that damn dog out of my field!" Jimmy and Timmy shrugged and wandered away in search of something more fun to do.

What Doesn't Kill You Gives You Colitis

Scholars regard Friedrich Nietzsche as the undisputed father of positive thinking. Here are a few of this nineteenth-century German Tony Robbins' greatest quotes and aphorisms that have inspired me since I was a lad.

- *Is man one of God's blunders or is God one of man's blunders?*
- *It says nothing against the ripeness of a spirit that it has a few worms.*
- *And if you gaze long enough into an abyss, the abyss will gaze back into you.*
- *God is dead. God remains dead. And we have killed him.*
- *That which does not kill us makes us stronger.*

Hearing Nietzsche's lyrical words is like the warmth of the sun's rays holding you in a loving embrace. Or the unadulterated joy of watching kittens tumble and squeak across a verdant field. Or the peaceful Zen of the ocean surf's eternal pounding against a sandy shore.

That said, a lot has been written about Nietzsche's influence on fascism and the thinking of saucy tarts like

Mussolini and Hitler. What a load of crap. Nietzsche was an invalid from tertiary syphilis thirty years before the wave of anti-egalitarianism swept through parts of Europe.

His dear sweet sister, Elisabeth, was the real peach. A known right-wing darling and anti-Semite, this aspiring Nazi served as her brother's editor and curator until he died under her care in 1900. His last years were lived in a nearly catatonic state of paresis and mental collapse.

While Nietzsche continued to languish, Elisabeth began reworking, and later publishing, some of his unfinished writings to align with her extreme support of fascism. She helped further the misconception of *Übermensch*, the Nazi concept of the superman, leading ultimately to Hitler's concept of a master race. Hell, she was so well-regarded in national socialist circles, her BFF and *Teppichfresser*, Hitler, even attended her funeral in 1935.

Teppichfresser, for those of you who lack sufficient German language skills, literally translates as "carpet eaters." According to William Shirers's book *The Rise and Fall of the Third Reich*, Adolf Hitler was so neurotic about the Czechs, he was frequently seen with nervous tics, often dropping to the floor in a rabid rage, literally chewing the edge of the carpet. If there was licking involved, Hitler may have been close friends with Eric Cartman's mom. (Sorry, could not resist the *South Park* reference.)

So, for Nietzsche, there is some bitter irony in the concept of "what does not kill us makes us stronger." Stronger? His body was stolen by syphilis, and his words were stolen by Elisabeth. And yet he lingered in a twilight existence, imprisoned in his own body, only to live on in posthumous infamy thanks to his Nazi *Arschloch* sister. No more free German lessons... look it up.

From my perspective, "what doesn't kill you makes you stronger" is rather bogus, too. The implication is that conquering adversity, at some moment in time, makes you more prepared to deal with future challenges. On one level, this can be true. But it does not speak to the new baggage, side effects, or residual impact that, having survived a catastrophic event, carries forward following the trauma.

Glass half empty? Maybe. But suffering makes you angrier. More cynical. Less trusting. More anxious. And, in my case, gave me ulcerative colitis. So, I would re-work Nietzsche's concept to more accurately reflect the nuances of trauma and its residual impacts to state, "What doesn't kill you gives you colitis."

You may ask yourself, "What is ulcerative colitis?" Well, David Byrne, thanks for asking.

Ulcerative colitis (UC) is an autoimmune disease. You develop long-term inflammation and sores (ulcers) in your colon. Some of the time, you are in remission and asymptomatic. Other times, you experience flare ups. A flare can be debilitating. Skip the next paragraph if you are easily grossed out.

We all normally poop each day. A UC flare can make you feel an intensely urgent need to poop twenty times per day. And each trip to the commode brings explosive diarrhea filled with little treats like mucus, blood, pus, and clots from your ulcerated intestines. And throughout, you are gassy and bloated with stabbing abdominal pain. And this can last for days, even weeks. You truly feel like ass (pun intended).

The only medical cure is to have your bowels removed completely and an ileostomy performed. A surgeon creates a hole in your abdomen upon which you hang a poop bag to externally collect your liquid waste. The practical upside is the fresh feces can keep you toasty like a hot water bottle on a cold winter night. My grandpa had his "poop bag," and oh, the cuddles we used to have!

Most times, through pharmaceutical experimentation – and not the good kind – you discover a regimen of meds that ultimately induces remission from a flare. Until the next flare. Gastroenterologists tell you it is equal parts science and magic, sprinkled with a little bit of luck. Throw in an annual colonoscopy, and you, my little Ricky Martin, are living *la vida loca*. Or, for Nietzsche, *ein verrücktes Leben*.

Part of managing UC is understanding your triggers. They are different for everyone. Stress for me seems to be the main culprit. Since I have always been a bit of a jacked-up spaz boy, often skating frenetically along a cliff's edge, you can imagine how heavy loads of stress can send me stumbling to the toilet.

Fun non-sequitur: in 2016, I had shoulder surgery to repair a torn rotator cuff and labrum. This was my first surgical procedure in my life, and I was knotted up with anxiety in the days preceding the first cut. Like clockwork, the day before the procedure, I erupted in a full-on, nasty-ass UC flare-up.

Sitting in pre-op, IVs hanging out of me like seaweed, floating in a sea of anxiety, I kept telling the nurses I needed to use the bathroom before going into surgery. They laughed it off. I was freaking out. The anesthesiologist came in to assuage me that in his twenty years, he had never seen anyone poop on the operating table, and he would make sure that did not happen to me. I was not assuaged.

Fast forward a few hours later, as I am sleepily and blissfully emerging from my anesthesia slumber, I hear an alarm going off and nurses yelling, "Oh my God! He's shitting! He's shitting!"

Laying on my non-surgical side, I then feel people packing towels against my back and butt. Yelling and bustling, the team worked to stem the brown tide. Still groggy, I felt my shame rise in crimson waves to my cheeks. I made eye contact with the anesthesiologist, and he simply mouthed, "I am so sorry." When he visited me in post-op, he, my wife and I had a grand laugh about it all. Last I heard, the nurses are still in therapy.

What was my trigger event for ulcerative colitis? Well, Lieutenant Columbo, let me tell you. My first UC flare-up happened randomly at the end of 2007, on a flight back to the United States from a visit with our manufacturing partner, Charlie Chan in China (discussed earlier in "Useless Pets" in case you're skipping around).

Given the symptoms, imagine the fun I had on a fourteen-hour flight from Beijing to Chicago. And airplane bathrooms? Barf. I can go on about that for days. So gross, made incrementally grosser by me.

My brother, best friend, and some high-net-worth angel investors owned our company at the time. While we skyrocketed in 2007 and 2008 – won Consumer Electronics Show Innovations Award, profiled on CNBC's *Squawk Box* – when the stock market crashed in November 2008, we slowly unraveled for the next eighteen months and never recovered. We filed for bankruptcy in May 2010.

The stress was inexorable. I was in a constant state of UC flares through this time, which further limited my ability to lead our business out of the abyss. To paraphrase Nietzsche, the abyss was gazing back at me. And I did not like what I saw.

The death of our business did not kill me. After a couchbound "Summer of Sadness" in 2010, I shaved my ZZ Top beard, trimmed my pterodactyl toenails, and got off the couch, forty pounds heavier. Yes, I ate away my feelings that summer. Eventually I broke eye contact with the abyss and looked to the light, and there was a shiny bag of Doritos waiting for me.

But was I stronger? Maybe. Certainly more laser focused. When I finally went back to work, I had a (nacho) chip on my shoulder. Something to prove. Having never experienced failure on such a grand scale in my life, I assailed my new job that year like Ragnar Lothbrook on a Norman castle. That hard work has been rewarded with a solid career ever since.

But I was so singularly focused on success at work that I lost sight of addressing the weight gain from the summer of sadness.' Living in airports and traveling every week reinforces lazy, bad eating habits, and the residual impact of maintaining that weight led to Type 2 diabetes.

The residual damage from the bankruptcy continues today with the UC and diabetes. The colitis is reasonably well managed. With my career doing great, I am now turning that laser-focus on to fitness and weight loss, seeking to reverse the diabetes before it has too much time to gain hold of me.

My closing thought is simple: unless you believe in reincarnation, you only have one life. Grab it by the haunches and hump it real hard, before it humps you. When it does inevitably hump you, take it. Endure. Unlike Nietzsche, if it does not give you syphilis, hopefully you will come out stronger. And at least *würdest du gefickt* along the way.

Erin Go Bragh

Part of growing up immersed in Irish heritage is an inborn, potentially inbred, proclivity to celebrate humor and craic.

Craic (pronounced "crack") is the Irish concept of fun and laughter, particularly in a social setting. Spend a Saturday evening in the Temple Bar district of Dublin, and you will understand.

Uncle Seamus was of the firm opinion that there were degrees of craic. "Like an onion, a good time has layers," he would whisper to me in my crib, baby bottle of Guinness in hand.

Pressing the rubber nipple to my rapacious little lips, he would add, "More vitamins than your poor mother's milk could ever hope to have." Even as a baby, that was good craic. But Seamus liked to delineate craic into very specific categories.

- **The craic was mighty**. Brilliant fun night out with the boys. Danced with some ladies. Drink was flowing. Everyone went home with a smile. Danny O'Hara may have hooked up.
- **The craic was deadly**. A grand night out with the boys for fun and debauchery. Literally fell into some girls after too many shots of Jameson. They fell back into us, and we all had a good laugh. Everyone hooked up. Gardai was called, and we all ran away, still laughing. Except Danny O'Hara, who was arrested for pissing on a cop car.

- **The craic was ninety**. Epic fun night out with the boys. Blacked out completely. Brief memory of hooking up. Flashbacks of *Caligula*? Woke up in jail cell covered in piss and lipstick. Danny O'Hara may have died. Not sure.

Implied in the spirit of craic is that those great times involve someone(s) of Irish descent, since we basically wrote the book on fun. The Irish possess a uniquely lyrical wit, sly and laid back, while gregarious and friendly, especially when Guinness or Jameson is generously applied.

Throughout childhood and over the years, I have learned of so many Irish characters that are fundamental to the concept of craic. I have assembled a few of my favorite Irish personalities in the hope that my fondness and amusement will tickle you in a loving, reasonably HR-appropriate way.

- **Two Fingers Ryan**. Ryan was a devout man. He attended mass every Sunday. But Ryan had a scratchy ass that plagued him relentlessly. He was often seen by my grandmother with two fingers down the back of his pants, digging his ass while waiting in line to receive holy communion. Grandma was horrified by both his sacrilegious and unhygienic public self-exploration. She claims she overheard Father Mick Herlihy once say to Ryan at the communion rail, "Body of . . . Christ, what's that smell?"
- **Orph & Clara**. Orph was cross-eyed and loved to drive his wife Clara around the village on Sundays after mass. Neighbors were known to complain to my grandparents over pie and coffee about Orph's car tire tracks in their front yards. Clara was born with her arms only grown

to the elbows, where an assortment of fingers grew directly from the malformed nub. Grandma always said that despite her limitations, Clara could crochet the loveliest scarves.

- **The Goddamn Man**. My grandfather tended bar for years at Jiggers in our hometown. He often spoke of The Goddamn Man. No one knew his name – he kept to himself and sipped his whiskies each night. All they ever heard him say was a single word, "Goddamn." Grandpa spoke highly of him as "a simple man with simple tastes and an economy of words."
- **Ass Ache McGee**. One of my grandfather's least favorite patrons at Jiggers was Ass Ache McGee. He always had something to complain about, and grandpa could not stand it, thus the nickname was born. Grandpa exacted his revenge one day when Ass Ache McGee was complaining about the weather and his sinuses. Retrieving a canned oyster from the kitchen, my grandfather stuffed it in his handkerchief and returned to the bar to commiserate over their sinus woes. Feigning a sneeze, my grandfather covered his mouth with the rigged hankie. Lowering it from his mouth, he acted surprised, picked up the oyster, and notoriously said, "Looks too good to waste." And tossed it in his mouth. The nauseous Ass Ache McGee ran out of the bar, never to return. On cue, The Goddamn Man winked, nodded and said, "Goddamn."
- **Erin go *bragh***. Uncle Colm, husband to third wife, Sky Cornflower, a.k.a. Nature (see prior reference) had a second wife named Erin. She passed away before my siblings and I were born. But, as he would often

nostalgically regale to us kids over some pints, Erin had a wonderful set of tits. She had never worn a bra in her life, and it was vividly clear when she was excited or cold. Colm was gobsmacked by them, and he wanted everyone to share in his enthusiasm. Every St. Paddy's Day, Jiggers would hold a wet t-shirt event for JUGS. Justice Under God's Sight was a community charity developed between the local Hibernian Society, Our Bloody Martyr Catholic Church, and the Masonic Temple Association. Through their philanthropic works, JUGS would provide food, clothing and money to widows of railroad workers. Given her coveted assets and the obvious irony, Erin was often the poster-girl for the JUGS wet t-shirt contest. Colm was fiercely proud. Mayor Pug Walsh and Father Mick Herlihy faithfully judged the contest each year, and the railroad workers packed Jiggers to ensure they gave generously to this worthy cause for the families of their fallen comrades. For years, the bartenders would honor St. Patrick by pouring a pitcher of beer down the front of each contestant as they danced on the bar and the menfolk cheered. Things went poorly for Erin the year Jiggers and JUGS tried to mix things up and use green beer. Turns out, Erin was allergic to the green food coloring they used, and she died hours later from anaphylaxis. To pay homage to his fallen breast friend, Colm had the epitaph *Erin go bragh* inscribed on her gravestone. And his ass.

- **Des Conway.** My wife and I honeymooned in Ireland in November 1994. I was obsessed with finding the origin of my family name and meeting some "real" Conways. We stayed at a quaint bed and breakfast in a remote northwest corner of County Mayo, near the little fishing village of Killala. Escaping a massive November gale, we sheltered and drank all night in a local pub. It was magical. The peat fire roaring pungently all night. The people welcoming us like family. The babies napping in car seats atop the cigarette machine. The Guinness flowing along with hot toddies (a drink of boiling water, lemon, currants, and Jameson). At 11 p.m., the pub closed, which meant the owners placed tar paper over the inside of the windows so the Gardai (McCops) could justify they were in fact 'closed.' The craic was mighty that night. I have always been told I "married up" as it pertains to my wife, who is a lovely lass, to be sure. An elderly gentleman at the bar that night, who said he knew a Des Conway, thought so, too. Well, maybe that's what he said. Not sure after all the hot toddies. Plus, he spoke more Irish than English. Maybe *he* was Des Conway? All I can certainly recall is that every time he said Des Conway's name, he snapped his fingers and pointed at my wife and me, then kissed my wife's cheek smearing his runny old man nose on it. He also drooled on her shoulder a few times. My wife is a true germaphobe and was horrified that I did not intervene. I could not help but laugh more than a few times. She had the last laugh when she kicked me in the nut sack on the 5am drunken trundle back to our hotel.

- **Uncle Seamus**. The last remaining family member with admitted IRA affiliation, Seamus lived in South Boston, aka Southie. Family legend holds that Seamus was a hitman for the Irish mob in Southie. Dad often warned my sister that he would call Uncle Seamus to "take care of" any boy who treated her badly. When we were teens, Seamus died while walking past an exploding car. Weird, right? It makes what my friend and I did for our senior Anthropology project in high school especially wrong. Tasked with interviewing a family member who best demonstrated our "ethnicity," we convinced my dad to act as Uncle Seamus, fake Irish brogue and all. Dad slayed imitating the slain Seamus. Since Seamus lived so far away in Southie, we tape-recorded the faux-interview over the faux-phone, thereby ensuring dad maintained his veil of anonymity. It was so authentic, our teacher held it up to future classes as the epitome of what an A-plus grade project looked like. That is until my brother took the same class five years later and snitched. The teacher was crestfallen. He resigned that year to a cabin deep in the woods where he ultimately died alone from alcoholism or starvation or bear attack. Or was he the Unabomber? I forget which. Regardless, my friend and I showed my brother the meaning of "snitches get stitches" that summer.

One of the best things to know about interacting with the Irish is to never take everything we say at face value. The twinkle in an Irish eye is the sun reflecting off a tear formed due to the pent-up laughter from having some sport with your gullibility.

A dear friend of mine is known for saying, "Never let the truth get in the way of a good story." And so 'tis with the Irish. Part of true craic, and why the Irish are such good storytellers, is that we nurture the ability of a speaker to capture a listener's attention with an appropriately long-winded mix of fact, humor, emotion, and fiction.

So, while we may be a wee bit full of shite, is it really our fault if our gift of the gab influences your beliefs or disbeliefs in our stories? Though our stories may sometimes be a load of Blarney, they are in fact a grand tease, an exaggeration of the truth meant to charm and entertain. And what is the harm in that?

Lá Fhéile Pádraig Sona Daoibh! Happy Saint Patrick's Day to all!

But Who is Man that is Not Angry?

Timon of Athens is one of William Shakespeare's least known, and out of fairness, least liked tragedies. Honestly, it kinda sucks.

There is an impassioned academic debate today whether the playwright and cynic, Thomas Middleton, co-wrote this play (and others) with Shakespeare. Scholars believe the distinctive style differences between The Bard and Middleton detract from the play's cohesiveness.

Interesting to note that Middleton also helped with *Macbeth*, yet you do not hear many scholars nitpicking that play, do you? Even intelligentsia play favorites, too.

Being a Bill Shakespeare enthusiast, I think *Timon of Athens* is deceptively underrated. The titular Timon (FYI – he does <u>not</u> have a friend named Pumbaa) is a character study and cautionary tale of excess, betrayal, and the profound bitterness that inevitably follows.

2 Angry Men

For simplicity's sake, let us winnow down the characters to two angry men – Timon and Alcibiades.

- **Timon**. After a lifetime of squandering his money on fake friends who abandon him in his time of need, an angry and betrayed Timon exiles himself from Athens, escaping this corrupt society forever. Ending up misanthropic and alone, Timon conveniently discovers some gold, which he ironically uses to exact his revenge. Money may be the root of all evil, but before he dies, it buys Timon the final word with all the parasites who wronged him. He even gives a small bit of his gold to some whores so they can spread their venereal diseases across the world he has come to loathe.
- **Alcibiades**. It is the general, Alcibiades, who always captured my attention. First, super cool name. Second, is his line, "To be in anger is impiety; But who is man that is not angry?" Alcibiades' defense of a soldier from the death penalty falls on deaf ears when pleading his case to the Senate. Because of his persistence and irreverence toward the Senators, Alcibiades is banished from Athens. Vowing revenge on Athens, Alcibiades finds the embittered Timon living in a cave outside the city, and Timon gives much of his treasure to subsidize Alcibiades' army and pending attack on Athens.

Shakespeare (and Middleton) present us with two angry characters. Timon, hateful and vengeful. Alcibiades, just and vengeful. One seeks to destroy, and the other seeks to rebuild.

But as Alcibiades says, and Timon personifies, are we not all just a bit angry? Don't we all have triggers that set us off and show our lower, more ignoble character?

I sure as hell do. Because you are my invisible friends, we need to develop this digital relationship based on my printed, albeit brilliant, words. So, please indulge me with the opportunity to opine on a brief, potentially quirky list of things that truly make me angry.

8 Angry Things

1. **Buffets.** Everything sucks about buffets. But my real flashpoint—aside from the cheesy ambiance, abject gluttony, and poor food quality—is those disgusting plastic sneeze shields that pretend to protect your food trough from the next zombie apocalypse. While the underpaid buffet workers sit mindlessly in the corner huffing the cleaning fluid instead of using it to create a germfree line of sight over the slop, Wayne-Doug is peaking underneath, dirty fingernails and overgrown nose hair and all, trying to figure out how to work a pair of salad tongs.
2. **Slow Drivers.** If you cannot drive the speed limit, call an Uber, grandma. Seriously, if your faculties can no longer afford you the ability to be a productive contributor to the interstate highway community, don't get mad at me when I am riding your ass to move out of the passing lane. This is totally your fault, Mildred. When I blaze by you, rest assured I relish you giving me the finger. It reinforces that I am a true Highway Alpha. And it is not just old people. That is far too lenient. A special "hate you" shoutout goes to truckers in the passing lane, Canadians in the passing lane, and Prius drivers in general.
3. **Like.** Overuse of the word "like" when speaking is like nails on a chalkboard to me. Not sure if this generation

has become amazingly inarticulate or irretrievably imbecilic, but this unconscious speech pattern needs to end. It is bad enough I watch *The Bachelor* at all (and maybe enjoy it). But by the end of the season, not only do I hate every twenty-something in America for being so vapid and self-absorbed, but I have also heard the word "like" used more times than a poorly applied simile in a stuttering contest. Since the current populist trend in politics seems to want to give everything away for free, why not give away some elocution and public speaking lessons as a precondition to graduating high school? I am, like, *soooo* done with it.

4. **Spitting.** This is so unhygienic and unnecessary on every conceivable level. Unless you are a conscientious porn star, I struggle to conceive where spitting is remotely acceptable. Watching baseball is difficult for me because of all the rampant spitting. It's like a side competition for who can be the biggest douche. Baseball is considered a sport, right? What other professional athlete can chew tobacco like a redneck at the Fair, guzzle mouthfuls of seeds like some starving chipmunk, or chew wads of gum like some lonely fat kid with halitosis? And then spit it all over the place? Disgusting. Basic rule of etiquette: if you cannot swallow something in your mouth, don't put it there in the first place. Am I right, ladies?

5. **Fairs.** Speaking of Fairs (and spitting), I hate going to them. I have commented about my intense fear of clowns (as opined in my *Quit Clowning Around* essay) and inability to connect with carnie culture. But our State Fair draws some of the most inbred hill-folk

that I only thought existed in movies like *Deliverance*. One ironic year, my wife finally convinced me to go to the Fair and spend some family time with her and our toddler daughters. It was a sweltering day. A thin layer of grime quickly adhered to us after jostling through the dense crowds who milled mindlessly about like a scene from *The Walking Dead*. The air was rife with competing smells of fried food, body odor, and cow shit. All this was marginally tolerable, until a drunken old hillman spit a massive mouthful of chewing tobacco across my oldest daughter's legs, replacing the dusty grime with his black saliva. After the fisticuffs were over, and the police escorted us out, we have (shockingly) never returned to the Fair since.

6. **Uncontrolled Children.** Whatever happened to parenting? The artful delivery of a well-planted bitch slap upside the head of a loud, unruly, mouthy child? I travel a lot for work. Air travel is particularly uncomfortable, stressful, and nasty, made infinitely worse by the caterwaul of an unmuzzled toddler. I am working on an invention: a sleeping pod where you insert a one-year-old child, and six years later, out comes a grown seven-year-old who knows how the hell to properly behave and communicate in public. Maybe mom and/or dad will take a few parenting classes during this hiatus, too!

7. **Everything Disney.** Happiest place on earth, my ass. Isn't a giant rat mascot a clear sign of infestation and decay? It is a documented, journalistic fact that beneath the Magic Kingdom, there is a secret lab (and temple)

where Walt Disney's reanimated head communicates plans for world domination to his adoring devotees. The whole experience is designed around mind control. Otherwise, how could we logically spend so much money on such a shitty experience? Disney is a Fair on steroids (maybe on psylocibin). Spoiled screaming children not getting overpriced trinkets, massive crowds melting in sweltering heat, and lame rides with wait times that defy the patience of even the hungriest crocodile in times of drought. Evil genius at work.

8. **Covidiots.** As I often tell my twenty-something daughters, it is not always all about you. We exist in a world of 7.8 billion people. We are only as successful curtailing the spread of disease as the shittiest person or the biggest idiot. As I watched these moronic children (raised by even more moronic, indulgent parents) ignoring warnings and partying on Florida beaches during lockdown, I thought, *what a great opportunity for a shark attack*. It will only take the bloody mutilation of a few Brookes and Addisons in front of a massive mob of shrieking Gen Z-ers to demonstrate the point: random shit happens. Is it the shark's fault for eating sweet Emily? Hell no. He was hungry, and the water was conveniently stocked with fresh food. Is it a virus' fault it infested thousands of asymptomatic spring breakers, and then it killed their at-risk grandparents when Brandon returned home? Think people. Funny not funny.

Sadly, most of yous, my deer fans, won't never get to see me stomp outta Athens like Timon. He an irate manchild who figured out life sucks. He shoulda buyed this here book.

Hell, most of you won't never even see me accept for my boyish good looks and smiling mug all over thee interwebs anyways. Some of yous been asking bout the possibility of a late-night talk show down the road. Write now, my righting is my priority, but yous never know!

Oh, I forgot! Bad grammer, pisses me off two!

Surviving Elephant's Foot

The Adirondack region of Upstate New York boasts over three thousand lakes and ponds spanning over six million acres. The mountains are low and ancient. The forests are dark and primal.

Locals refer to the Adirondacks as the North Country, extending from the eastern shores of Lake Ontario to the western shores of Lake Champlain, separated from Canada by the Saint Lawrence River to the north.

"Smell the north."

Truer words were never spoken as you enter the North Country. The air is fresher. Cleaner. There is a pungent pine smell that permeates everything due to the abundance of conifers. Pine trees thrive in the colder weather and rockier soil of the mountains, taking root in the most amazing places.

While pine seems to be ubiquitous, you realize how prolific the deciduous trees are when you visit in the autumn. Sugar maples and red oaks explode in a spectral array of gamboge, auburn, and crimson as they prepare to drop their ornate leafy mantles for a long winter's nap. Truly breathtaking to behold.

Quaint towns and villages pepper the landscape, interconnected by single lane roads. There are very few highways in this wild place. It is not uncommon to see moose striding along the road, glancing sidelong at you as they meander toward a nearby wetland. It is Henry David Thoreau's wet dream.

Exiting one of the single lane roads, you see dozens of potholed dirt roads leading to homes and camps, typically along a shallow river or a timeworn lake. The isolation is both fantastic and intentional. A refuge from the hectic modern world. And a guaranteed alignment job for your car when you return to civilization.

Down one of those bumpy dirt roads lies Muskellunge Lake. The Walden Pond of this adventure.

The forest grows claustrophobically close, reaching out for your car, subtly scraping the doors as you slowly roll by. It tries to impede your progress in entering its inviolable sanctuary.

As the forest finally relents, you round a curve, and down a slight incline lies a few camps scattered along the sandy shoreline of Muskellunge Lake. The lake is small and mysterious. Black water holds the cloudy sky's reflection, still and somber. Dense pine forest and small rocky cliffs engulf the far shoreline, framing the lake, protecting it from overdevelopment. You are nowhere and everywhere all at once.

One sweltering summer, my godparents had rented a camp for two weeks on a slight rise above the shore of Muskellunge Lake. A ramshackle structure, nestled in interloping trees and overgrown grass, designed only for sleeping, crapping, and eating.

The ratty roof and stained shake shingles yielded entry through a peeling red door into a turn-of-the-century kitchen and a small adjacent bathroom. A white peeling archway opened into a large living room—a literal barracks—framed with metal bunk beds, a few moth-eaten couches, and a chafed dining table. As kids, we thought this was the coolest place ever!

Our first week at camp was heaven. My family and my godparent's family were a gang of ten. Tight quarters, but who cares? We were outdoors swimming, fishing, boating, and exploring every day with our cousins from dawn until dusk.

(Yes, the same cousins discussed in my prior masterwork, *Jeux Sans Frontières*. We were far less destructive this summer, as we had too much to occupy ourselves and no weapons to make it more interesting.)

When each day ended, we would drive to the camp garbage dump in the pitch black and, from the safety of our locked cars, watch the cautiously foraging black bears illuminated by the headlights. It was so much better than the TV we did not have at camp!

The second week at camp was when shit got real. Real bad. The Monaghans arrived. Party of two, Aunt Curl and Uncle Art thankfully never had children. Where Colm and Nature were dirty, lazy people, Curl and Art were poor. The kind of poor that only unemployment and alcoholism nourish. They lived in a blighted city neighborhood in a house that made the Muskellunge Lake camp look like a luxury resort.

My mom's sister, Curl, smoked constantly. A fiery skinny redhead, a cigarette always hung from the corner of her mouth. Ashes fell haphazardly like nuclear fallout in the wake of her explosive movements. Smart and garrulous, Curl engaged and opined on any literary topic. When not drinking, she read avidly. F. Scott Fitzgerald stoked her passions, as did their shared love of the sauce.

But those moments were few and far between, and the grip of alcoholism was vicelike. Irish stereotypes are deeply, sadly grounded in historical fact. As a race, we have a very tempestuous relationship with drink. Curl changed after just a few beers. Angry and cruel, she honed her intelligence and wit as a weapon to eviscerate everyone in earshot. Arguments and fights followed her like cigarette smoke.

Curl's husband Art was a mess. A discharged navy veteran, Art had never—candidly, could never—hold a civilian job. He was drunk all the time. A short, slight man with a comb over, Art was wiry strong. He was a regular at the local neighborhood city bar where he was a known pugilist. Again, an Irish stereotype in the flesh.

A few years before camp, Art stumbled home from the bar, drunker than a peach orchard boar. Houses in his hilly ghetto rose ten feet above the street, with broken concrete steps the only means to access them. In his attempt to climb the steps, Art fell and fractured his skull. The VA repaired it with a metal plate.

Art was never the same after the fall. His speech had been somehow permanently slurred, only made worse to the point of unintelligible by his frequent intoxication. The best we could discern, he repeated the phrase "Woozhie, woozhie" in varying inflections and extensions as a primary form of expressing himself.

Of course, brain damage is never funny. But we were kids, and kids are evil by nature. So, Art was thereafter nicknamed Uncle Woozhie Woozhie. To lessen word count, I will refer to him as Woozhie.

Curl and Woozhie arrived at the Muskellunge Lake camp on a rainy, muggy Sunday. Having borrowed a friend's car and driven from the city, Curl was somewhat sober and needed to move post-haste to the kitchen for a beer. In her moment of need, with the driver's door open and Woozhie sitting in the passenger seat, Curl left the neighbor's car running.

From the kitchen window, we had a birds-eye view of what happened next.

Woozhie hollered something unintelligible after Curl. Trapped under a clinking heap of empty beer bottles after the long drive to camp, it appeared he was pissed she left him alone in the car unassisted. Lunging to the side, he toppled over toward the open driver side door, lying sideways across the driver's seat.

Cursing and mewling, he tried to raise himself back up by grabbing the shift stick on the steering column. Thrown into gear, the car surged forward, down the incline, splashing heavily into the lake.

Woozhie screamed a muddy string of curses as Curl rushed to the car to save him, beer in hand. As she dragged him through the open driver side door, they both fell backward into the shallow water, thrashing and soaking each other.

My dad and godfather leaped into action, hooking some chains to the waterlogged car, towing it with the pickup truck back to safety. Curl and Woozhie continued to flounder in the shallows, splashing and cursing at each other for quite a while longer. Dad was overheard muttering in a faux brogue, "Feckin eejits."

In the following days, we avoided Curl and Woozhie like the plague. Plus, we had discovered a real treasure further down the lake along a wooded deer trail: a cliff we later learned was called Elephant's Foot.

Elephant's Foot presented some thrilling conundrums for our preteen brains.

- The cliff appeared fifty feet high. As an adult, I can acknowledge it was probably no more than ten feet high.

But the drop to the water looked terrifying from a kid's perspective. Would we (could we?) break bones from the fall?
- The lake had its fair share of water moccasins. We knew these water snakes could bite you, and we had no clue how venomous they could be. And they were fast, wriggling across the surface of the lake. Could we outswim them? Would we die?
- We had no idea how deep the water was below the cliff. By observation and exploration, this was a shallow lake along most of the shoreline, which seemed dangerous. But our fathers had spoon-fed our voracious imaginations with bullshit legends about glacier-filled depths and undertows. What was fact? What was fiction?
- We did not want to get eaten by the muskellunge (aka muskies) that had lived in the lake for millions of years. Our fathers told us these ancient beasts were a type of little-known freshwater shark that grew fifteen feet long with razor sharp teeth. If we ventured too far out into deeper water, they would rip us to shreds. The danger was intoxicating. The craic was 90.

The top of Elephant's Foot was a wide rocky clearing. We imagined Native people created it as a holy place to perform ritualistic human sacrifices to appease the muskie and snake gods of this primordial bottomless lake.

My cousins, my sister, and I gathered on this hallowed ground, arguing over who would jump first. It was a heated negotiation, full of name calling, schmoozing, and horse trading. No one could show their fear. That was weakness.

My one cousin's testosterone was almost fully amped for takeoff when, from the tree line, we heard a massive crashing sound. Woozhie came tottering through the overgrowth hollering something at us. He moved inconceivably fast, given his condition.

Turns out too fast. Apparently, he could not slow his acceleration. Was he drunk? Was his damaged brain misfiring? Maybe both. In an instant, Woozhie rushed by us ... right off the edge of the cliff!

I swear he fell like Wile E. Coyote falls in the Road Runner cartoons. Arms and legs splayed to the side, only to belly smack with a massive plume in the black water far below. His body bobbed back to the surface, face down in the water, not moving.

Proud to say, completely freaked out, our heroic rescue skills kicked into high gear, casting off all our imagined fears. Several of us leapt off Elephant's Foot into the abyss. We turned Woozhie over onto his back and swam him into shore. The snakes fled before us. The muskies stayed in the deep.

My oldest cousin knew CPR and cleared Woozhie's lungs with a few hard puffs into his mouth. Coughing and gagging, Woozhie stood up and punched my cousin squarely in the face. He went wild, trying to slap each of us as we scattered from his waterlogged reach. We ran away at full-panic kid speed, far outpacing him. His strangled cries of *Woozhie! Woozhie!* were fading behind us as we ran through the wooded deer trail along the shore of Muskellunge Lake. We bypassed camp completely and swam out to a sandy island in the middle of the small lake until nightfall.

Not knowing what we did wrong, we were certain the inescapable blame would invariably fall on us, and we would get an old school ass-whooping from our moms. Christ, our handicapped uncle had fallen off a cliff. Could it get worse?

To this day, we still do not know the *why* behind Woozhie's actions that day. That secret died with him years later. But that glorious day, it dawned on me. We had survived Elephant's Foot. We had lived in the moment so fully and completely that we could never possibly feel this alive again. And that was worth all the ass-whoopings in the world.

Finding Jesus in the Easter Bunny

Growing up Catholic, Easter was always the most confusing holiday for me. On one hand, Easter was a celebration of the death and resurrection of Jesus Christ. He was born, God made man, to a virgin. He preached and performed miracles. Brutalized and crucified, he died for our sins. Three days later, he rose from the dead and ascended into heaven. God sacrificing His only begotten son opened the doors of heaven to us, if we would believe and have faith.

On the other hand, the Easter Bunny secretly invaded our sleeping home in the middle of the night. A freaking rabbit. EB hid treats all over the house, which we children had to sluggishly search for on Easter morn. The grand prize was a large individualized Easter basket, also hidden, with our names written on it. Then we would gorge ourselves on chocolates and Easter eggs until we were puking in our sweet pre-diabetic mouths at Easter mass.

This never computed in my child brain. How could something so sacrosanct and something so commercial coexist on the same holiday? To make it more confusing, historians remain conflicted as to the origin of the term "Easter." Why not call it "Resurrection Day" or "You Go, Jesus, Day"?

Most researchers agree with the findings of the seventh century monk, St. Bede, that the Anglo-Saxons named the month of April after the pagan goddess, Eostre. Also spelled Eastre, her festival commemorated the arrival of spring.

Over time, as Christianity supplanted ancient religions, the English term "Easter" helped smooth the transition from pagan to Christian. By retaining remnant names and dates, the Saxons could retain some cultural identity, even as they replaced the many old gods with the one new God.

And what about the Easter Bunny?

Some blame the German tradition of a mythical bunny named *Osterhase* crapping out colored eggs in a basket as the root infiltrator of Christian traditions. Not sure that theory scratches my intellectual itch. But let's run with it, because EB clearly shares the holiday with Jesus today. One could also argue EB inappropriately steals the limelight from JC. "And that's not right," he said in his favorite Kevin Meaney imitation.

After rigorous academic debate over many years, historians and theologians have pieced together four hypotheses that support how the Easter Bunny could exist on Christianity's most holy day.

1. **Jesus knew kids were dicks.** Jesus had been a kid. He should know firsthand. Growing up poor, there is some scholarly debate that Jesus may have had a chip on His shoulder. If true, then it stands to reason that Jesus himself created the Easter candy tradition to punish future "rich kids" with gluttony and diabetes so that they could sample a chocolaty piece of His suffering on the road to Calvary. In general, Jesus was keenly aware that kids were born dicks and needed to remedy that

design flaw to prepare them for grace (recall the lessons learned in *Jeux Sans Frontières*). Pulling together an elite team of jaded apostles to deliver him a plan, Jesus made history by introducing candy at Easter. Although that same history has lost track of which apostles, I have my guesses. Judas and Thomas were the more rascally apostles. Only makes sense that Jesus would require their unique set of skills. The final plan that continues through today provided for such an obscene quality and quantity of candy that kids felt nasty and exhausted for days after Easter. And the irony of having a fuzzy, innocent bunny deliver the poison makes His revenge even more delicious. Lesson learned. Do unto others.

2. **Jesus needed to give kids relief after Lent**. To Catholics, Lent is literally a living purgatory. Giving up things you love for six freaking weeks in preparation for Easter is beyond the pale for a child. Add to that the Catholic tradition of not eating meat on Fridays during Lent? I still heave a little bit when I think of my mother and grandmother's Lenten tuna noodle casseroles, one with peas, one without. The chocolate we gorged on Easter Sunday was scant remuneration for such abject cruelty for forty days prior. But it was at least something. Jesus was smart, maybe prescient. Oh wait, he was God. Definitely prescient. He foresaw the value of this ultimate carrot and stick system for making it through Lent. Lent was the stick, and Easter was the carrot. Because it was a carrot, the messenger must be a bunny. Because bunnies love carrots. Obvi. Amazing how kind yet logical God can be, isn't it?

3. **Jesus was lactose-intolerant**. Although the technology did not exist at the time to prove it, science seems to indicate that Jesus was not a fan of dairy. A tall glass of milk on a warm desert morning would wreak havoc on His digestive tract before he preached to the masses. Not once in the Bible did Matthew or John discuss His flatulence, as they ensured he adhered to a strict diet of wine, bread, and fish (quantities of which they never ran out of). In support of His healthy Mediterranean diet, Jesus created the tradition of Easter eggs, delivered by the Easter Bunny as a healthy snack to kids. As early Christian history goes, the bunny stole them from the Easter Duck, because ducks are miserable creatures and bunnies were Jesus's favorite. Jesus did not really tolerate eggs well either, but it was better than an Easter Cow bringing kids Easter Milk. That made no sense. And then the Germans screwed things up, as history shows, AGAIN, by creating chocolate eggs sometime in the early nineteenth century. *Nicht gut.*
4. **Jesus had a holy pet rabbit named Reg**. Much has been said about the gnostic scriptures discovered nearly two thousand years after Jesus's resurrection. The chapters of the modern Bible we read today were edited to fit the canon of the Roman Catholic Church in the first few centuries after Jesus died. The remaining scripture was excluded – some would argue discarded – because it did not all neatly fit a digestible story of Jesus. The oft ignored *Gospel of Reg* was one of them. No one is sure who wrote *Reg*, but there are fringe thinkers who believe Reg wrote it himself. That seems silly to me, but miracles

do happen. From his first days in the manger, Reg was at Jesus's side gently nibbling carrots. According to the gnostic tomes, several of the apostles were jealous of Reg. Especially John. He was always Jesus's fave. There is a vague reference to John intentionally falling on Reg, crushing his little body, killing him. Jesus was recorded as saying, *Reg, veni foras*; and the wee reanimated rodent leapt with a squeak into Jesus's arms. Historians now wonder whether this was the real story of Lazarus. There may also be some confusion about the translation errors around the term "Lamb of God." It may in fact refer to Reg, the "Lapin of God." Either way, Jesus truly adored Reg. He clearly could be the Easter Bunny. Explains a lot of the Santa-esque magic EB can pull off, too.

It all makes so much more sense to me as an adult. Irrespective of which theory you subscribe to, Jesus irrefutably enabled the Easter Bunny legend to share His biggest day.

Jesus was all about love. This probably best supports the *Gospel of Reg* theory. He sure loved that rabbit. Not sure why the early church decided to edit Reg out. Bad marketing on their part. The story is a delight.

It's fun to solve historical and religious conundrums. I've been restored to normal life but will never forget our Easter holiday of sheltering in place during the COVID plague, watching loved ones eating ham on Zoom, basking in the confidence we have no problem with a bunny sharing the limelight with the Savior.

Amen.

DARK SHORTS 2:
DINGLE SNEEM

Dingle Sneem McCarthy had an unfortunate and unlucky name. Daughter of unwed Irish parents, her father was from Sneem and her mother was from Dingle. In a cruel twist of fate, their car was swept over a cliff by a mudslide along the Dingle peninsula during a blustery November storm just one day after they brought their yet-to-be-named baby home to Dingle's parent's farm. Raised by her grandparents, she was named Dingle Sneem in honor of her dead parents. Try telling that to the other ten-year-old children at Our Lady of the Bleeding Jesus Crucified Catholic School in Killarney. One day, while Dingle Sneem sat sullenly on a high green hill looking over the black lakes of Killarney, a leprechaun visited her. Grandpa told her never to trust the fae, and especially this brand of trickster. So, Dingle Sneem took luck into her own hands. She grabbed the leprechaun by the collar and beat the shit out of him until he took her to his pot of gold. Leaving him for dead, she went to the bank that held the deed to her grandparent's farm and purchased the property from the bank. Returning to the farm with the Garda, she evicted her grandparents for giving her this dimwitted feckin' name and lived out the rest of her days as Betty.

Manscaping with Occam's Razor

When reduced to its simplest form, Occam's Razor is an analytical principle that posits when two or more theories predict the same result, the simplest solution is generally the right solution. A scientific variant of *keep it simple, stupid.*

The fourteenth century philosopher, William of Ockham, was an English Franciscan friar and theologian. While famously contributing to social, scientific, and religious thinking of the time, William ironically never used the phrase Occam's Razor in his writing. But ol' Billy was not without controversy.

William of Ockham is best known for his work on *nominalism*. Heretical during the High Middle Ages, nominalism tackles the ontological and epistemological issues of the nature of reality being absent of "*universals.*" These abstract concepts do not exist in the same way as physical, tangible material. According to nominalism, reality only exists in "*particulars.*"

Nominalism flies squarely in the face of *realism*. Upheld by Plato and Aristotle for over a thousand years and furthered by Thomas Aquinas not even one hundred years earlier, realism relies on both *universals* and *particulars* coexisting for a comprehensive explanation of reality.

For example: a nominalist views *orange* as an abstract concept, a universal. A clementine is orange. A sunset is orange.

Donald Trump is orange. These objects (clementine, sunset, Trump) labeled by the same term (orange) have nothing in common other than the fact they are all the same color.

Orange, therefore, does not exist, as it is too subjective and general. It is simply a verbal abstraction and convention of language. A realist view would accept that the universal descriptor (e.g., orange) can comfortably exist alongside the particular object (clementine, sunset, Trump). Fascinating and heady shit, but not really the point of this screed.

Here is the bottom line: Occam's Razor was the natural byproduct of William's nominalist thinking. By accepting and studying the object itself versus the descriptors or generalizations about the object, we then develop theories that can whittle reality down to its simplest, most logical form.

We all must reach conclusions about things in our lives based on the evidence presented to us. Let's examine ten practical, common scenarios that life presents us with on a daily basis and the conclusions we reach by applying Occam's Razor. As you consider each of the following observations, ask yourself: which is the simplest conclusion? A or B?

OBSERVATION 1: *A bicyclist lies bleeding on the side of the road in front of my car.*

- **CONCLUSION A.** The bicyclist cut me off, and I ran him down in a fit of psychotic road rage.
- **CONCLUSION B.** A giant pterodactyl swooped down from the sky, mauling the bicyclist after escaping from a secret island research lab. I slam on my brakes to snap a pic of the gruesome (yet captivating) aftermath.

OBSERVATION 2: *I have terrible explosive diarrhea that seems to move on its own in the toilet bowl.*

- **CONCLUSION A.** I ate raw pork bacon when I was super high. I have worms.
- **CONCLUSION B.** I am witnessing the creation of life in that my healthy diet and rigorous exercise regimen have now enabled me, as a man, to birth a new form of life. From my ass. *Howdy Ho!*

OBSERVATION 3: *Garbage cans are knocked over in my open garage.*

- **CONCLUSION A.** Raccoons battled over my discarded Chipotle from three nights ago. Third try at making carne asada this month. Still cold. Still sucked.
- **CONCLUSION B.** Oscar the Grouch hitchhiked from Sesame Street after a gentrification-driven eviction, saw my garage door open, and tried to make himself at home. Can was too small, and a pissed off Oscar ransacked the place in a fit of spurned Muppet rage.

OBSERVATION 4: *My daughter fails her college Statistics test.*

- **CONCLUSION A.** She did not study enough, opting for keg stands and bong hits instead.
- **CONCLUSION B.** Her mousy brown-haired professor detests gingers and, in a fit of jealous contempt, writes a particularly difficult, nasty, and personalized test for her that even a Florence Nightingale-esque obsessive on Crimean War infographics would fail.

OBSERVATION 5: *Japan canceled the 2020 Olympics.*

- **CONCLUSION A.** Coronavirus global plague spreading out of control. Japan is protecting the world's top athletes.
- **CONCLUSION B.** Reanimated Godzilla returns to battle in Tokyo with Rodan, Mothra, and Ghidorah on his way to refuel by eating the North Korean nuclear arsenal. Japan keeps the decimation and devastation hush hush out of shame and dishonor.

OBSERVATION 6: *My niece is suddenly pregnant.*

- **CONCLUSION A.** Her boyfriend's "spray and pray" birth control technique was an epic fail. Good job, Chad.
- **CONCLUSION B.** This is the second immaculate conception in known history. Except this time Chad is sterile, and the father is Satan. Their son, Damian, is due in six weeks, six hours, and six days.

OBSERVATION 7: *My car has a flat tire in the driveway Sunday morning.*

- **CONCLUSION A.** I ran over a nail when I drove home buzzed from the bar through the construction site, avoiding the police roadblock down the road.
- **CONCLUSION B.** My dickhead neighbor, Gary, stole my weed whacker. Honestly, I kinda forgot about it for three years, but then when I remembered, I asked Gary to give it back. He said I never gave it to him and told me to get off his property. But Gary didn't know I saw it in his wife's *she-shed* behind their house. So, I snuck

out Saturday night after avoiding the police roadblock and burned down her stupid *she-shed*. Gary definitely slashed my tires. I don't care, I win. Up yours, Gary.

OBSERVATION 8: *My man bits are bleeding. I'm scared.*

- **CONCLUSION A.** Need to work on my manscaping skills with either duller tools or a steadier hand. Maybe watch a little less *Sweeney Todd*. Painful date with a styptic pencil is next. Ruh roh. Does this need stitches?
- **CONCLUSION B.** I probably need to stop having sex with Contagion Chloe, the homeless lady who sleeps in a cardboard house under the overpass. I thought it was just kinky foreplay and smack talk when she said she was hiding a mousetrap in her lady clinic. Apparently not.

OBSERVATION 9: *I gained five pounds this week.*

- **CONCLUSION A.** Eating assuaged my corona anxiety while I sheltered in place from the plague. Don't judge me! It is important to feel assuaged. Some habits are hard to shake.
- **CONCLUSION B.** Hostile aliens bombard the earth with thousands of dense metallic asteroids seeking to create a *mass extinction event*. All these new asteroids increase the mass of the earth, thereby increasing its gravitational pull, thereby increasing my weight. Ha! Eat a dick, Susan. I told you I'm not getting fat. It's science. $W=m*g$

OBSERVATION 10: *Two trees fell in my yard on a windy Sunday night.*

- **CONCLUSION A.** The old, dry trees were easily felled by the powerful wind.
- **CONCLUSION B.** The loud windstorm gave me the proper sound cover to chop the trees down and then into smaller logs, perfect for burning with this dry summer heat. Slash my tires? Bite me, Gary. See what it's like to wake up to your house burning down around you.

See how easy it is to take something hard and make it easy in application?

Whether you ascribe to nominalism, realism, conceptualism, barbarism, Taoism, or cannibalism, you must still use your brain and arrive at decisions to exist in this life.

Arguing that nominalism ultimately has resulted in modern nihilism (see discussion on Nietzsche elsewhere herein) it is logical to conclude that life is without objective meaning, purpose, or intrinsic value. Given this existential quandary, who really gives a flipping flip about my musings? Kind of pointless. Class dismissed.

Back Toward Safety, Forward Toward Growth

"One can choose to go back toward safety or forward toward growth. Growth must be chosen again and again; fear must be overcome again and again." – Abraham Maslow

Abraham Maslow pioneered the field of humanistic psychology. He was also a famous University of Wisconsin-Madison Badger. Quick shout out: My youngest daughter graduated from UW-Madison in 2021. *On, Wisconsin!* #JumpAround

Best known for his Hierarchy of Needs, Maslow was also a fascinating character:

1. Oldest of seven children, as a child, Maslow was labeled "mentally unstable" by a psychologist. Perfect grounds for becoming a psychologist.
2. Anti-Semitic gangs in Brooklyn chased and threw rocks at Maslow after school. He was known as a loner. Explains a lot about his quotes on overcoming fear.
3. Poor grades and poor family steered Maslow to several colleges, finally landing an affordable, achievable degree in psychology at UW-Madison. Affordable is *not* a word I would use for UW-Madison these days.

4. Maslow married his first cousin, Bertha. His parents did not approve. Love is love, right? No matter how cringeworthy? They loved playing Twister, too.
5. While jogging in Menlo Park, Maslow died of a heart attack at 62 years of age. It's always the fit ones. Reinforces why I stay home, eat butter by the stick, and nap frequently. Chewing is exhausting enough.

Maslow's Hierarchy of Needs posits that once a person attains their physical and safety needs, they can continue to develop as a person to the ultimate level of achievement: self-actualization.

Let's focus on the Safety level in the pyramid, as this is what most deeply concerns so many people these days.

The base of the pyramid is physiological need. While sheltering in place during COVID lockdown, many people had these basic physical needs met. We drew breath if we were COVID-free. We had shelter, food, and water. We could take a shit when needed, although maybe we saw more of a splatter spectrum depending on anxiety levels. Sleep occurred, albeit in nightmarish fits and starts.

The second tier of the pyramid is Safety, encompassing security and protection. It focuses on people having order and control over their lives and environment. Societal structures like police, fire departments, health systems, et. al., must function reliably for individuals to feel safe. Family structures like insurance, property, health, and well-being of loved ones, et. al., must exist to ensure stability.

According to Maslow, we cannot advance to higher levels of personal progress without reasonably satisfying the core needs of this level. Holy shit. No wonder we are such a steaming pile of hot mess these days. When the actual frig is the last time you felt truly safe?

My job as writer, shaman, and healer is to help you develop coping strategies during times of anxiety and uncertainty. Detailed below are some ideas to help you feel safe and return to your path of enlightenment and self-actualization. You are most welcome.

1. **Safety Division Reunion.** My high school rock band: Safety Division. Talking about getting the band back together. Not to brag, but we were a big deal. Like, a really big deal. In our own minds. Jeff (vocal), Paul (guitar), Bill (keyboard), Chris (bass), and me (drums) laid down some of the best music the eighties had to offer. We covered Duran Duran, U2, John Waite, Journey, Springsteen, Ozzy, and so much more. Fans jammed into crowded high school gyms and run-down bars to witness our greatness. Girls swooned. Especially for me. Because we all know girls like to listen to the guitar, but they all want to feel a drummer's rhythm. Yeah, baby. We brought so much love and joy to our community. Imagine what we could have done for the world during lockdown! We would have been like a giant hug across the globe, spreading collective feelings of community, all done from our individual houses, over the internet. Yikes... that sounds very technical. And hard. Yeah, glad we skipped that. Damn! Being useless ruins everything.
2. **Global Safety Dance.** Think about it. Take the best band in the history of Canadian one-hit wonders, Men Without Hats. Next, take their epic 1983 hit *The Safety Dance*. Not the radio version, but instead the extended

play (EP) version. Their low-budget MTV video was the first time I ever knew that Little People terrified me (back then we could say "midget," but I have evolved). Actually, I have Tyrion Lannister to thank for overcoming that fear. Props, Peter Dinklage. You helped me through some rough times. Returning back to the topic at hand: "The Safety Dance." It was such a beautiful sign of solidarity during the COVID plague to see the images on the news of people around the world clapping as one for our healthcare heroes. Imagine instead if we all cranked "The Safety Dance" at the same time. First, we could have continued clapping, as there are some sick clap tracks in that song. Second, singing songs is so much more fun than clapping. Third, think of the choreography opportunities. You can envision social media blowing up with different countries developing their own steps and moves and grooves. Think of the unifying effect this would have had to help us feel safer, part of a more predictable global community at 7 p.m. local time each night. Amazing. Never happened.

3. **Family Horcruxes.** Okay, my fellow Harry Potter nerds, get stoked. I am finally incorporating a reference to the Potterverse. Know this: I have a future essay in development about Harry Potter characters that never made the final cut. Rowling's world-building extolled for all in search of a succulent reading treat. For those of you not dorky enough to know, a horcrux is "the word used for an object in which a person has concealed part of their soul." Very dark magic—a horcrux can only be created after committing murder, the ultimate act of

evil. So, we may need to think through that killing bit. But, if we can, imagine how safe you and your family would feel against future plagues? A family of five would simply need to commit five murders to ensure their survival. And not just for some short mortal life. For eternity! Even if coronavirus found its way into your life today with negative effects, you could not technically die! Think of the confidence that would create. Maslow Level 3? Yes, please.

4. **Universal Safety Word.** I think we can agree there are a lot of fake gods. My fake god is a dominatrix named Ingrid. She is truly a sadistic little strumpet. Ingrid gets off on putting humanity's nipples in clamps with wars, plagues, famine, and endless other forms of devastation and depravity. You know, the light stuff. COVID is her most recent masterpiece. But sadism binds her by universal rules. She must allow her masochist partners a safety word just in case shit gets too intense. What if we all agreed our universal safety word would be *Armageddon*? Just like the discussion in *Useless Pets*, where the gay couple used that as their safety word when gerbil felching ran amok. What if we all united and yelled *Armageddon!* Three times in succession (because three is always a magical number in fairy tales)? Ingrid would have realized we'd had enough, and life would have instantly turned back to normal. No more coronavirus, just some freaking sore nipples. Worth it.

5. **Safetynet.** *Author's note: This vital section was penned during COVID lockdown, but would it really be any different today?* Remember Skynet in *The Terminator*? Like that.

But different. Instead of an artificial superintelligence that becomes self-aware and nukes the earth to destroy humanity, Safetynet will execute its own Judgment Day . . . focused on *Covidiots*. Because Safetynet will be so wicked smart, it will know how to identify and eliminate these jackballs. C'mon. Don't be naïve. The government has chipped us since the 1950s and tracks all our movements anyway. Since liberty died seventy years ago, let's at least put our tax dollars to use. Safetynet can identify Covidiots in several ways. First, low IQ. Should be self-explanatory. Second, MAGA hat. Similar to low IQ, but more of an advertising thing. Third, self-centered douche. This is the biggest group: Social Darwinist Governors, zealous esurient preachers, beach-going Gen Zers. You get the gist. Safetynet could use the lasers in *Space Force* to precision target each Covidiot and zap them into oblivion. That feels unsatisfying to me. My preference would be to use the space force's tractor beams to pull each Covidiot into outer space to suffocate like the people they infected. Imagine your satisfaction when you see protesting Covidiots rising, body and soul, like the Rapture, into the sky! What fun. We could all do The Safety Dance each time it happens. The good news? Fake data analysis indicates that Safetynet needs to eliminate approximately 40 percent of the U.S. population to truly make us safe. In truth, it is only 15 percent. The other 25 percent are a bunch of pussies who follow the political pollen wherever the culture wind blows. We should be able to carefully reintegrate these lemmings into our new healthy, safe world. Feeling safer?

Think about it. You have a new favorite band committed to making the eighties cool again. You have a dance that arguably is the greatest form of art ever created. You have made use of Harry Potter in a far less dorky way than making normal people guess what in noncapitalized god's name a fucking Hufflepuff is. You have a blasé goddess turning her kinky predilections onto some other unfortunate cosmic creature's nipples. You have the ultimate Safetynet ready and available to deliciously eliminate the threats to your peaceful existence. And if any of these strategies work, we can all move along to Maslow's third tier of attainment: Love and Belonging.

Sheltering in place made us resent our families more than ever. We were on each other's last nerve living in such close quarters. Our social connections became almost completely digital. Even after this much time, not sure I ever want to shake someone's hand, let alone accept a hug from their germy carcasses.

Let's get safe first, and *stay there*. We have a lot of work to do to fix the third level. As said, I am a writer and a healer. For now, you're welcome. Resume your journey. Self-actualization awaits.

BRIDGE STREET RUN: A TRADITION OF OSWEGO DEBAUCHERY

Oswego, New York is a sparse city of around 20,000 people, nestled on a craggy stretch of shore along the southeast corner of Lake Ontario. The Oswego River bisects town, running south to north, rapidly rushing into Lake Ontario.

Bridge Street (NY Route 104) is the major thoroughfare in the area. A highway in bygone days, Route 104 connects Oswego to Niagara Falls, paralleling the southern shore of Lake Ontario across Western New York. The eponymous Bridge Street bridge is the primary connector between the west (college) side of Oswego and the east (townie) side. Standing over fifteen feet above the rocky, rushing Oswego River, the bridge spans nearly one hundred feet across.

History shows her age in this tired little town. Turn of the century buildings in varying states of blemished antiquity stand in sharp contrast to the intensely striking natural setting. Instead of a record player, Oswego is a gramophone. Loved with age and memory, but tinny and scratched.

The sunsets from the Oswego shoreline are breathtaking. Urban legend purports that *National Geographic* claimed that

Oswego had the second-best sunset in the world behind Hong Kong. I have not been able to find hard evidence to prove this claim. But evidence aside, stand along the lakeshore on a summer evening and watch crowds of people stand and clap like fans at a rock concert as the sun finishes her encore below the purple horizon. Breathtaking.

The lakeshore climate favors only the sturdiest folks. Its location primes the pump for Lake Effect snow each winter. It is not uncommon to see (what feels like) 15,000+ inches of snowfall in a single winter. And the winds! With no land barriers, Oswego experiences gale force winds on a regular basis. The local college, SUNY Oswego, strings thick ropes between buildings during the winter for support. It issues warnings regularly for small, petite people to not walk unaccompanied at the risk of being blown away like a human tumbleweed. Usually to their death.

The State University of New York (SUNY) is a mélange of 64 state-run college and university campuses. Middling academic rigor combined with affordable pricing makes the SUNY system a tremendous value for the 96,000+ students who graduate each year.

SUNY Oswego is where I finished my last five semesters of college. Attending the prestigious University of Rochester for my first three semesters, I had an academic scholarship for a Pre-Med track. I intended to change the medical world with my genius and charisma. In hindsight, I was arrogant and untested. I did not know myself. I was a god among a pantheon of rival gods – all as smart as me, and far more disciplined.

With that pressure, my educational priorities shifted like Donald Trump's opinion of injecting disinfectants to cure coronavirus. I discovered the pure hedonism of self-gratification. Not masturbation, you perv. My babysitter taught me that many years earlier.

This was pleasure-based distraction on a scale I could never have fathomed. Pledged Sigma Chi fraternity (donned Captain Piss Puck, president of the pledge class), played rugby, drank constantly, and smoked more weed than I care to admit. It was a contest to see how many girls I could hook up with in a month, let alone a semester. In short, I was a douche.

And my bong-hit-crisped brain could not keep up with the intensely competitive and uncompromising classes. Grades reflected it. Intelligence completely focused on the wrong things. I failed my white privilege and dropped nearly every science class until my academic scholarship disappeared. My dad's phone call still sticks with me today. "Military or SUNY, your choice." I considered the military for literally five seconds and knew immediately I was too much of a pussy. With that, I transferred to SUNY Oswego.

I transferred as an English major because my only A grade at University of Rochester was in an English Lit class. I also transferred to SUNY Oswego because one of my best friends from high school (and former Safety Division bandmate) attended there, loved it, and I could land with social connections from day one. Douchery still intact.

SUNY Oswego was a brief oasis in a desert of lifetime pressure to succeed. The English program was exactly what I needed to thrive academically. For the first time in a long time, I could feed my ego with nourishing accolades and honors in my coursework and writing.

My personal life was still an utter shit show of debauchery and substance abuse. Great example: at the beginning of each semester, we played a game I have since named "Forty Days in the Desert." Unlike Jesus's winsome ecclesiastical adventures, our exploits involved getting blown-out drunk every night for the first forty nights of each new semester. Then praying for death the following forty nights from how sick your body became while recovering.

Oh, the friends I made! Friends to this day, nearly thirty-five years later. I love them with all my soul. Most of us lived on the seventh floor of the same dormitory my first transferred year. What a cast of characters. Names of course changed to protect the guilty. Facts are mine to omit, edit, or fabricate as I see fit, so please no emails after the fact, Oz gang.

Here are a few samples:

- Trip captured a feral dog wandering campus and broke into the tyrannical Resident Assistant's room while she was at a weekend ROTC camp. The dog trashed the room and then mauled her upon return, giving her rabies. She transferred to another dorm.
- Buddha's room was famous for its nightly pregaming before heading to the bars. One Oswego claim to so-called fame is they have one of the highest per capita rates of bars to people in the United States. The Drooling Green Monster was a horrific shot mixed with varying available alcohols and enough Scope mint breath freshener to turn it green. Rancid.
- Our core girlfriends were the Booze Hags. Never has there been a more gloriously deviant and fun group of ladies. They were always up for an adventure and could outdrink and outlast the biggest, fattest alcoholics you can fathom. Several of them stood watch as my anus

overflowed with a bottle of yellow mustard while passed out. Worst yet, my visiting cousin was the culprit who turned my Hershey Highway into the Yellow Shit Street.
- "Frolicking" became a phrase our psycho crew coined for what happened upon returning from bars on the weekend. The elevator door would open, and there would be a pile of men and women (the "Freaks") in a heaving pile, beating the living shit out of each other. Punching, biting, hairpulling in some surreal hellscape of reckless abandon. And we loved it.

But the Bridge Street Run was the capstone of sin and depravity, essentially a bar-crawl along the two-mile length of Bridge Street. Starting on the East side (townie) bars, participants head west and need to drink a beer (or a shot) in every bar along the route back to the terminus at the SUNY Oswego campus. Or until you either barf, blackout, or both.

Props abound and vary. Depending on your group's "leader," which in and of itself is a joke, there may be plastic whistle used to rally your team when it is time to depart each saloon. This level of organization usually lasts for the first five or six bars until it all starts falling apart from rowdy drunkenness.

White t-shirts and Sharpie markers are a must because you need to get a signature from each tavern on your shirt to document every bar you visited along your sojourn. Souvenir shirts lined an entire drawer of my dresser at one point. Devastating to admit, but I think they were turned into dusting cloths at some point.

For most normal Oswego alumni, the Bridge Street Run recalls an annual celebration after Final Exams to mark the end of the academic year. By tradition, it usually occurs the first

Friday in May. For the Freaks? Not so. A typical semester would consist of three, maybe four, Bridge Street Runs. Yeah, I know. We had problems.

One BSR stands out above them all for me. It started like any other Run, except instead of twenty or more people, there were only eight of us. Our fatal error may have been breaking the rules at each of the first five bars by having a beer *and* a shot instead of the prescribed beer *or* a shot.

Already sloppy from the east side bars, the Bridge Street bridge loomed ahead of us like a talisman on our westward journey home. Father Joe ritualistically mumbled to himself as he walked next to me, eyes on the next three bars across the bridge, early evening lights twinkling along the river.

Father Joe was quite possibly the stealth king of The Freaks. Sober, when he spoke, his soft voice teetered on the edge of inaudible. Quiet and unassuming, Father Joe was like a shadow with mass. You always felt him nearby, but his thoughts were imperceptible. Father Joe loved drugs. The more the better. At a Grateful Dead concert, the police hogtied him naked to a plank of wood for hours after the cops rode him down on horseback while tripping on acid . . . after streaking naked through the parking lot.

The Father Joe nickname stuck after a Halloween where he dressed like a barefoot priest, took three hits of acid, and disappeared. We received a call at 3am from the Oswego police that they had arrested Father Joe for home invasion.

Allegedly, this barefoot priest walked into a local family's home after kicking in the front door, yelling "Trick or Treat!" The dad hit him in the head with the butt of his shotgun as Father Joe walked up their staircase toward their bedrooms. He tumbled backward down the stairs, laid on the floor for a few moments, then (in the dad's own words), "sat up like Michael Myers in *Halloween* and started back up the stairs." The second blow from the shotgun knocked Father Joe out cold until the po-po came. Thankfully, the family did not press charges. The dad was an Oswego alum and understood the concept of Freakdom.

On this dreary spring twilight of the Bridge Street Run, Father Joe ambled next to me in stewed silence as we approached the bridge. I would now pay anything to know what was going through his elusive mind at that exact moment. Father Joe placed his pink plastic whistle in his mouth and winked at me. Blowing it loudly, he broke into a full sprint toward the bridge, screaming, "Charge!"

As he separated further from our group, we stopped to watch what happened next. Just before the bridge, a small abandoned tire store with a large display window and a few tires still on display beckoned. Father Joe lurched low to the ground, scooping a large rock without breaking his stride. He launched the rock at the display window, shattering it into a thousand shards.

But that was not the end of his athleticism. Father Joe grabbed a tire and ran to the middle of the Bridge Street bridge. He tossed the tire over the railing into the bloated, roiling Oswego River fifteen feet below. In a single deft motion, he then launched himself over the edge.

Holy shit! The seven of us, sobering quickly, sprinted toward the center of the bridge. As we looked over the edge, we could see Father Joe sitting in the tire, giving us the finger as the raging current rushed him toward Lake Ontario. "Hasta la vista, assholes!" These, the last words we heard from Father Joe that night echoed as he howled like a wolf in the fading distance. Waterlogged and exhausted, Grifter Grady fished Father Joe from the shoreline the next day. This act of kindness was ironic, given that Grady killed his mother a few years after college and drove around in her stolen car with her dead body in the trunk until the police caught up with him. I wish that story weren't true.

I had some of the best days of my life at SUNY Oswego and maintain dear friendships to this day. Those memories are still so vivid, emblazoned in my memory like a Lake Ontario sunset.

Oswego needed to end for me. That level of excess and insanity combined with that level of frequency was a path trodden with great peril if I had continued. And the Bridge Street Run was the apex of all that unmitigated chaos.

My wife and I started dating in my last semester at Oswego. Our story and adventure began at that time. We have had our fair share of crazy moments that may certainly fuel some future brilliant compositions. Until then, my dear invisible friends, please hug your friends and family tight. And thank god every day I survived the Bridge Street Run. Otherwise, how could you have ever known about it?

WEIGHT A MOMENT. AM I DYING?

The food industry plays us for suckers and fools every day. Or so we tell ourselves. The funniest, most ironic part of that statement is that we blame them because we are *fat*. Ha! Did they force that extra Big Mac down your gullet? Did they coach you into that marathon sitting position for gaming 24/7 while you guzzle a 20-Liter Mountain Dew? The simple answer is NO.

We blissfully traipse through the mall of life, sucking down sugary frappa-fatty-fat-fats and greasy filet-o-fat-fucks in all their processed glory. We allow commercialism, consumerism, and convenience to drive our behaviors, tottering through the maze of life like the brainwashed, voracious lemmings we have become. In short, we make choices. And all choices have consequences.

Anyone with common sense knows that, at its most simple form, weight loss is a function of calories in and calories out. 3500 calories of input or output results in a gain or a loss of one pound of fat. It's science. Distilled into a tasty soundbite we can all digest: *Move more. Eat less.* So, Slim, what is your excuse for dying quicker each day, consuming the wrong things, and not moving?

As a fellow Chubs, I have known for a long time I need to drop 25-30 pounds. In particular, as I have gotten older, I have gotten sicker because of it. As discussed in my prior hit essay, *What Doesn't Kill You Gives You Colitis*, my ulcerative colitis flares far more regularly.

Excess weight does not help with inflammation. I have developed Type 2 diabetes, after a long runway as a plus-size model, knowing I had pre-diabetes and not doing anything truly meaningful to reverse it. Weight loss might have been my one shot.

So, of course, now it is deadly serious for me. I eat a little better, drink somewhat less, exercise a ton more. Amazing how fear of death can focus your thoughts and sculpt your actions (along with your abs). I literally have zero interest in learning through experience if there is a god or not.

I am but a doughy little grain of sand in a desert of fat people. What the living hell is wrong with us? I have a very fit wife and a lot of fit friends. Why do I not model their behaviors? Why do I continue down this icy mountainside of doom on freshly waxed pepperoni skis?

For me, it took the real consequence of "hitting bottom" to learn I am not invincible. The accompanying apathy truly did not help. Mix that altogether with a heaping teaspoon of anxiety and fear of death, and life seems a hell of a lot shorter and more precious these last few months.

What is your excuse? Here are some thoughts that might help you take that hard look in the mirror and commit to affecting some change in your life before you die.

- **You are ignorant.** There must be some portion of the population out there that has not been exposed to basic health concepts. Right? They can't help it; they just don't know! You know the person – no internet, no TV, no public-school education, no fat role models in their family to be disgusted by. I call bullshit. The real reasons are below.

- **You are stupid.** "The math is too hard," he whined. Shut up. Christ. Buy a calculator, mathlete. Even if not customized to you, your body, or your metabolism, the average male requires approximately 2,500 calories of input per day to maintain weight. The average female requires approximately 2,000 calories per day to maintain weight. If you decrease calorie intake by 500 calories per day, then you will lose 3,500 calories per week, or 1 pound of fat. That's 50 pounds per year! But this requires counting the calories for every electron of Dorito dust you huff down your gullet. What about output? If you just went for a walk for an hour each day, that could burn 250-500 calories. Another 25-50 pounds lost per year! Maybe more if you are extra porky. If your time in grandma's basement has made you averse to sunlight and fresh air, just march in place in front of your video games. Either way, there are dozens of apps out there that do all the counting for you. Continue being dumb; give Technology the wheel.
- **You are disorganized.** Time management is the most teachable skill in the world. But it requires you to stick with it like the Cinnabon frosting on your chubby, glistening fingers. If you lack the basic discipline to keep to a schedule, I would love to see how your checking account looks! "Where did my money go for rent?" he whined to his mommy. Safe bet: the Taco Bell drive thru. Planning meals takes some forethought, for sure. Before

you disappear into grandma's dark basement to flog the bishop for eight consecutive hours, start your day with a quick journaling of your planned meals and mealtimes for the day. Keep it around 2,000 calories. Bonus for you! There must be some sort of calorie deficit created by such egregious chicken choking. And please stay hydrated!

- **You are apathetic.** Zig Ziglar taught, "It is your attitude, more than your aptitude, that will determine your altitude." So now you are fat, waving your hands in the air like you just don't care, drowning below a waterline of apathy. Your altitude is below sea level, Amelia Earhart. And even all your newfound blubber will not keep you afloat for long. Here is a thought to wake you up and perhaps motivate your callous ass – Death is nigh. You heard me. Death is coming for you in the form of Karma. Throw your douchey blasé attitude into the Universe, and Karma will deliver you an eighty-liter Coke enema. The worst part is She is patient and sadistic. There are millions of disenchanted dickheads out there just like you, and She can reckon with you whenever your turn comes. And when it does, I promise, you will suddenly care. A lot.

- **You are invincible.** The curse of the young—their naïve perception of invincibility. This was me. Bad things only happen to other people because I am . . . me! I am a unique individual adrift in a universe of shit, but because of my sheer me-ness, no harm can befall me. Why worry about the future when everything is so awesome in my life today? And if there is a problem, if I get fat, I can fix it. I will have time. Ask Ozymandias where that level of hubris got him. One certainty I have as I continue along the denouement of my own life: we are all born dying. We were endowed with the free will to make choices that will impact the rate of that celestial discharge, but die we shall. And the more I shower that free will with arrogance, pride, and delusion, the bigger the flood I need to navigate. Consider me your own personal Noah. Not much room left in the ark.

- **You are impatient.** Weight loss takes time. Sorry to burst your bubble, Bubble Butt. You have spent a lifetime reaching a 45 BMI and morbid obesity. If you have 80 pounds to lose, it may take a year or two to get there. We all need a little patience, sayeth Axl Rose. Our world surrounds us with false promises and magic pills. Internet hucksters sidle up in their digital chuckwagons, peddling their Pirelli's miracle elixirs (shout out to Sondheim). We consume and consume ad nauseum, repeating the same failing behavior, expecting a quick fix and a different outcome when there never has been one. When Jesus resurrected his bunny, Reg (as told in the gnostic *Gospel of Reg*), that was a real miracle. They're rare. Time to roll up your sleeves and get to work, Mr. Creosote (shoutout to Monty Python). Practice the line, "No. Fuck off, I'm full."

- **You are lazy.** My wife and I had a custom-made sectional sofa delivered to the house right before the Plague descended like an unwanted third testicle. A gift to ourselves as Empty Nesters. Something decadent and sexy. And comfortable? Oh, my word. This couch absorbs your fat ass in a cloud of cooling yet supportive leather, whispering her siren's song of *stay with me forever* in your ear as you fade in and out of a take-out food coma, sometimes called a nap, while Anderson Cooper's sexy dulcet tones lull you into further submission with stories of the End of Days. If you could shit in a dirty pail nearby, this might possibly be heaven. Yeah. That kind of lazy. Our creature comforts and animal pleasures trump the harder things in life – like niçoise salads or jumping jacks. As Robert Heinlein said, "Progress isn't made by early risers. It's made by lazy men trying to find easier ways to do something." Well, that's just asinine. And I love Heinlein. But flip that statement around, and you're beginning to get at the essence of the truth. Life is hard work, effort, and challenge. If you are sick and tired of being the laughingstock of Fatsville, it's time to get off that leather sectional.

For me, this whole conversation is deeply personal. I figure, best case, I have another thirty years orbiting the sun if I get my shit together and drop some weight. But as it stands, I want at least sixty more.

One of the myriad reasons I write is to leave a part of me behind. Something that recalls me and reminds the world this pudgy yet funny bastard existed, albeit a smidge pudgier than desired. My writing is like a murder-free horcrux immortalizing a piece of my soul.

Closing thought, my little pandas: use Occam's Razor. The simplest solution is the correct solution when presented with comparable facts. If you are fat, you will die early. Losing weight could help prevent that from occurring. William of Ockham just did a medieval cartwheel.

Just drop the bullshit excuses and watch all that excess weight drop off you! In the immortal words of White Goodman in the vastly underrated movie, *Dodgeball: A True Underdog Story*:

"Ugliness and fatness are genetic disorders, much like baldness or necrophilia, and it's only your fault if you don't hate yourself enough to do something about it."

Colonoscopies: Show Your Inner Beauty

"We all poop. Don't be such a damn baby." – Plato

"Let's talk about poop, ba-by." – Salt-N-Pepa

"Howdy ho!" – Mr. Hanky, the Christmas Poo (love you, *South Park*)

Now that elective medical (maybe medieval) procedures have been fully resurrected from their death during COVID lockdown, it is time for me (for us all) to think about a colonoscopy.

As you may recall from my clinical and philosophical masterpiece, "What Doesn't Kill You Gives You Colitis," living with ulcerative colitis sort of makes me a colonoscopy pro.

Like any professional athlete, your full preparation is essential to continued success. Rest his soul, but Kobe Bryant exemplified that blue-collar work ethic of practice makes perfect, too. Speaking of clichés, ignorance is not bliss. Colonoscopies play a vital role in the detection and prevention of colorectal cancer. It is better to be safe than sorry. If the attitude you bring to the table is not positive, how can you expect to not be left down in the "dumps"?

Knowledge is power! Let's take a few moments and define some key terminology so you can best rationalize this indispensable event.

1. **Colon** (a.k.a. large intestine) – last five feet of intestine before your butt hole. After your small intestine has absorbed all the nutrients, the colon dries and processes the remaining waste until you're ready to poop it out. This is where the cancer hides.
2. **Colonoscope** – the tube and camera that your gastroenterologist inserts in your butt hole and inflates with air to create space for the five-foot, cinematic journey of insertion up your colon. Remember: that air has nowhere to go but out when you recover in post-op.
3. **Colonoscopy** – the procedure of inserting the colonoscope up the length of the colon, looking for cancer and polyps, taking biopsies along the way. Your doc may have pics available for sale in the lobby after the procedure.

Just to keep it real . . . colorectal cancer is the second leading cause of cancer deaths in the United States. 140,000 new cases are diagnosed every year with 50,000 estimated deaths. According to medical research, at least 30,000 lives each year can be saved through awareness and screening. Shit just got real. (*I couldn't resist*)

Now that you understand what a colonoscopy is and how you could die without it, let's have some fun and make lemons out of lemonade.

Top 7 Tips for Colonoscopy Preparation

I would be remiss if I failed to address the joys of colonoscopy prep. Your life-affirming colonoscopy could never be so enjoyable without putting in some work in the day(s) leading up to it.

But I want you to really dig deep and focus on the psychological and spiritual benefits of this unique process. As you suffer, even as you persevere, you will emerge stronger. You may even see the face of god and hear her shimmering countenance say, "You are my beloved and most wondrous creation."

I hope these prep tips from a colonoscopy pro help you (and your colon) thrive.

1. **Anal bleaching.** While optional, this is the truest of clinical courtesies. No muss, no fuss. Fill in the blank: "If eyes are the window to the soul, then the anus is the _____."
2. **Forget 24-hour fasts.** Perform minimally 240 hours (yes, 10 days) of "spiritual fasting." Hold the pink rabbit's hand when the hallucinations kick in. Think of Jesus's bunny, Reg. He is your spirit guide. And so is Grace Slick in her immortal song, "Remember what the dormouse said / Feed your head."
3. **Practice proper toilet etiquette.** Respect the 3 Ss ... **sound, stink,** and **splatter** ... they should all be controlled and/or confined with the proper requisite level of shame. Bowel prep is disgusting and therefore you are disgusting whilst participating. Internalize that mantra as your insides spill out.
4. **Deal with the discomfort.** This process is your cross to bear. Act like Jesus and shoulder that burden. Don't whine. Keep moving up that hill. When you are feeling selfish, ask yourself, "What would Jesus do?"
5. **This next tip is in the same vein as Tip 4.** "Do unto others" .... If you don't like being abused by a grumpy dick, don't be one. Stand strong. Hide your feelings.

Create visual images of Jesus slapping a leper or telling Lazarus to get back in his cave.
6. **Judiciously use flushable wet wipes**. God's gift to clean. Plus, they can really make that bleached anus shine! And they might be good for the environment, too.
7. **But the crown jewel of bowel prep** is to enjoy that short term weight loss! All that misery and mess are psychologically flushed away when you drop thirteen pounds of pent-up turd weight.

Top 7 Tips for the Colonoscopy Itself

Uncle Jimmy was one of my older coworkers. He was a legend in the world of medical sales. He looked like your favorite white-haired uncle, and thus, the nickname was born.

I thought I would share some pearls that I had shared with Uncle Jimmy's wife, Karen, a few years ago so she could truly optimize her first-time colonoscopy and dig deep into the world of medical buggery.

These procedural tips should be taken seriously, as they will truly enhance the overall adventure.

1. Make sure they use no anesthesia.
2. Tell the anesthesiologist you want to be keenly aware to ensure vivid memories of the event.
3. Also tell the anesthesiologist you want them to firmly hold your hand and maintain intense eye contact throughout the event.
4. Tell the OR nurse to hold your hips and whisper your name in an assuaging ritualistic chant throughout. Focus on being assuaged.

5. Upon insertion, ensure the gastroenterologist keeps repeating, "That's my girl. What a champ." A tousle of your hair means they are super proud of you. Bonus.
6. Safety words are optional and, candidly, frowned upon. If you must acquiesce, some popular choices are "Armageddon"! or "Moo!" Oinking like a piglet is taking things way too far. Control yourself, you naughty little heathen. No one likes a Furry.
7. As with any good record album, you should always buy the EP version, if available. Like the secret menu at In-N-Out Burger, this is a little-known treat with colonoscopies. You will never forget the event if they can prolong the procedure as long as possible.

Your adventure is almost complete. I have detailed the quasi-religious experience to optimize your prep and pre-op knowledge. You understand expected conduct, protocol, and proper behavior during the procedure. But what about post-op and recovery?

Alas, there are not many words of wisdom to impart. Recovery is simple: fart. While post-op can sound a lot like the baked beans campfire scene in the Mel Brooks' classic movie, *Blazing Saddles*, don't be dismayed. Join in! The louder and prouder you can let 'em rip, the faster the nurses will let you go home to feed your starving body. It is their clarion call.

Grandma Healy's Hooley

My family is an exquisite and complex Irish American amalgam.

A Conway dad married a Healy mom. Both sides of the family date back to the Eire motherland, with Gaelic surnames like Callahan, Maroney, Barry, Clark, Waters, Burns, and Silverstein salting our genetic potatoes.

But the Healy side takes the cake (or soda bread, if you will). My mom is the thirteenth of thirteen children. I have dozens upon dozens of cousins and second cousins. Alcoholism runs rampant through both sides of the family like a pestilence. Every page of history you turn seems to reveal a new scandal or controversy or tragedy. I have a ferocious love for and loyalty to the Healy clan. Spoilt cabbage and all.

The family hub rested in The North Country of Upstate New York, an hour west of the Adirondacks, in the small village of Carthage. Carthage is a declining paper mill town along the Black River, rapid waters bisecting the town into Carthage and West Carthage. As with so many North Country towns, Carthage endures, careworn and age-worn like the rocky hills and bucolic countryside that encase it.

The family hub "rested?" What about "rests?" Great question (you were certain to ask).

My Uncle Deak (short for The Deacon) lost the family home for not paying taxes, squandering the money instead on a gambling addiction after my Grandma Healy died. My father and godfather tried to keep the house by giving Deak the money for taxes, which he in turn also used for gambling. This created a permanent, irreparable rift in family relations. The house was one of the many victims of addiction.

Built in the mid-1800s on a military plot of land originally owned by the Marquis de Lafayette, the Healy family home was a traditional house for its time. Originating in County Cork, Ireland, the wealthy Clark family first emigrated 'sud' to The North Country after landing in Canada. Settling in Carthage, they constructed this two-story home with a wide wrap-around porch that greeted you with a weathered but loving smile when you arrived.

The home passed down through several generations of Clarks. As their wealth dwindled over time, the old house continued to wane into infirmity along with the family. A fierce pride of their Lace Curtain Irish heritage stood at odds with the steady decline in affluence and social standing. The house held ghosts and memories of better days. It creaked and groaned, feeling its age. By the time my mom was born, the house was divided into front and back.

In the back, lived Hattie and Maggie Clark, my Grandpa Healy's spinster aunts. The aunts protected and coddled him like a fop. He lived in the back of the house with them. For reasons still unclear, the crones limited and tightly regulated his interactions with his wife and children in an assumed effort to maintain some connection to the Clark family reputation and legacy.

The front of the house was occupied by my Grandma Healy, and in varying cycles, thirteen children. The space was entirely too small for so many residents. A single bathroom with a clawfoot tub and a pedestal sink sustained the hygiene of everyone. Grandma was constantly busying herself with the upkeep of her children and the home. She tended the coal furnace in the basement several times daily. She was meticulous and did her best to stay the relentless decline of time and money. All were slowly slipping away.

So, given these physical, social, and psychological barriers, how did my grandparents have so many children? Turns out, they would sneak away and meet for romantic trysts in the third-floor attic. Et voilà! In the grandest of Irish genetic traditions, a never-ending assembly line of children.

When Maggie died, she deeded the home to Hattie. Hattie died with no will, throwing the estate into chaos, with her nieces and nephews clamoring for a piece of any remaining affluence. Think of the Sacksville-Baggins raiding of Bag End when Bilbo departs for his adventures in *The Hobbit*. Like that, only greedier. In the end, the house and assets went equally to all the nieces and nephews until they died off, Grandma Healy the ultimate benefactor.

Grandpa Healy died soon after Maggie and Hattie. Uncle Deak was the oldest male and a supervisor at the local paper mill. He lived at home, a bachelor his entire life. As the other kids moved on with their lives and families, Grandma and Uncle Deak continued with their unadorned, simple lives, along with the spirits of the home. For all his vices, The Deacon cared for Grandma, the best he could do, until she died.

As I grew up, Grandma Healy was the matriarch of the Healy brood. A petite wisp of a lady, she weighed maybe ninety pounds. A sweet little bird, she gave the best hugs. Her loving talons would grab you and pull you in tight. You could feel her false teeth shift as she squeezed tight and pecked a trembling kiss on your forehead. When she released you from her love vice, you simply craved more.

But Grandma was always busy puttering around, doing something. Cooking bacon in an ancient cast iron skillet, stoking the coal furnace, running errands (she walked everywhere), hanging the clothes on the line to dry in the backyard in the summer. Everything smelled like sunshine and fresh air in her house.

In the harsh, snowy North Country winters, she would hang the wash (she would say warsh, so cute!) in the third-story attic where she and Grandpa had rendezvoused so many years before. Talking to the ghosts, you could hear her clear as day carrying on one-sided conversations with Grandpa or Hattie. We guessed likely not Maggie since she had been deaf in life. Never sure if heaven relieved Maggie of that burden or just used divine sign language.

I always imagined that was how my mom and her siblings felt about their mother: a deep abiding love and respect, but at a distance. Not because grandma was consciously dismissive. She was just so damned busy all the time. Managing thirteen kids and a husband with aunts who never allowed her the space or time to connect for too long with any one person. The impact was a loved but lonely feeling, wishing she could give you a smidge more, maybe one more amazing hug.

Although living very modestly, Grandma Healy always had a never-ending supply of quarters for us as kids. She would take you to a little coat nook under the front stairs, where her purse hung. So adorable, she would hold her little finger to her mouth and whisper *shh shh shh* as she furtively found her hasped coin purse and bestowed a secret gift of silver unto you. Oh, the candy cigarettes we would buy with those coins!

Grandma loved the New York Yankees. She would sit in an upstairs front bedroom, dark room dimly lit by the yellow streetlights below, cold Budweiser in-hand, listening to her radio, nodding in and out of sleep. I would peek around the corner of the doorway and watch her, thinking how much she had earned this simple pleasure in her life. A moment of rest in a life full of frenetic motion.

Her big treat when we would visit was to have dinner at the West Carthage McDonalds. Every time, she would order a hamburger, small fries, and a coffee. Like the little bird she was, grandma would luxuriate in her meal, savoring slowly, never finishing even half the burger. No wonder she was so little! But such seemingly small gestures provided her with such deep contentment. Another sigh in a long life of short breaths.

Grandma eventually died of natural causes a few days before her 89th birthday.

The family converged on Carthage for her Catholic wake and funeral to pay their respects. For those unfamiliar, Catholic funeral rites include three parts: the wake, funeral Mass, and committal (burial). Since the wake—also called a vigil or a viewing—is the first of these rites, it's also the first opportunity to offer prayers for the deceased the day before the funeral.

For our purposes, let's add one part: the Irish hooley, in between the wake and the funeral Mass. Bundy's funeral home did their best to make grandma look presentable at the wake.

I have always felt uncomfortable viewing the dead in an open casket. We lie to ourselves to say how good they look. But they don't. They look dead. I guess it gives some people more closure to see for themselves that the person is, in fact, dead. Not sure why a death certificate from the funeral home cannot suffice.

Grandma's wake lasted several hours, and hundreds of people came to pay their respects. At least half of them were the extended Healy clan. With absolute impiety, after paying our requisite respects to our dearly departed grandmother, the cousins spent the next few hours scheming, planning, and hyping up the party we would have that night to celebrate grandma: the hooley.

By definition, a hooley is "a lively party." But it's so much more than that. It is storytelling, singing, music, dancing, and some mighty craic, enveloped in alcohol consumption at such a level it reinforces the Irish stereotype of overindulgence, burning itself into the annals of folklore and legend. And that night was legendary.

Van Halen came to Carthage that night. Figuratively. No chance Eddie would ever come to a backwater town like Carthage. And not the syrupy Van Hagar version either. Oh hell no. We are talking about the kind of crazy that only a drugged-out, nutty David Lee Roth version of Van Halen could bring, with all the destruction and ruination implied.

The evening began at a local pub. Packed with Healys and assorted other family surnames, the music blared with tin whistles and banjos. The exuberant energy pulsed rhythmically after spending so much time with so much solemnity all day at the wake. We laughed and told stories. We drank shots along with our pints. And more shots. And still more shots.

Then someone pulled out their penis and showed it to the bartender. Neither impressed nor happy with the direction of our inebriation, the bartender bounced us all from the bar.

Someone yelled *"AFTERHOURS!!"* and dozens of us headed backwoods to the Pineview Motel, a rat-hole dive that should have paid you to stay there. Total rundown dump, now out of business, ideally demolished. A few of my cousins and I stopped to get some beers for the afterparty. By the time we arrived, all hell had broken loose.

As we entered one of the two adjoining rooms, my aunts were all sitting on a bed, throwing bottles of empty beer against the walls, shattered glass everywhere. Laughing wildly every time a new explosion cut through the noise of the bedside clock radio blaring ... something. Had to be Van Halen. Only makes sense. *"Running with the Devil"* feels apropos.

What followed was the single greatest party I have ever attended, even after surviving the Bridge Street Run at SUNY Oswego. The night resulted in thousands of dollars in damage that, once again, my dad and godfather paid for. But it was so worth it.

Still a blur, I can only provide a highlight reel of events. Some version of 3am Conway vs. Healy basketball (yes, the Pineview actually had a court in the parking lot out back), so drunk it devolved into some bastard pugilistic hybrid version with punching, kicking, name calling, dirt throwing, and biting. No one left the court without a little blood drawn.

Inside the motel, the rooms were in utter devastation. Debris was everywhere. The bathrooms were unusable from all the vomit and flooded water. A cousin lay passed out in a dirty puddle, blood flowing out of his nose from the beating he earned on the ball court. I pulled him by the hair out of the water so he would not drown. He smiled and hugged my calf. Carpet was smoldering by the back door.

I stepped out for air and ran across my dad smoking a fat doobie. In a brain-damaged, primal father/son bonding moment, we shared some Mother Nature as the birds began to greet the earliest dawn with songs of glory to the revelry and debauchery they witnessed that evening. I wish I spoke bird to hear their recounting. But I was too high.

As an exclamation point, my naked brother pedaled feverishly around us on a stolen Big Wheel, laughing insanely.

The next morning, we woke up like rock stars for the funeral Mass. My cousins and I spent the thirty minutes before Mass puking up our sins behind the church, forming a small river of peccancy that drained down the hill toward the gutter. But we posted. Proud pallbearers for grandma's casket, we did our duty with split lips bleeding, black eyes forming, scraped heads banging with vicious hangovers.

Grandma Healy would have utterly loathed how we celebrated. She had experienced more alcohol abuse in her years than most people could in several lifetimes. But she would have loved knowing her family was together, united in love for her, celebrating her life (albeit too raucously) and honoring the importance of family.

After the Mass, as we headed to the cemetery, one cousin looked at me and said, "Cathargo delenda est." *Carthage must be destroyed.* Marcus Cato spoke these famous words to the Roman Senate at the conclusion of every speech prior to the Third Punic War with Carthage, Rome's great adversary. We should have made t-shirts.

Dark Shorts 3: Rosebud

Freddy had a gender-fluid fruit fetish. Freddy was not fussy. On certain days, a buxom blonde banana or a plump perse eggplant sent him into pure ecstasy. On other days, a pudenda pink papaya or pap smear puce pomegranate scratched his prickling perversions. But nothing, not even a succulent ass-shaped squash, came close to his infatuation with mangoes. Freddy would spend hours in the produce section of his grocery store. Damp hand gliding gently along every piece of produce, delicate fingers exploring nooks and crannies, sketchy smile spreading over his face. Thank god no store allows black lights on their produce. Freddy was not a handwasher. One of his many pervy proclivities. Above all other fruits, Freddy loved mangoes. And while all mangoes were a guaranteed trip to Bonerville, nippled mangoes took the grand prize. These unicorns of fruit sported a natural deformity, an additional hard protrusion on the tip of the mammary-like mango. Freddy would whisper *mango, mango, mango* to himself, just loud enough for children to hear, and rub the mango hither and thither across his face. One Sunday, a protrusion burst open, and a poisonous tropical spider emerged, biting Freddy's face. As the neurotoxin took hold, Freddy folded fluidly to the floor of the store, neck craning toward the mango display, his last whispered word: *Rosebud*.

Are You There, God? It's Me, PS.

Judy Blume's timeless codex, *Are You There, God? It's Me, Margaret*, was a groundbreaking Young Adult novel when it released in 1970. Among the first books of its genre to address major adolescent themes, *AYTGIMM* wrestled directly with the truth that I have discussed for years: kids are evil little shits.

While dealing with smaller pubescent derivatives like crushes and conformity, Blume's novel also dealt with some taboo themes rarely (if ever) tackled in the YA genre of a half century ago: menstruation, teen sexual feelings, religion. *The horror! The horror!*

Margaret grapples with so many teen rites of passage: first kisses, teen cruelty, acceptance, trust, friendships. She talks to god about anything. The intransigent, prejudiced behavior of adults, especially her estranged grandparents who disapprove of Margaret's parents' interfaith marriage, triggers her appalled but brief hiatus from god. Coming-of-age at the end, Margaret ceases to wish she were someone else and learns to be satisfied in her own skin. Starting her period, she is a little wiser to the ways of the world and reestablishes her conversations with god.

Universally celebrated in the world of literature for its derring-do and candor, *Are You There, God?* captured numerous awards over the years.

- 1970 – *New York Times* Outstanding Book of the Year
- 2005 – *Time* Magazine's All-Time 100 Novels
- 2011 – *Time* Magazine's Top 100 fiction books written in English since 1923

Not without controversy, this book frequents the American Library Association's Top 100 banned books due to its frank sexual discussions and purported anti-Christian ideas. Heck, abstinence groups have had an existential hard-on for Blume's wherewithal to address teen life as it is: masturbation, loss of virginity, and all. In fact, four of her other books have made the ALA naughty list as well.

Unless you think this intrusion on intellectual freedom is a byproduct of fifty years ago, welcome to the "woke" world of censorship in which we reside. Alive and well in all its tyranny.

With post-truth populism trends taking hold during the pandemic, people were now joining tribes based on doctrinal beliefs. It was not merely political; it was also religious. You could not simply believe in god. You must believe in my god, the way I interpret god, and the form and fashion I deem necessary to attend to the tenets of that belief. Anything different was wrong and open for judgment.

For some zealots, violence is somehow not acceptable in YA literature. Are you freaking kidding me? Our 21st century world guzzles graphically violent images on the internet, in video games, in the movies, on the news, and in television shows like they are super-sized blood Slurpies. In truth, there is nothing new at all with these mediums. Recall Elmer Fudd shooting Daffy Duck point-blank in the face. Hysterical! What is new, however, is how glorified the visual violence can be. I have yet to find a YA novel that celebrates and encourages violence.

If anything, it is a means to an end or a cautionary tale of what not to do.

These tribes coalesce around facts distorted to match their opinions about literature. Somehow, if you read about LGBTQ life as a teen or you support queer lifestyles, you may turn out gay. Probably a pedophile, too. There is so much wrong with that sentence, so much ignorance and hatred. As older generations continue to die out, I pray their ignorant, racist, homophobic thinking dies with them. Any redneck remnants can get sucked into space by Trump's Space Force SafetyNet tractor beam to suffocate and die along with all the other Covidiots, all of whom are likely kinfolk or fellow Klansmen.

I know I have personally had to contend with censorship impacting my own daughters and some of their favorite books. Their ravenous little minds gobbled up YA books as soon as they hit the bookstore shelves, especially the world-building fantasies of Rowling, Pullman, Meyer, and Collins.

But confusion prevailed with the barrage of adults telling them how books would change them – make them gay, make them witches, make them atheists, make them violent. They just wanted to read, likely in part to escape from the idiot adults scaring and judging them.

I often would buy an extra copy of their beloved childhood books to read along with them so we could discuss together. Incredible bonding experience aside, my feeling was that if they heard from me that it was okay to ignore the outside morality interlopers, they could truly consume the literature for pure enjoyment. If they had questions, challenges, or concerns, we talked about them. Most importantly, they could express their curiosity, thoughts, feelings, and opinions before others told them what to think or how to feel.

So, upon further inquiry with my now adult daughters–none of whom, by the way, have joined the Church of Satan after stuffing their heads with such sinful material–I have comprised a list of their favorite YA books or series. For each, I will explain the common complaint by the would-be censors and purity police. Then, I will provide commentary as to how I would modify some key plot points to really give those fanatical jack-wagons something to freak out about.

His Dark Materials series (Philip Pullman, 1995-2000)

- Complaint: anti-Christian institutions
- Commentary: Turns out, god is not dead. God is gay. She was on vacation in Boca. But she is back, and she is out of the closet, bitch. Big time. Her first order of business is to convert any straight people remaining in the Magisterium, few though they may be. Second edict is to stuff everyone's daemon back inside the body where it belongs. That was a big kerfuffle during Creation. Third is to change all "dust" to "glitter" and sprinkle it across all dimensions. Everyone deserves *total consciousness*, and not only *on their deathbed*, Carl Spackler.

Harry Potter series (J.K. Rowling, 1997-2007)

- Complaint: magic, witchcraft, spells, violence
- Commentary: Voldemort convinces Harry to become a Death Eater, and together they imprison all Gryffindors in Azkaban for agonizing torture, forcing them to breed with magical creatures and get sucked off by Dementors. Ravenclaws and Hufflepuffs are left to their own devices because no one ever cared for them anyway. After that,

the evil Dynamic Duo actuate the genocide of all Muggles and Mudbloods. Like the Wonder Twins, they activate this extinction event with combined superpowers and a mighty killing spell (*Avada Kedavra!*). Sorry, Hermione, but this new world order has a certain look and feel. You're out.

Twilight series (Stephenie Meyer, 2005-2009)
- Complaint: sexuality, occult material
- Commentary: Remastered by Stephen King who once claimed that Stephenie (pretentious artsy spelling) Meyer "can't write worth a darn. She's not very good." As we all know, King can rest on his vaunted Nobel laureates to critique others so publicly lest we forget such masterpieces as *Rose Madder* and *The Tommyknockers*. This Twilight reboot takes place near a creepy *sematary* in gloomy Washington state. Cokehead vampire Eddie Van Cullen regularly beats the shit out of his goth wife Bellatrix Cygnenoir, a mute half-human who kinda likes it. Sometimes they get extra kinky when meth head Jack White the Native American panda shapeshifter jumps in the sack for a little ménage à trois between drugged-out dullards and malcontents. After all the teen sex, they sometimes say mean things to each other and stare deeply into each other's eyes.

The Hunger Games series (Suzanne Collins, 2008-2010)
- Complaint: anti-family, occult, violence
- Commentary: The story opens in District 69 of the dystopian future world of PanAm. This is the hooker

district where teenage girls graphically pleasure fat old men from the Capitol. With plenty of graphic underage sex between minors and adults to rival even *Twilight*, we meet Katpiss Everpeen, the madame of District 69, and her pimp, Peeter "Pumpkin Eater" Malarkey. Resources are scarce across PanAm. Annual tributes are offered where the handicapped and disabled are transferred to and hunted on the Island of Infirmity (District 00) for sport. The annual event, the Encumbered Games, receives universal television coverage for everyone to watch and have a good laugh in this Social Darwinian rom com for the ages.

It feels like I need to apologize after writing such shocking and truly horrifying words. But I won't. If you are incapable of understanding satire, sarcasm, or irony, what in god's lowercased name are you doing reading my work? Go read your bible and pray for me.

In my own awesome way, I am paying homage to the legacy of other great satires like Swift's *A Modest Proposal*, where he suggests that the Irish poor might assuage their economic challenges by selling their children as food to the rich. And that was 1729 cannibalism!

In that spirit, I will end with an excerpt from my daily conversations with god:

Hi, god. It's me, PS. Are you there? Maybe you can unmute? Or we can try Zoom. Anyhoo, wanted to express a concern. I am entering manopause, so I'm a little less tolerant of dim-wittedness than normal. And I'm sweaty all the time. Like back-of-the-knees, soaked-through-my-jeans sweaty. People are starting to ask questions. I left a wet ass print on a leather chair the other day. Just sayin'.

Point is, what the hell? I am one of your singularly best creations–arguably the best–and yet I have diabetes, ulcerative colitis, skin cancer, and other crosses to bear. Oh sorry. Bad idiom. But you get the point.

I truly understand that free will is a gift. And that censors and zealots have the free will to act in your name and misconstrue your words to harass children and make them feel less for who they are or what they think or what captures their imaginations. And I am sure you are going to punish the snot out of those cads in burning effigy when they die.

But for now, can you please throw a little wisdom their way? Grant them the discernment to worry about their own lives, their own families, their own beliefs. You know - mind their own business. If that doesn't work, perhaps some sort of debilitating fall or traumatic head injury? A lesson of some kind? Guessing the tractor beam suggestion was a bridge too far, eh?

Thanks for listening, god. I will assume you're still stuck on mute. I'm signing out for now. Need to go change my clothes. I'm drenched. Conway, out. Amen.

Moby's Dick

Call me Pig Shit.

Some years ago—none of your business how long exactly—I was poor and needed money. So I thought I would travel around for some time and explore our wondrous land by working as a farm hand.

I was always a dour young man. Born Pygmalion Shitake after my farmer father's penchant for mushrooms and the fact my mother was a mannequin breathed to life, we grew up in the little rural hamlet of North Learville. Our Quaker teachers were far more interested in schooling us in the bible and agronomy than in the 3 Rs – reading, writing, or 'rithmetic. My full name was simply too hard to spell. As a joke, one of those damnable Stubb kids dubbed me Pig Shit during a malodorous Fertilizers class, and the name stuck.

It was all I could do to leave North Learville for good. I was so restless and full of morbid angst. When I was not doing chores, I liked to play with dead things down by the crick. If you used your eyes – and nose – you were certain to find a washed-up fish corpse, a gutted black bear, or a dead foreigner who just couldn't keep to themselves.

Turns out, the life I thought I wanted wasn't but a few miles from my parent's farm, as the bébé crow flies. Owned by Old

Farmer Baha Baal and his wife, Jessie Belle, Pequod Acres was the exact elixir needed to assuage my wanderlust. Occupying 500 verdant acres at the end of Cordelia Lane, Pequod Acres was the pride of North Learville. Baha grew corn. A shit ton of corn for Kellogg's and other major breakfast cereal brands.

Farmer Baha was a good man, the captain of his own tractor, and maybe a little batshit crazy. He did not seem to farm much but was always scheming to kill the Big Bwana. Racist Tarzan references aside, the Big Bwana was a prehistoric sized deer, an albino manifestation of all malignancy and evil. The alabaster buck had a giant rack, not unlike Jessie Belle.

According to legend, Bwana's rack regally adorned his head like a crown of deadly thorns, at least thirty razor sharp points, the width of a condor's wingspan. He wielded his rack like Bjorn the Norseman carved Saxons, cleaving through Farmer Baha's crops, decimating his livelihood like a boss, desecrating the fertile ground with his massively odious hooves, red eyes glowing like an Irish *púca* somehow magically transplanted by the *fae* to Upstate New York.

Baha's right-hand man, Dip, was the crew boss. He had the unfortunate christened name of Dipshit, but he was a certifiable psycho due to some mysterious boating accident, so no one dared call him anything but Dip. Dip was nuttier than squirrel crap and about the same size. When he wasn't hollering at me and the boys or standing on a stool trying to have some butt sex with a goat named Azazel, he was whispering in Farmer Baha's ear about killing the Big Bwana.

Dip had brought on an eclectic crew to work the October corn harvest, and they were the oddest fellas I ever done seen. There was a dark-skinned, tattooed chap named Queeki,

Quinten, Queenie... ah, screw it, I couldn't pronounce it. Useless Quaker education. I just called him BeerKeg. Close enough, and he seemed to care less than Judas at the Last Supper.

BeerKeg wasn't a Christian. Not sure what he was, but it was surprising that Old Farmer Baha let a pagan work on his farm. Though as I think on it further, there was always something not-Jesus-like about Jessie Belle, too. Plus, she always seemed to be a little extra friendly around BeerKeg, oiling up his muscles after a hard day's work and whatnot. A little too familiar if you asked me. She even tucked him into a wood coffin he used as a bed. Weird, I know, but he fit in that box real good. I just kept my head down and did my work.

Tim Horton, in contrast, was a Canadian and a devout Christian. We called him Timbo, cuz it sounded cool, and he used to hold prayer sessions each night in the barn around a kerosene lantern with some of the lesser characters too boring to describe in this short story. Enough to know that Timbo and his boys loved our Lord and wasn't afraid to tell you so. Especially wasn't afraid to whisper about BeerKeg, either.

The barn was where we all slept that Fall. One cool gray afternoon, BeerKeg and I was working the end of the field closest to the forest where supposedly the Big Bwana lived. And that's when I saw him the first time. The creature burst from the brush in an explosion of twig and leaves, much like a mammoth white whale breaching the sea for air. He exhaled a wet, rheumy snort, and you could feel the malevolent heat from him. With one athletic leap, he entered the cornfield and began using his giant antlers to tear and shred corn with reckless abandon.

We stood dumbstruck. But nearby, you could hear Dip yell, "Bwana!" and Farmer Baha came bursting out of the corn like some elderly Zulu warrior, pitchfork in hand, yelling a battle cry akin to a Confederate soldier at Antietam. With similar results. The Big Bwana leapt to the side, dodging the deadly stabbing, and kicked Farmer Baha squarely in the chest, sending him flying back into the corn. The ivory beast reared on its hind legs, all of ten feet tall, its mighty rack blotting out the weak autumn sun. And, with a final dramatic huff, it bound noisily back through the brush into the trees.

The next day, an injured but motivated Farmer Baha called off the harvest and handed out shotguns to the crew like Tic Tacs at a halitosis festival. This would be the second time I saw the Big Bwana, and we were conscripted to hunt him. Dip even said it. The prey was now the hunter. Oh, how wrong he was.

A thick briar patch grew along the roadside of Cordelia Lane. Generations of deer runs had formed a natural tunnel through it over time. Baha and Dip were certain this was Bwana's daytime hidey hole. They walked in front, whispering with each other, as I walked between BeerKeg and Timbo, keeping their bodies—and prejudices—physically separated, lest sectarian animosity derail our quest. An assorted cast of filler, nameless, disposable characters brought up the rearguard. Shotguns at the ready.

It was an ambush. As we advanced deeper into the tunnel of thorns, dappled light dimmed as the thicket thickened. The Big Bwana attacked from behind in the half light, throwing the Disposables like rag dolls into the thicket. His mantle gored in thick crimson blood, bodies flung into the barbed bushes, tearing flesh from skin. It was blood and chaos and screaming. BeerKeg grabbed me around the waist and threw us out of the way. Timbo dove to the other side, hellbent not to land atop a heathen.

We covered our heads as the screaming subsided, waiting for the hellish wrath to abate. Only one scream remained. It was the agonizing pain of a Disposable; I think his name was Medulla Oblongata. Something close to that. Let's call him Medulla. Quite a diverse group of farmhands for the boondocks, eh? Bwana's antlers had eviscerated Medulla, and his intestines were caught in the demon's majestic horns. As the monster fled to escape, he dragged Medulla behind him by a gruesome intestinal rope, spraying bloody agony and howling nightmarish wails in his wake.

And then it was over. Not a shot was fired. Dip hissed something in Baha's ear as we all stood. Their eyes were wilder than the moon over the Atlantic after a blustery Irish gale on a gray November solstice. The Mourning Moon, according to Pagan tradition.

That night, we sat in the barn around a centrally situated fire pit, mourning the dead bodies covered with tarps that rested outside the firelight's warm touch. BeerKeg sat quietly in his coffin, which he had dragged into the circle of corpses. Not sure if he was honoring the fallen Nobodies or protecting the coffin as his place to sleep. Timbo sat as far away as he could, sipping fresh-brewed coffee, intense eyes locked on BeerKeg. His expressionless face masked his thoughts completely.

Farmer Baha blustered like a tempest, pacing around us, cursing the pale colossus to the nine circles of hell. Dip chittered in circles around him, flitting like a moth around the heat of Baha's rage. On and on Baha raved, with the passion of a ritual and the intensity of a mind lost to an incurable obsession. The flames leapt to his beckoning, reflecting in his dilated pupils, adjoining to the stoked conflagration in his soul.

Then Baha paused, freezing in place. All fell silent. The silhouette of a diabolical behemoth stood in the open barn doorway. Eyes glowed like embers in the blackness of the night. Antlers barely cleared the width of the threshold. The only sound was the crackling of the fire and the muscular breathing of the impossible incubus. This was the third and final time I encountered the Big Bwana.

In unison, we all sprung for our guns as the devil hurdled its mass an inconceivable distance, directly into the middle of the flames. It kicked and flung logs and coals with its rear legs in all directions, spraying tidal waves of combustion to rags and hay, catching fire to the remaining people, both living and dead. The barn burned hotter and hotter as the hellscape crescendoed. Everything was aflame. All the people were burning and screaming in agony as they died.

Timbo and BeerKeg lay charred and entwined near the coffin, so disfigured from burning that it was unclear whether they were fighting with each other or shielding each other from the Machiavellian massacre. Or making love? That might explain a lot.

Dip released a final scream of terror as the Big Bwana crushed his skull with his hooves. All that remained was Farmer Baha, who was crawling toward a shotgun a few feet away. The buck sauntered toward him and used his rack to roll Baha over. In one violent motion, Bwana smashed his horns through Baha's scorched body, impaling him in a gory spray. Raising his neck, Bwana lifted Baha into the air, crying out in mortal pain, Baha's purple blood staining Bwana's ivory fur. With a final snort, the Big Bwana ran into the darkness, Baha dying in his antlers.

I am sure you are curious. *What about you, Pig Shit? What happened to you? How did you survive?*

As I swatted out the flames erupting on my shirt, burning pain seared me with panic. The brute attacked me, spearing my arm with a particularly large spike. I shit you not, it dragged me, bleeding and shrieking and flailing across the barn floor to BeerKeg's coffin. With a shake of its mighty pate, it dislodged and deposited my broken and bloody body into my sarcophagus. It stared at me for a moment, eyes full of wrath and vengeance, then turned to finish the carnage.

The barn burned down around me as I lay unconscious in the coffin. Apparently, the Brazilian Ipe-wood beerkeg used for material has some sort of flame-retardant quality, and the coffin never truly burned.

Blacking out again, I awoke in the hospital, physically recovering but my mind and soul forever scarred from the events of the last few days. I had simply wanted to work the land and escape the naïve notions of home. Instead, I encountered a nightmare of supernatural dimensions, of such ferocity and violence that the scars etched upon my soul would never fully heal.

As I convalesced in the hospital over the following days, a music video from Richard Melville Hall—aka Moby—and Gwen Stefani played on the television. Was it *South Side*? Cool song. I think I could see his dick through his jeans.

Manopause: A Treatise on Aging & Severus Snape

One of my favorite characters across all of literature is Severus Snape from J.K. Rowling's Harry Potter series.

So many Potter fans are right now asking, "What is wrong with you, bro?" Don't "bro" me, nerd. You live in a glass house of shame, too. But I do feel a little bit guilty for admitting it. Almost naughty. And not in the way that somehow means your opinion on the topic matters to me. It does not. It is more of a sinister, wicked delight that makes me giggle drolly to myself that it might bother or irritate you. There is something milk chocolatey delicious in that.

Buckle up, bitches. I am in the driver's seat. Or step out of this flying Ford Anglia now before a Whomping Willow of alternative character study crushes your brain.

For those of you who live under a rock or have chosen to censor Harry Potter books because it has turned us all into violent, malevolent witches, here is a quick snapshot of Severus Snape.

A Potions Master and temporary Defense Against the Dark Arts professor at the Hogwarts School of Witchcraft and

Wizardry, Severus Snape is a cruel, snarky, arrogant dick. His contempt for everyone is evident, but particularly for Harry Potter. Harry is an ever-present reminder of Lily Potter, Harry's mother, who Snape loved deeply as a teen. Ironically, Snape revealed the prophecy to Voldemort of a July-born child whose birth would lead to his destruction. The Dark Lord assumed it was Harry Potter. He killed both Lily and James Potter to destroy the divination, setting Harry's story in motion as *the boy who lived*. Wracked with guilt, this explains so much about Snape's bitterness toward Harry.

Many complex ironies exist with Snape's character:

- Snape is cold and calculating, but his capacity for a soul-aching love when it comes to Lily Potter is genuine. I also believe his friendship with Dumbledore was based on love and loyalty, far more than just respect.
- Snape is a bitter bully, but he was also bullied horribly by James Potter and Sirius Black when he attended Hogwarts. Harry's character grows when his idols—father and uncle—have their flaws revealed, arrogant teens themselves, breaking their angelic Gryffindor image. *gasp*
- A prominent Slytherin, aligned with the pro-Pure Blood movement, Snape should detest any non-pure magical being. But he is in fact a half-blood, born to a Muggle father, leading to the moniker "Half-Blood Prince," honoring his witch mother's maiden name. Harry idolized the mysterious Half-blood Prince until he discovered it was Snape.
- Snape served the Dark Lord as a Death Eater, then later joined the Order of the Phoenix, serving Dumbledore as

a secret agent. The Snape in the first half of the Potter-series is truly a douche canoe, or at least seemingly to Harry before he knew of Snape's dual agency; but the richness of his character is truly revelatory in the back half of the series.

- Snape must kill his bestie Dumbledore because he was coerced into making the Unbreakable Vow with Narcissa Malfoy to kill Dumbledore himself if Draco could not handle this assignment from Voldemort. When Snape tells Dumbledore, Dumbledore insists Snape kill him to maintain the illusion of Snape's continued Death Eater loyalty.
- Voldemort believes the turncoat Snape was the master of the Elder Wand (a Deathly Hallow), which leads to Snape's death at Voldemort's hands/snake's fangs. In many ways, the other Death Eaters acknowledged that Snape was powerful but with questionable allegiances, representing a threat to their evil plans of genocide and world domination.

There is no doubt that Snape is oily and selfish. He is both good and evil. He is a small man who wields power like a boss. Fear, jealousy, and loss govern his every move. But I have my own theory about Snape: he was in the early stages of manopause. As am I.

Women steal a lot of the limelight from men in their later adult years with menopause. All the glory and celebration and kibitzing. Vast social networks of women share this common experience with each other, offering support, and a gentle listening ear to each other's relentless bitching and moaning. Book club, my ass.

Yet little discussion occurs about how men suffer with a comparable manopause. Expected to "nut up," men endure in silence. When a man complains, he is weak. And gods forbid we try to share how we feel with each other! Pop another Viagra, Captain Flaccid, and everything will be okay.

Fulfilling my role as an innovator and groundbreaker, I will share my symptoms and experience with you in the hopes that you can find some damn empathy for men in their fifties. Maybe men can learn to drop the macho bullshit and give each other a massive, empathetic hug. And maybe save a kind word for Severus Snape.

- **Loud noises.** I am not sure if this is related to manopause or not, or if this is some undiagnosed form of PTSD. What I do know is that my tolerance for loud, startling noises has found its nadir since I entered my fifties. I am a musician (a drummer for Chrissake!), and I am intolerant of loud music (especially in the car). It makes me angry. Literally. Loud noises at home? Oh hell no. My incredibly tolerant, patient wife is probably laughing right now recalling the times I scream, "What the fuck is that!?" if a pan falls in the kitchen or the dog barks suddenly. My flare for the dramatic might differ from Snape, who was a pretty chill cat, but I can picture him snapping his finger and glaring at Harry Potter for making a loud noise.
- **Profuse Sweating.** As mentioned in "Are You There, God? It's me, PS," I am sweaty all the time. Like back-of-the-knees, soaked-through-my-jeans sweaty. People are starting to ask questions. Traveling with a friend for work on a frosty North Carolina morning, I left a full

sweat ass-print through a thick pair of blue jeans on the leather seat of his rental car as we arrived at the office. It was cold. There was black ice. The look on his face was of utter horror and disgust. Snape had clearly pasty skin that had a nasty sheen to it, unmasking his perspiratory proclivity. I am guessing under those heavy-ass wizard robes was a smelly, salty sea of damp nether regions.

- **Aches and pains**. Jesus, seriously. Most of my life has been pain-free. I played rugby for years. But since turning forty-five and now after fifty, what the heck doesn't hurt on a given day? Get out of bed? Shoulder pains. Shovel the driveway? Back pain. Sit immobile for too long? headache. Total bullshit. Up yours, manopause. I devolve into the character, Roseanne Roseannadanna, from early *Saturday Night Live* days, "Well it just goes to show you, it's always something . . . ." Alan Rickman, rest his soul, sported a sneer when performing as Snape that clearly descended from some early onset joint pain due to manopause. No question about it. Disdain for his nemesis certainly contributed, but there is no chance his sciatica wasn't nagging the nice out of him during some of the more intense scenes.

- **Low tolerance for stupidity**. During the COVID prison camp, it was a revelation how much I hate dumb people. All my life, I have dealt with being smarter than 99.9 percent of humans. It was just something I knew and accepted. I never judged or compared myself to other people. As I age, and manopause digs its talons deeper into my psyche, it is so obvious how truly gifted I am – and that minimally 25 percent of the population is a moron. Covidiot stupid. Donald Trump stupid. *Tiger King* stupid. Insipid and selfish, COVID revealed the haves and have-nots in the brains department. Unwavering faith in god or the government or their youth or their freedom, these intellectually inept mouth-breathing knuckle-draggers make me thankful every day that my death will occur in the next thirty years. Snape's take on this subject? Do you even need to ask? We both weep for this world.

- **Hate visitors.** This issue was magnified during COVID ... and now manopause. Home is my sanctuary. I deal with people every day in the public to varying degrees of enjoyment or lack thereof. But when I am home? *Ahhhh.* It is quiet. There is a furry dog to snuggle. There is an interesting, insightful, sexy spouse who makes me laugh. We remained safe from the plague because of the near-fascist lockdown protocols my brilliant wife enacted to protect us. Even now, the thought of anyone else coming through those sacrosanct doors is pure anathema. Before COVID? Honestly? Kinda the same, but not as obvious. Not sure if it is the pressure to be "on" in my "off" space. Not sure if it is the mess and clean-up. Not sure if it is that I simply want to visit others outside of my home. Lately, one of my daughters said I reminded her of a codgety curmudgeon, like Clint Eastwood in *Gran Torino*, yelling, "*You kids get off my lawn!*" Thanks for that, manopause. But you can also imagine Severus Snape sitting in his office, buried in books of potions. Everything is quiet and peaceful. His thoughts are dark and scheming. Then Harry Frickin' Potter bursts through the door with one of his damn dramas to deal with. Hate you most, Harry.

For those of you reading this because you are young, and it is about Harry Potter stuff, don't be so annoyingly insipid. Heed the wisdom of your elder and do not succumb to aging. As Dylan Thomas warns, "Rage against the dying of the light."

Maybe instead of accepting aging and feeling sorry for each other, we push back. We refuse to let our changing minds and bodies be a rate-limiting factor, and instead, we dig deeper to embrace these changes with passion and exact more joy from our fleeting existence before we take our final dirt nap and go to the void.

My motto since starting this book: If life sucks, laugh at it. Snape had the right attitude, made all the better with his symptoms of manopause.

Your Pain. My Pleasure. Thanks, Schadenfreude.

Germany has contributed voluminous amounts of beauty to world culture.

Listen to the great German classical composers like Bach, Brahms, and Beethoven. Taste the malty beers, the decadent sausages, and marvel at the hedonistic joys of Oktoberfest. Think with some of the greatest philosophers such as Leibniz, Kant, or Hegel.

Then consider the German language. At times, not necessarily the gentlest sounding diction for the tenth most spoken language in the world. It tends toward throatiness. Certain words are heavy and thick with guttural sounds reminiscent of snarling, buzzing, and/or throat-clearing.

There is a hysterical video on YouTube entitled *How German Sounds Compared to Other Languages* that humorously shows how words sound so bright when spoken in other languages while perhaps sounding a little harsher in German.

Obviously, German friends, the joke is *grob übertrieben* and stereotyped. It is not reflective of your entire language. And, of course, I'm obliged to say this because everyone knows Germans have no sense of humor whatsoever.

Although this joke floats around the interwebs and is hysterical, hopefully likewise to Germans. *Tell someone you love them today because life is short. But shout it at them in German because life is also terrifying and confusing.*

Germans have always had a fascinating world view that shapes the meaning of some rather awesome words, too. For example,

- **Zechpreller** – closest concept in English is a person who performs a *dine and ditch* or a *chew and screw.* They leave the restaurant after eating without paying their bill. Some college friends from SUNY Oswego may recall a night at Sal's when I left to pee, and upon return, the table was empty, sticking me with the tab. You know who you are. Dicks.
- **Verschlimmbesserung** – English equivalent would be attempting to improve something only to make it worse. Next time hubby tries to rewire the basement, ending in a full-house power outage, perhaps a small electrical fire, you now have a new choice word that sounds like cussing. Dickhead or Shitbird falls on deaf ears when used a lot. They'll never forget this one.
- **Warmduscher** – English equivalent is comparable to a wimp or a pantywaist. This person is a bit of a pussy and will not step out of their comfort zones. Reminds me of a time in 1990 when I accompanied our restaurant's pastry chef from Montauk to NY City to get 'flour' at midnight. By flour, he meant cocaine. As he grabbed a handgun and left the SUV, I cowered on the backseat floor until he concluded his dealings unscathed.

But my favorite German concept word is *Schadenfreude*. It is the concept of malicious pleasure derived by one person from the misfortune of another person. Wicked, right? Love it. It literally translates to 'harm-joy.' Delicious. In English, I like to think of it as gloating – on Machiavellian steroids.

Not to be confused with sadism, Schadenfreude is pleasure in the *observation* of someone's pain whereas sadism is pleasure in the *infliction* of pain on others. On a still finer note, Schadenfreude insists the injured party deserved the pain; some cosmic justice meted out.

To further elucidate Schadenfreude, I have concocted five commonplace scenarios, and how you can increase the kinky pleasure depending on the level of harm inflicted. I labeled those consequence as GOOD, BETTER, and BEST.

Schadenfreude #1.

A redneck in a rusted Ford F-150 cranking 'Sweet Home Alabama' cuts you off on the highway, then speeds off, flipping you the bird, resplendent in their own mulleted douchery.

- **GOOD**. You pass him a few miles up the road, pulled over by the police for speeding, arms waving, arguing with the cop that he never speeds. You chortle to yourself at how just the universe can be sometimes.
- **BETTER**. You pass him a few miles up the road, pulled over onto the median, flames and thick black smoke billowing from his engine. With panicked, flailing arms, he tries to flag you down for help, but you just keep on keeping on. Was his mullet on fire? Who cares? You're a boss and this highway is your bitch.

- **BEST**. As you drive down a hill to a severe curve in the road, you can see a gas tanker jackknifed across the highway on a bridge. Roll Tide does not seem to notice until too late. Slamming on his brakes, he plows full throttle into the tanker, causing a massive explosion, collapsing the bridge and its occupants to flaming death in the canyon below. About to dial 911, you set your phone back down on the passenger seat and hug yourself warmly.

Schadenfreude #2.

The Sunday paper has a headline about yet another pedophile priest abusing young altar boys for over forty years, and the Catholic Church had hidden the details until now. Wait. This was your parish priest. The one who baptized your kids. The one your sons had served as altar boys. Oh no.

- **GOOD**. The Vatican hid the perv away in a dank papal hidey-hole, not far from the remaining gnostic Scriptures the church edited out of the original bible. He weeps as he reads the Gospel of Reg, left alone in the damp dark, his guilty thoughts collapsing his miscreant mind into madness. This image makes you grin outwardly.
- **BETTER**. The priest dies slowly from pancreatic cancer in a hospice facility, where Nurse Betty, whose son just disclosed the bastard molested him, pretends to give the rotting kiddie diddler his morphine, keeping it instead for her own Fentanyl addiction. Her glassy eyes smile, as his cries of agony echo through the halls.

- **BEST**. Justice finally served, the church miraculously cooperates in prosecuting him, and the convicted shitbag goes to prison. Tiny Terrence, and his gang of convicted felons, treat Father Fresh Face to a daily taste of his own medicine, which is one dose of beating, two doses of fellatio, and ten doses of anal rape. They don't let him die or kill himself, despite his pleas. His agony continues to this day. You wonder how much worse hell could be. Then take a nap.

Schadenfreude #3.

Your three-year romance ends when you discover your boyfriend, Crispin, is a serial cheater. Turns out, his philandering knows no limits. That sleazebag has been living off your charity, squatting in your apartment, delivering pizzas between bong hits, playing video games, and fat-shaming you when you know you look fly. Plus, what a dickwad name!

- **GOOD**. Crispin put a baby in Cinnamon's belly. "Cinn" is a stripper at a truck stop "rub-n-tug" joint that Crispin and his boys like to frequent. Apparently, his seed found purchase during some productive lap dancing. Cinn wants the child and expects support from Crispin. You wish her luck as you gleefully throw his clothes off the balcony into the street.
- **BETTER**. Crispin contracts syphilis from Cinnamon. He is starting to go blind, challenged to advance his delivery career due to driving restrictions. He calls you every night, sobbing in terror, from his new home on his bro, Clint's, couch. Much like the nihilist German philosopher,

Friedrich Nietzsche, Crispy knows tertiary syphilis symptoms of paresis and mental collapse are imminent, and he has no medical insurance. Your heart heals daily.

- **BEST.** Crispin and Cinn try to make it work. Cinn gets COVID and dies, losing the baby in the process. Crispin catches COVID from Cinn but is asymptomatic, spreading the plague throughout the seedy underbelly of strip clubs and other sordid establishments, which in turn spreads throughout the massive population of johns in the metro area, which in more turns spreads to their friends and family. Decimating an entire city for generations, the losses in wealth and life are incalculable *Uhhh*. You shake your head. That may be too far. The syphilis is enough.

Schadenfreude #4.

Un-costumed ten-year old Tommy saunters onto your front porch on Halloween, rings the doorbell, and holds out his bag without even saying Trick or Treat, then proceeds to complain he doesn't like coconut when you reward his ill-mannered behavior (and attire) with delectable Mounds candy bars.

- **GOOD.** You point and laugh at the little prick when he falls off the porch in the dark, flesh shredded in your rose bushes. Closing the door slowly, savoring his tears, you turn off the front light.
- **BETTER.** While pruning your rosebushes the next day, your neighbor, Wanda, asks if you had heard from Tommy's mom. Tommy went to the hospital last night when he had anaphylaxis after consuming candy containing tree nuts. Coconut is a tree nut. You blush wickedly.

- **BEST**. As the little shit reaches the end of your driveway, he is mowed down by a speeding delivery truck who is running late due to longer than normal delivery delays caused by COVID. The driver, who knew he should have fixed that damn broken headlight after his cheating lover, Crispin, left him, cradles the boy in his arms crying out, "Where is the justice, god? Why?" You sigh, knowing god is in her heaven, and all is right with the world.

Schadenfreude #5.

Joe Biden got so tired of Donald Trump making him look creepy. A little shoulder rubbing, finger licking, and pelvic grinding is fun, and the ladies really seem to dig it, man.

- **GOOD**. Trump lost the 2020 election in a bigly victory to Biden. Joe thumbs his nose at Trump in victory, then puts his hand down his pants to adjust his erection. Popularity makes him happy.
- **BETTER**. Trump has a Peter Griffin-esque stroke from gluttonously eating thirty consecutive hamburgers and gets disqualified from running. Mike Pence, burdened by the crucible of his complicity in perpetuating lies and evildoing, returns home to Mother's bosom, never to be seen again. Joe licks a baby.
- **BEST**. Trump reveals himself to be the true Antichrist, Jesus returns, and an epic Armageddon ensues. After vanquishing Trump to eternal damnation and returning the earth to its original tranquil Garden of Eden lushness, Joe Biden poses for a photo op with Jesus, and tries to finger his ass.

These different scenarios evoke varying levels of Schadenfreude. Could you feel it?

Vengeful thinking is liberating. Visualizing perilous consequences and taking joy in that is a coping mechanism that helps us resolve our feelings of hostility internally versus expressing them externally. It is a psychological "big red button," stopping our lowest impulses.

Schadenfreude prevents us from picking up an AR-15 and shooting up a concert because those other people could afford the tickets, while we can barely make ends meet supporting our loser boyfriends or dealing with our entitled neighbors or bickering over partisan politics.

At the end of the day, Schadenfreude illustrates our own insecurities. As discussed in prior pages, we have failed to self-actualize; and it is our own bullshit and low self-worth that allows us to revel in the failures of others. It passive-aggressively prevents us from looking inward at our personal shortcomings. And by being a snarky dick, stalls our own personal development.

Ouch. Truth hurts.

I mentioned early in this piece that Germans have no sense of humor. Untrue. German humor is deeply sarcastic, biting, and dour. Schadenfreude, in that sense, is the highest form of German art: pure comedy.

A Tale Told by an Idiot

Let's kick off this party with a Shakespearean word hug. Language so perfect in its construction and application that the pantheon of gods gives a standing O when it's read or spoken. I just make the O face.

> Tomorrow, and tomorrow, and tomorrow,
>   Creeps in this petty pace from day to day,
>   To the last syllable of recorded time;
>   And all our yesterdays have lighted fools
>   The way to dusty death. Out, out, brief candle!
>   Life's but a walking shadow, a poor player,
>   That struts and frets his hour upon the stage,
>   And then is heard no more. It is a tale
>   Told by an idiot, full of sound and fury,
>   Signifying nothing.
>   -Macbeth, Act V, Scene V, Lines 19-28

Shakespeare digs deep with this sublime illustration of poetic nihilism. Easily one of the most quoted soliloquies in literature, Macbeth has reached the brink of the abyss, haunted, teetering on the edge of madness. Time and existence have all been reduced to nothing. Life is a grand illusion, a tale told by an idiot.

Tough word, idiot. When our daughters were little, their two worst "swear words" were "stupid" and "idiot." Uttering those words was anathema that resulted in them sucking in their breath and chastising me with a horrified, "Daddy!"

It was adorable to our friends and my parents that the girls, particularly as toddlers, had no problem with words like "c*nt" or "f*ck" (for clarity: * = u). Brings a tear to my eye recalling their delightfully precocious little cherub voices. Like little British football hooligans. Angels from heaven's finest working-class pub.

Meh. They turned out OK. Maybe a little vulgar, but hell, it's only words. We all know it is someone else's problem if they allow simple little words to really bother or offend them (*he said provocatively*).

All joking aside, words have power. Words can wound. They require a sensitivity in application that my daughters understood at a young age. Using words like "idiot" or "stupid" or – god forbid – "retard" is cruel, judgmental, and irresponsible. They are words that seek to lessen others or suggest inferiority due to some form of intelligence deficit.

So, let us use "idiot" as a literary construct. That way we can work this discussion from a common language, without having to revisit the ugliness of implied offense or superiority. It is also synonymous with "fool" for this discussion.

Since the beginning of recorded history, idiots and fools have been used as an archetype. Although dull of wit, many supposed idiots in literature provide wise insights and revelatory truths that contradict their real or supposed mental or societal deficiencies.

Shakespeare made use of these fools precisely to allow his audience deeper understanding of surrounding character flaws and shortcomings ... even madness.

- **Feste** in *Twelfth Night* delivers some of the most intelligent and witty vivisections of other more foolish preeminent characters, warning Lady Olivia, *"the cowl does not make a monk."* i.e. don't judge a book by its cover.
- **Touchstone** in *As You Like It* personifies practical cynicism. He is bawdy and vulgar, constructed to judiciously deconstruct the courtly conventions of love and its adherent mythologies for great comedic effect.
- **The Fool** in *King Lear* is my favorite. Intentionally unnamed, the Fool functions as Lear's conscience. Where the king is foolish and unwise, The Fool is ironically his alter ego. In his final moments of clarity, Lear comprehends the magnitude of his unwise decisions. The fool's purpose fulfilled; he dies.

Modern literature is also rife with examples:

- **Lennie Smalls** in John Steinbeck's *Of Mice and Men*
- **Benjy Compson** in William Faulkner's *The Sound and the Fury* (great nod to Macbeth)
- **Boo Radley** in Harper Lee's *To Kill a Mockingbird*.
- **Charlie Gordon** in Daniel Keyes' *Flowers for Algernon*.
- **Forrest Gump** in Winston Groom's novel (or better yet Robert Zemeckis's movie *Forrest Gump*).

Forrest Gump, for me, is the best modern example of an idiot who has something to say, something that means something. His words are Hemingway-simple yet so poignant. His hyperbolic life story of perseverance, acceptance, and love makes us examine ourselves more deeply. Through the eyes of this simple man, we see ourselves and our own unrealized potential. We are inspired.

During the pandemic, the last few months of quarantine and social distancing helped the real-life idiots, the Covidiots, to evolve.

Sadly, these people are not wise. Covidiots are not acting dumb. They are choosing dumb. We do not learn more about ourselves from their foolish behaviors, other than how not to behave. Our world is not bettered by them, in fact, it's made far riskier. They are the weak link in the chain of our existence. The faulty bulb in your mortal string of Christmas tree lights.

Let's ensure we have the characteristics of a Covidiot clearly outlined. They are selfish. They lean Socially Darwinistic. They are impatient and impulsive. They do not follow science, favoring institutional religion (or the words of President Cheeto Christ). They defy data, fact, and basic safety rules to expedite emerging from quarantine.

Forrest Gump had some timeless quotes. Perhaps exploring a few of them might help clarify the problem Covidiots present us with today? I think yes. Shall we?

Gumpism #1: "Stupid is as stupid does." I don't care what your political beliefs are about Donald Trump, the Chairman of the Covidiot Board. Narcissism and thin-skinned personality aside, he was nothing short of thoughtless, reckless, and dangerous in his handling of COVID. His micropenis ego refused to allow him to lead by example. He was the Anti-Leader.

Quoting Shakespeare from *Julius Caesar*, "*What a terrible era in which idiots govern the blind.*" Stupidity was and remains his choice because the political calculus of intelligence would deprive him a reelection. He would not wear a mask, he would not socially distance, he would not follow the guidance of top scientists. Trump has neither care nor regard for others. His reelection obsessions superseded the good of all.

Gumpism #2: "I don't know if we each have a destiny, or if we're all just floatin' around accidental-like on a breeze. But I, I think maybe it's both." This is part of the ironic Trump network effect on the MAGA mob. Operating without a plan, unencumbered by strategy, reacting based on feeling vs fact, the Covidiots followed the word fiddle of their fearless leader out of their homes while Rome burned.

They set down their bibles on their davenports, bored with safely praying to their god in isolation, and migrated *en masse* to church following the clarion call of destiny. Trump, a faithless mongrel himself, said it was okay to closely assemble for long periods of time without masks. And he said god wanted—nay, required—hordes of potentially sick people to risk their lives to adore her. It is their First Amendment right, darn it.

A diabolical calculation was made by Covidiots. Their freedom to gather and worship was worth risking the lives of the infirm, elderly, or vulnerable. The weak were expendable. I seriously cannot think of anything more Christlike. Hopefully I am not misquoting Jesus, I think from the gnostic *Book of Reg*, Reg 661:666, where he says,

"*Yay unto thee I say abandon the weak. Feed them not, lest ye go hungry. For thou hast toiled for the fruit of thine labors, and thine toils are thine and thouest's alone. Share not thine fruit.*

Horde instead like Egyptian toilet papyrus. Also, thou must gather in great throngs, from sea to shining sea, casting asunder the poor and aged, to visibly show thine neighbors thou art true to me, and thine family is truer to me than their family, yada yada, yada; and, thusly, verily thou rejects the ugliness of the poor and grossness of the infirm. Maranatha."

Gumpism #3: "Mama always said life was like a box of chocolates. You never know what you're gonna get." You know when you are wiping your ass with cheap toilet paper and your finger goes through the paltry paper, giving you a stinky fingernail of poo, and of course, you sniff it, because, well, just because? That smell is the taste of that random piece of surprise, nasty chocolate in this plague-infested candy box of life. Covidiots are the puke that follows consuming that rancid pink goo in the middle of the defective chocolate.

Let's unpack that metaphor. No one ever thought we would live through a real plague in our lifetime. That is so freaking Old Testament. But now that we have managed through it, and we know what it takes to stay safe, who would have ever thought we were so selfish? That a few months of isolation and boredom could reveal our inner sociopathy so vividly? That we ate that skank chocolate and puked out Covidiots?

This is not about the absolute rock star heroes who necessarily ventured out into the unknown and continued working while we hid at home. No. That was necessity. This is about the unconscionable losers who attended massive pool parties in Missouri, packed bars in college towns, or flocked to the beaches like they had never witnessed water. For what? Some distorted sense of entitled liberty.

Deep, cleansing breaths. *Ahhh*. Fools and idiots, as literary tropes, help us grow. They opine wisdom where it is absent in title characters. They warn us of behaving as our lesser selves. They add clarity where only ambiguity stands apparent.

Morons and Covidiots, as real people, are dangerous. They shun wisdom when others try their best. They embody our lesser selves. They live for their emotional self, illogical and senseless in their decisions.

Did we emerge from the COVID pandemic a better society? Is it so wrong to doubt it? Society is really an illusion, a false construct to control the mob with bread and circuses. The relevant, controllable question: did we emerge as better *individuals* following the plague? Can we try to put the needs of others above our own selfish desires?

It scares me. What have we learned about ourselves after the pandemic? How are we using what we have learned to develop personally, and in turn, come together in shared caring and empathy to improve the world for others?

To conclude, in the inimitable words of Mr. Forrest Gump, "That's all I have to say about that."

DARK SHORTS 4:
DIGBERT & EGBERT GO TO **MARS**

Digbert loved robots.

Since his childhood, Digbert dreamed of creating his own robot. A friend. A companion. But his dreams were bigger than building a new toy. Even at an early age, Digbert laid out under the stars behind his family farmhouse, dreaming of creating a sentient being. Something with the ability to think and feel.

But Digbert developed a problem that diverted him from making even his first human friend. He relentlessly needed to scratch his ass. As the compulsion worsened with age, Digbert found deeper places to itch in the dank recesses of his Cadbury canyon. Until the day he struck turd gold. Wrist deep, Digbert's finger seemed to snag in a recess that heretofore remained undiscovered.

And then he heard the voice in his mind's ear, as though his finger was a microphone, "You have found me." Digbert froze. "Who are you?" he whispered. "I am Egbert," came the response.

Digbert spent the next few weeks getting to know Egbert. They were inseparable. And Egbert had a plan. He helped Digbert design an external robot Egbert, powered by an anal interface embedded into anal Egbert. The robot resembled a Roomba with an articulating eye stalk, two claw arms, and an antenna. The only downside was the fifty feet of wire that hung from Digbert's butt cheeks that connected Egbert to the robot.

But why sweat the small things? Digbert finally had a best friend! That month, Digbert and Egbert enrolled in MARS, the Midstate Anal Robotics Show. The amazed judges awarded Digbert and Egbert first prize. As the tethered friends approached the stage to collect their winnings, an alien ship's laser blasted through the roof killing everyone inside. Two gray aliens walked up to Digbert's smoldering corpse.

One Gray pulled on the wire until Egbert came free. "See, Xander," I told you I left my anal probe behind." Xander looked incredulous. "It's about time," said Egbert. "I've been stuck with this asshole for too long."

STUPIDITY:
THE BUCK STOPS WITH EVERYBODY

Albert Einstein may have infamously quipped, "Two things are infinite: the universe and human stupidity; and I'm not sure about the universe."

Infamous, in part, because no one is sure Einstein said it, so the attribution's veracity is in question. Was it some nameless, famous philosopher-astronomer? Perhaps renowned Gestalt therapist Frederick Perls? Sounds a little Mark Twain-ish to me. Honestly? Who cares.

What matters is that some very smart people arrived at the conclusion that stupidity knows no bounds. And, scary though it seems, certain social circles celebrate stupidity in these times of COVID.

For context, I think it is important to reveal that I was, until Trump, a registered Republican, not some big-government, anti-military, tax-and-spend apparatchik. I believe deeply in a small Federal government favoring the States for most governmental decisions, a strong military, and spending only the money we have available, which should be lessened by lower Federal taxes.

Sadly, in my own party, I am a unicorn who failed the party Purity Test: a social liberal and fiscal conservative. A middling soul stuck in political limbo. I persist in the belief that the character (e.g. integrity, empathy, open mindedness, communication skills, et al) of a leader matter as much as, if not more than, their accomplishments alone. Our greatest leaders achieve the right results, the right way. And we should never expect less from them.

Let us begin with our erstwhile Covidiot-in-Chief: your messiah, Cheeto Christ. You know the guy, right? The very stable genius, the guy who is like, really smart. That one.

Recent studies compared presidents back to Herbert Hoover and concluded that, once off-script, Cheeto has the lowest vocabulary of any modern President. By far. Two different studies land Him at an either fourth or fifth grade vocabulary level. And that's compared to Biden!!!

Read any transcript from Trump's tweets, press conferences, or campaign rallies where He tries to vamp. Lies, inanities, inaccuracies. Please keep in mind: this was the President of the United Fucking States of America speaking. How many can I quote?

- **"Two Corinthians"** versus Second Corinthians – but Trump and Jesus (and Yeezy) are bros. Thankfully, His deep Christian faith and principles have shaped His conduct so admirably throughout His storied life of infidelity, porn stars, and "doing anything" to women including "grabbing them by the pussy."
- **"The buck stops with everybody"** version of "the buck stops here." Cheeto's Harry Truman misquote shows His true views on integrity, leadership, and accountability. An unfeigned upholding of the Founders' social contract.

- **"They say the noise (from windmills) causes ear cancer."** Cannot make it up. With such a conscientious and data-driven outlook for the world, sign me up for more. Hell, make it a lifetime appointment.
- **"Who's doing the raping? Somebody's doing the raping?"** Uh, Mr. President, thou hast proclaimed the Mexicans are doing the raping. Please pay attention to thyself. And also thine track record – dozens of claims of sexual assault and liability for millions of dollars in damages. Oh, and 34 felonies.
- Was it **"the Blacks"** or **"Pocahontas"** or **"kung flu"** that clued us into His race-baiting? Or was it the **"very fine people"** among the white supremacists in Charlottesville? Cannot imagine how anyone would think He is racist. Baffling.

Even though "the buck stops with everybody," we all know that leaders and their words can affect how their lesser, inferior followers behave. Voicing cruel, ignorant, racist, unaccountable, and *wrong* utterances shaped an environment that enabled the Covidiots to emerge from lurking in the shadows. It normalized repulsive behavior and dumbed down the dialogue.

Cheeto is not the first. Just the worst. Lying is certainly not new to politics, but He hath perfected it into a complex symphony with over 18,000 documented lies since he left office and an uncountable number since he has started to run again.

All things heal in time. And it will take time to return to informed civil discourse and unifying language at some future date post-Cheeto, post post-truth. For now, my wish is that we approach communications with linguistic incrementalism. Let us aspire to pronounce a handful of words correctly. Screw the truth and political correctness and the soul of America and other such heady bullshit for now. Baby steps.

Clearly, if you cannot properly pronounce a word, you discount your intelligence further than necessary. Why discount your credibility with words? Your actions will more than explain your rampant idiocy. At least sound smart, pretty boy. Meanwhile, can we please huddle up as a team of native English speakers and agree that we can minimally commit to the pronunciation of the following ten words? A small ask, really. Ten words, said identically from a common damn language, to make us all sound at least slightly less dimwitted than the most orange Cheeto on the planet.

10 Mispronounced Words

1. **Supposably**

    The intended word is supposedly. Another reason to hate adverbs more egregiously. I think adding the *-ly* confuses dense people. Remove the suffix, and what remains is the core word of "supposab" or "supposed." Hm. I wonder which one is an actual word? A clue. Unless there is some suppository to enhance core strength that I have never heard of, let's use some common damn sense, shall we?

2. **Irregardless**

    The intended word is *regardless*, but ironically, "irregardless" is still a non-standard word. The problem is the prefix *ir-* and suffix *-less* mean the same thing, and therefore negate each other, leaving *regard* as the remaining word. Technically, irregardless is the opposite of regardless and means something akin to "concerning" versus the intended "not concerning." Sentences help to clarify the proper use of irregardless for those of us above a fourth grade education: "*Irregardless* of her chronic *flatulation* problem, Dingo humiliated her family with her noise and stink.

3. **Nucular**

    The intended word is "nuclear." I think the first time I ever truly noticed another human being saying "new-kyew-ler" versus the correct "new-klee-er" was former President George W. Bush. It gobsmacked me at how hick it made him sound. It was simply an exclamation point for a man who struggled with hard multisyllabic words like "strategery" and "misunderestimated" anyway. Consider: If your second-grade teacher's directions were *unclear*, would little Dipdip raise his hand and proclaim, "Teacher, I am *un-kyew-ler* about what to do." Dumbass needs to go back to first grade or smartass needs to visit the principal's office. Either way, here is your F.

4. **Expresso**

    The intended word is *espresso*. How? Why? What? Listen, if you cannot pronounce the word correctly, you lack the requisite refinement to drink a piping Italian nectar so delicious and sophisticated. Three-syllable words may be overkill for you. Try ordering milk or tea. Oh shit, wait. Chances are you'd spell that as "tee," and then we would have to go into some lengthy diatribe about golf. If we are feeling adventurous, we could expand to two-syllable words. Coffee? Given the prior concerns about tea/tee, just please don't embarrass yourself by ordering it in writing as "Coffea" Derp. Above all other things, avoid all Cheetoisms. Never ask for "*covfefe.*"

5. **Prespire**

    The intended word is "perspire." This error should self-correct when you make yourself feel as dumb as you sound. Break your mistaken pronunciation into its two component parts *pre-* and *-spire*. Literally, your nonexistent word means "before the tower." So, Shrek, unless you plan to work up a stanky ogre sweat before scaling the tower to rescue Fiona, think before you open your giant gaping gob. Or you'll wonder how you ended up living as an outcast in a swamp.

6. **Jewlery**

    The intended word is "jewelry." Confusing an *-el* sound with an *-le* sound is very common in English. Why? Because we are lazy in our speech patterns and/or we are remedial in our spelling. Think sensibly, geniuses. Do you recall the adorable, homeless singer Jewel? Fetching voice, needed some orthodontics? Would her name now be Jewle? Call me crazy, but that sounds oddly anti-Semitic or references some fabricated Welsh Princess who led her pagan troops into battle against eighth-century Mercia. Either one. You pick.

7. **Libary**

    The intended word is "library." The irony is delicious. You cannot correctly spell nor pronounce a place of words and books. Too yummy. Said aloud, this mistake is absolutely cringeworthy. "Lie-barry." Sounds more like what a dominatrix says to Barry as their instructional bondage session begins. Hey! How about a great library joke? "Ziggy walks into a library and asks for a book about cliffhangers. The librarian says..."

8. Mute

The intended word is "moot." Reminds us of when Joey on the sitcom *Friends* said, "It's all a moo point. Like a cow's opinion. It's moo." Equally as puerile. Far less funny and far more inane-r to say mute ("myoot"). Aside from sounding absurd, this suggests that the point is silent versus irrelevant, which unless you are in a heated debate with a mime, is plain silly.

9. Fustrated

The intended word is "frustrated." Why people drop the 'r' is beyond me. I envision Lucretia, a blubbering child with a speech deficit, gasping between sobs, "I'm so fustwated," when Morticia refuses to share her dolly. Even then, they have the excuse of early age Elmer Fuddisms as a crutch. What's your excuse? You're a grown-ass adult and, as everyone knows, baby talk is not cute and only has its place in the bedroom. Change your diaper and grow the hell up. Or get in bed and warm the lube. Your call.

10. Calvary

The intended word is "cavalry." Both are nouns; one is a place (where Jesus was crucified) and one is a thing (bunch of soldiers riding on horses). I bet, in hindsight, Jesus's predicament may have looked a whole lot brighter if Paul and John had mustered a cavalry to rescue him. The Romans had plenty to spare. It's history. I may need to confer with the gnostic *Book of Reg*. Maybe it did happen, and the early Magisterium erased the records. Now that's some believable gossip!

This is not particle physics, my friends. Just a modicum of focus to raise the bar in the quality of our speechification will go a long way to repairing the damage to our collective intelligence caused by the Reign of Cinnamon Hitler.

Hair Führer will disappear sooner or later, and his tide of Covidiots will hopefully ebb with his demise. Worst case, they will scamper back into their secret communes of obscurity, stock up on more automatic weapons, and continue plotting the next armed American revolution. Dreaming of *The Handmaid's Tale*. Out of sight, out of mind, eh?

At least our little enclave of invisible digital friends will have greater mastery over our linguistic skills and show the world how smart we are with our refined and most excellent pronunciation competencies. We will never fall trap to sounding unintelligent when, by evidence of reading this book, you have proven that you desire to walk a path of enlightenment.

Better said, in the prophetic words recounted after caddying for the Dalai Lama himself ("the flowing robes, the grace, bald ... striking") by Carl Spackler in *Caddyshack*, for the effort, "You will receive total consciousness." So, you've got that going for you. "Which is nice."

Reflections from a Midsummer's Walk with Hairy Kerry

I love my dog. His name is Hairy Kerry. We tried to be clever with his name.

A Cubsession

I love my wife. She loves baseball. And she is arguably the biggest Chicago Cubs fan who has never lived in Chicago. Every year we purchase the MLB package. She watches all 162 regular season games from April to September. A grueling 26-week season of 3+ hour games that relentlessly persists until the October Playoffs. If a dirge were a sport, it would be baseball.

As only true Cubs' fans can appreciate, September tends to be the end of their season most years. But, in recent years, play has extended into *Cubtober*. And, of course, who can forget 2016 when they broke the Curse of the Billy Goat? My wife has been notably quoted as saying, besides our wedding day and the birth of our children, the Cubs' World Series win on November 2, 2016 was the best day of her life.

I like baseball. I do not love baseball. Putting aside all arguments about whether, like golfers, baseball players are real athletes or not, the relentless spitting makes me want to puke. Like going to the Fair. *Ewww*.

To fill the tedium of baseball's plodding pace, the TV cameras always seem to land on fake left fielder, Jose Sciuridae, hawking a wad of sunflower seeds down his drool-slick chin like some chipmunk colossus on steroids. *GAG* Or fabricated first baseman, Ryan Kotmund, spitting black tongue cancer from his chewing tobacco-packed gob. Usually the sticky, stringy type of saliva that sticks to his lip like a graphic scene from some black-market German porn. *BARF*

But my wife adores her Cubbies. In particular, she treasures legendary Cubs sportscaster, Harry Caray, who called games for the Cubs beginning from 1981 to 1997. As much caricature as maven, Harry Caray delighted baseball fans when singing "Take Me Out to the Ballgame" during the seventh-inning stretch. Renowned for his trademark eyeglasses as well as his love of Budweiser beer, Harry liked to drink. A lot. Rumor has it that employees of Wrigley Field had to hold him by his feet during that stretch to prevent him from falling out of the press box.

Etymology of Hairy Kerry

With my wife's *Cubsession* now firmly established, we thusly bestowed the honorific of the sportscaster Harry Caray four years ago on our new fur baby. Here is the etymology of how we landed on Hairy Kerry.

- Too clever for our own good. We felt "Hairy" was the fuzzy puppy version of human Harry. Made even cuter when you know his full forename is *Hairold*. I know! Totes adorbs.
- Caray was Harry's stage name. His given surname was Carabina. Neither epithet really fit for our little man, whose breeder first called him Kanye. After Kanye

West. Three reasons why we did not stay with Kanye. One, Kanye West is a nutjob. Two, a rural white breeder naming a black dog "Kanye" felt... mmm... kinda racist to us. Three, reminder that Kanye West is a nutjob. Fourth, Kanye Conway? Aurally insufferable.

- As you may recall, my wife and I have a mild obsession with our Irish heritage. We have sojourned to the Motherland several times in our lives, and we feel very connected to County Kerry, the Ring of Kerry, The Dingle Peninsula, and the town of Killarney. Some of the most scenic places on earth. And for the inexperienced American driver, a feckin' white-knuckled driving experience you will never forget!
- Kerry sounds identical to Caray. But it becomes more wistfully nostalgic when spelled as the Irish "Kerry." Again, behold our satirical sagacity. As the character Rocket in Oscar Wilde's short story "The Happy Prince" says, "I am so clever that sometimes I don't understand a single word of what I am saying."

Welcome to the world, Hairy Kerry Conway.

WTF is a Cavachon?

Hairy is a Cavachon. This designer dog is not an American Kennel Club (AKC) recognized breed. It is a mutt. A lady in Ireland once referred to her scruffy mongrel as a Bitsa (*bitsa this and bitsa that*). But dumbasses like us fork over a lot of cash to know that a purebred *Cava*lier King Charles Spaniel father and a purebred Bi*chon* Frise mother humped out some adorable progeny. Ergo, Cava-chon.

This is the breed's curb appeal: cuteness like a curly teddy bear come to life. Cuteness like a petite Ewok transplanted from Endor. The attraction is instantaneous. Hairy ratchets the cute up to epic levels with his eyebrows. Because he is a tri-color—black, white, with some tan markings typically along the face—his distinctive dirty-white eyebrows are quite prominent. They give him a range of facial expression from excitement to contempt. It took us an adjustment period to acclimate to his uncanny eyebrows. Even when he relaxes, his eyebrows sit naturally lowered, and he looks concerned. Maybe even pissed off. It's intense.

Eyebrows aside, that suave exterior is a manifestation of his sweet personality. All licks and snuggles and wags. His sole raison d'être is to give and receive love. When I am home, he is my furry shadow. As I type, Hairy lies inches behind the wheel of my office desk chair, waiting for me to back over him *again* as though it never happened before. I said sweet. Not smart.

And for dog lovers with major pet allergies, the Bichon bitch passes along low-dander (quasi hypoallergenic) qualities that allow most allergy sufferers to tolerate the plush Cavachon fur and copious licks without anaphylaxis closing their windpipe. Hairy and I can get down on the floor and tussle without me worrying about exploding in hives post-play. And we have some epic scraps with each other, the likes of which make *Beowulf*'s heroic battles with Grendel and Aglæcwif seem as exciting as attending a yawning symposium.

Pre-Walk

Hairy is content to chillax all day—eating, napping, and shitting— provided he gets a walk. He knows this daily ritual usually occurs between four and five p.m. every day. Hairy can tell time? Yes, only because we bought him a watch for Christmas.

It begins with him sitting and staring at me to the point where I can feel those intense eyes on me. His tail cranks audibly back and forth like a whip. He mumbles and grumbles. He is too pretty to whimper. Eyebrows at full furrow, the face says, "C'mon, ass hat. Time to walk." And then the real fun begins. The dance of joy. Hairy dances. His long tail acts like a rudder, balancing him for long periods on his hind legs. And he smiles. A giant, shit-eating grin spreads across his face as he shimmies his shoulders like a professional rumba dancer. If god exists, the utter elation Hairy emanates must be an earthly reflection of her love. Radiant. Pure. Bliss. Harness and leash donned, we're off.

The Walk

For the first ten minutes of every walk, Hairy smiles over his shoulder every minute at me as though to say, "This is the best. Right, daddy?" He prances. Proudly strutting, head held high, tail erect and curled. The neighborhood dogs go bat shit, running back and forth across their yards, barking hysterically. Hairy could not give a tinker's damn. He barely graces them a sidelong glance as we parade by.

As his jubilance luxuriates over me, I enter a Zenlike state. The warm summer sun swaddles me in a hug. The breeze cools my sweaty brow. My senses heighten to absorb the birdsong, consume the smells of barbecue, watch the bees buzzily cavort. I am one with my dog.

The physical activity enters autopilot as we subconsciously meander our suburban trails. For me, it is the perfect time to think. Clear my mind and reflect on the deep questions the universe presents. Questions that require us to ponder the nature of our own existence. The big questions. The deep stuff. Real important shit.

But sometimes Hairy has a way of shredding those moments like an unguarded Sunday newspaper. Let me share a few such deep questions and the ensuing interruptions.

Reflections

- **What is the value of your dignity?**
  Hairy just took a dump in his favorite grassy spot off the trail in our nearby park. He performed his ritualistic "Circles" routine, where he spins in circles as he makes waste, spreading his little fertilizer all over the grass. My little gardener. Oh wait. Oh no. A final turd is stuck by what appears to be a . . . hair? Is he eating hair? Dangling midair from his bunghole. He looks confused and continues to spin in circles, seeking to see the abnormality he so clearly can feel. What to do?

  No one can see my handsome dog sporting a dingleberry. Panic sets in, and I reach for the hair to free the turd. I am not wearing my glasses. Manopause sucks. I miss the hair and grab full wet turd. It smushes moistly between my fingers. It's still hot. I scream, "You little BASTARD!" and start violently wiping my hand in the grass as Hairy starts barking at me. An old couple passes by on the path, once smiling at us, now gaping in horror at our literal shit show.

- **If a tree falls in the forest, does it make a sound?**
You bet your sweet bippy it does. The trail takes us through a massive copse of thick forest. The air gets cooler and the ambient light dims. All is quiet. Something is moving in Mirkwood. Hairy and I freeze, and he looks up at me. We know what it is. Spiders. Giant spiders. I reach for Sting and realize I do not have a sword. Nor am I Bilbo Baggins.

At that exact moment, a tree falls in the woods with a thundering crash. As god is my witness, I swear Hairy screamed like a panicked goat, as did I. Ok, maybe it was just me. Either way, he leapt into my arms, eyes wide with abject terror, and I ran as fast as I could, carrying my traumatized canine papoose to the safety of the park beyond this clearly haunted wood. Nothing could stop me from saving my boy. I could change my piss-soaked pants at home.

- **How do you know you are not dreaming right now?**
Hot Mom is walking her purebred poodle, Lady, toward Hairy and me down the path. While I am happily married and Hairy has no scrotum, we still don't want to look like schlemiels in front of the ladies. Chests puffed; we approach. Hot Mom and I stop walking an appropriate social distance away.

As the bipeds commence mindlessly chit-chatting about the weather, the quadrupeds warily approach each other on their leashes, closing the gap between us. A few sniffs of each other's butts, and Lady haughtily finishes with

Hairy. Apparently, the fun has just begun for him. As she turns away, Hairy lifts his leg and begins pissing all over her. Hairy! NO! Chaos ensues.

Lady goes ballistic and plows into Hot Mom, knocking her off the trail into some thick plants. Uh oh. Poison ivy? Startled, Hairy barrels into me. I bend to settle him, and rip a fart, the majesty of which can only be explained by a snarfed lunch of three bean burritos at *Taco Bell* a few hours earlier. *No quiero, Taco Bell.* Heavier than air, the rancid fart wafts across Hot Mom's flared nostrils as she extracts herself from the brambles. "What the holy hell is wrong with you and your filthy dog?" she screams. Perhaps a smidge dramatically if you ask me. And storms off.

Whoa, Bro!: Hot Dad, her seven-foot-tall husband, shoves me in the grocery store parking lot later that day and says to stay away from his wife and dog. *No hay problema, jefe.*

Closing Thoughts

Existential humorist Jack Handey once commented that if dogs ever rule the world and crown a king, he hopes it won't be based on size because there are some pretty smart Chihuahuas out there.

Not sure what that has to do with anything. Just a witty quote about the potential of small dogs. Why do you care? Indulge me. I love my small dog. My small dog loves me. Our walks are essential for him. They have become essential for me. His endless capacity for love helps me fleetingly forget the raging insanity of MAGA Nation, American post-truth politics, and the anxiety of managing so much uncertainty. It is a metaphysical symbiosis. Love sits squarely in the center of it all. Love so limitless, pure, and unadulterated that you grow certain that god must be a dog. I mean, they are *heteropalindromes*, after all, a string of letters that form a word when read backwards of forward. Coincidence? I wonder.

Which leaves us with the biggest philosophical question of all: Which would you rather be, an unhappy human being or a happy dog?

Sneak Peek:
10 Reasons I'm Better Than You

I am contemplating a book. Writing one. Another one. A *New York Times* best seller. Because, candidly, I wouldn't know how to write anything less. You see, dear friends, I am awesome. And I believe that revealing my ostentatious splendor to the world would be a gift akin to god sacrificing her only begotten son for your sins.

Consider this a gift. From me to you. All of you except maybe that nasty idiot reading my work while watching midget granny porn. Walk away, sicko. Yes, it is a sacrifice of my valuable time to produce another book imparting such profound wisdom. So, for now, I am simply providing you a sneak peek at each chapter to gain some initial buzz.

I am supremely confident you will find value. How could you not? The book's title is *10 Reasons I'm Better Than You*. Read on and learn.

Reason #1: Fat is temporary. Ugly is forever.

When I was younger, a so-called friend would tease me and tell me I was fat. While thin, this guy was fucking ugly – aka fugly. The kind of fugly that makes you question why his parents didn't hit him with a shovel and bury him with a crucifix when he clawed his way out of his mother's womb. Wearing the moniker of *pudgy* or *husky* or *chubby* hurts. You know what hurts more? Knowing that fat is temporary. Ugly is forever.

You see, in terms of cuteness, I am effin'adorable. A solid 8.5. I can lose weight when I choose. I can diet. I can exercise. I can have surgery. None of those options fix ugly, because ugly is incurable. So, while my heft might collapse a folding sports chair at Dabney's soccer game, I won't crack a mirror when I stare into it longer than ten seconds. The mirror is so essential for me.

Reason #2: Don't be stupid. Money *can* buy happiness.

Money *can* obviously buy happiness. By its very nature, money buys things. Why not happiness? People who argue money doesn't buy happiness fall in one of two camps—lazy or Commie. Laziness sickens me. I buy things with the scads of money I make because I bust my ass 80 hours per week to earn it. Nice house, nice car, nice exotic trips. Yup, all titillate my chubby man titties.

Lazy people? Bitch and whine about their hard life, knowing they are working a dead-end, low-income job but too lazy to work a second or third job. My grandfather was a bus driver, a janitor, and a bartender to make ends meet. Worse, Lazies are covetous. They denigrate wealthier people like me out of petty jealousy instead of the commensurate deference they should show their Betters.

And Commies? Don't get me started. They would rather squat in their equally sized huts in a dirty Siberian alfalfa commune, subsistence living off what lichen they can grow or vermin they can kill. Like John Lennon (note the similarity to Lenin) once wrongly challenged us, "Imagine no possessions." Commie. Total pinko. The hard reality, comrades, is equality in personhood does not equate to equality in contribution. Without innovators and producers like me, who do a lot more, and therefore earn a lot more, your piddling little Prius would never exist.

Reason #3: Sleep is flawless for an unburdened mind.

"O coward conscience, how dost thou afflict me!" Shakespeare's king in *Richard III* laments over the murders he committed in his ascension. His nightmares wake him. What does that feel like? I sleep like a baby, unmolested by this so-called conscience thing. What a horrible burden! Out of fairness, to the best of my recollection I have never murdered anybody, let alone ten people like Dick III.

There was the one time I hit a kid on his bike. Came out of nowhere. Startled the ever-loving shit out of me. Through my rearview mirror, it looked like he was moving. Hard to tell at such a high rate of speed and with so much alcohol in my system. But I distinctly recall seeing no noticeable blood stains on the car hood when I hosed it down. And that cracked windshield was certainly the byproduct of some windblown debris or errant pelican. A child would have caused a lot more damage. I'm not a physicist, nor an oddsmaker, but I'm 90 percent sure that kid survived.

Reason #4: Drummers are the highest form of musician.

I am a drummer. Factually speaking, a humble drum god. Little known fact, but on his deathbed, Neil Peart had a tear-stained picture of me sitting at my drum kit hidden under his pillow. Respect. Peer superiority aside, drummers in general are the highest form of musician for three distinctive reasons.

Firstly, only drummers (and gods) control time. Oh, and Time Lords, too. Bands implode without the steady beat laid down by drummers. It's a known fact that guitar and keyboard players would recklessly meander into artsy, self-adulating chaos without the firm, guiding pulse of their drummer.

Secondly, drummers are athletes. Musicians are generally nerds. Not drummers. We're cool. Jocks, really. Playing the drum is a full-body muscular experience. Keyboardists sit for hours. Guitarists pace around and only exercise their fingers. Singers? Do they even count? Next!

Finally, drummers are the life of the party. Find me proof that women (and some men, too) don't fantasize about having sex with a drummer. Rhythm, baby. But it's more than that. It's that bad boy persona. Drummers die from excessive drugs and alcohol abuse more per capita than any other rock musician. Ask Keith Moon or John Bonham if they were smiling when they drowned in their own vomit. Too cool.

Reason #5: "Humor is mankind's greatest blessing." -Mark Twain

I am thankful every day that I am so funny. It's yet another reminder of how much better I am than other people. Think of what humor does for you. Humor leads to laughter. Orgasms aside, can you think of any release better than laughing so hard your laugh muscle in the back of your neck starts to seize? Laughing so hard you cough up pieces of your lung in a choking fit from your last bong hit? Laughing so hard you go temporarily blind and nearly rupture that undiscovered aneurism in your cerebral cortex?

Laughter, in turn, leads to happiness. If you hate happiness, you hate puppies and candy. Think of that warm bliss cascading around your body like some rare hemorrhagic fever. Much like a yawn, smiling is contagious. And that dumb, shit-eating grin you get from being happy is transcendent. The network effect of smiling takes over and can change the mood in a room. Nay, it can alter the course of history.

I am funny. And you are welcome.

Reason #6: Friendship is worth the wait.

All my life, I have combed the world like a doctor for pubic lice to uncover that one rare person worthy of my friendship. The search continues. My wife is awesome, so I guess you could count her as a friend, though I don't recall having intercourse with a lot of my friends. So maybe we share something different? Who knows? Life's mysteries, right?

The moment when I think I have made a new non-wife friend, that I have found a worthy cerebral and spiritual compadre, they disappoint me. They wear the wrong clothes or say something irretrievably obtuse or stop calling me back. Even when I text them hundreds of times, they give me the cold shoulder. Worse, they often respond with the standard *navacancha* like, "You're such a psycho," or with comments like, "Never contact me again, I hate you." Their jealousy of me is quite apparent, proving once again, they are not worthy of my superior sodality.

Reason #7: The Law of Self-Attraction: My Abraham is Balaam.

The Law of Attraction is simply another bunch of bullshit sold to gullible, sad people. According to channeler Esther Hicks, it relies on an unseen, alien collective intelligence named "Abraham" to help you get what you want. That's just plain foolish, bordering on insane. Instant loss of credibility. Follow my inimitable lead here.

I practice the Law of Self-Attraction. My spirit guide's name is Balaam. Well, Balaam and his talking jackass. (Yeah, literally. Not figuratively.) The Law of Self-Attraction begins by looking into a mirror, admiring the splendiferousness that is you. In this case, me, ogling myself. If I repeat *donkey, donkey, donkey* three times, an incorporeal Old Testament seer named Balaam appears in the mirror astride a large, grinning donkey. The strange part is that the donkey does the talking, and he sounds identical to Eddie Murphy's Donkey from *Shrek*. Or maybe I imagined that?

Either way, the talking burro reminds me of my daily affirmations, plagiarized from SNL's self-help guru, Stuart Smalley, "I'm good enough, I'm smart enough, and doggone it, people like me."

Reason #8: Parenting is unnecessary with good genes.

My sperm is genetic gold. With its Midas touch upon my wife's ovum, our zygotes experienced rapturous mitosis. Twenty-three perfect little chromosomes each to create two perfect little beings in my daughters. So why bother parenting a goddess? They were born with sufficient hereditary advantage and white privilege to ensure their dominance in life.

I feel so bad for my lessers. They give so much of their lives to their kids when they could be napping or tweeting or watching *Tiger King*. The conundrum is their imperfect progeny require teaching, and mom or dad barely qualify to instruct their child how to punch its way out of a paper bag. So, they rear their kids so utterly flawed that they next require proxy parents in schoolteachers to further develop their children. And when the asinine system of those mediocre intermediaries finally craps their kids out into a society-stained toilet bowl of a job market, managers assume the role of surrogate parent.

When your full-grown children return home from a day of meaningless, unfulfilling work, they interact with their final substitute parents – the television or video games – killing whatever remaining motivation, inspiration, or imagination was left in their uncultivated brains. Damn, that's dark. Listen, for $50 you can have my sperm. Call me.

Reason #9: Experience beats education.

Either you have natural intelligence like me, or you do not. It's science. Formal education is a massive social experiment in Nurture. Nature vs. Nurture has been debated for eons, and according to science, Nature wins every time. Imagine a world where we all learned as we did stuff. The mean streets of hard knocks, taking your lumps, and pulling yourself up by your bootstraps are your classroom.

By directly engaging with life at an early age, you will develop the survival instincts and skills necessary to contribute as best you can to the world, in your own intellectually limited way. Look at these PhD and MBA toffs who hang their reputations on their ability to master specific topics. Smart? Sure. But to what end? What does all their ivory tower, elitist years of thinking and studying and ideating meaningfully contribute?

So, I propose disbanding formal education and putting everyone to work. Real work. Let your natural inborn intelligence guide your ability to thrive. If everyone became a producer, the takers would eventually go extinct.

Reason #10: God believes in me.

I listen to religious people all the time telling me about their belief in one god or another. Their faith in their god helps them compartmentalize their dull, pointless lives into bite-size, digestible chunks. They cling to the promise of something bigger to follow this life which will makes suffering through this existence more bearable. How nice. Shoot me now. I am so thankful to have a radically different worldview. Shit, more of a different cosmic view.

You see, god believes in me. Not only because Balaam's talking ass says so (although he most certainly does). But also because my life is so full and perfect that I am content. I have no need to pine for an eternity beyond this world because I am a god here. I sleep flawlessly because I have led an unstained, unvarnished life, give or take possibly killing one kid. On Maslow's Hierarchy of Needs, I am the tip of the triangle, a little-known, pin-prick space called Fucking Awesome. Comes way after self-actualization.

All I ask from you, dear readers, is to appreciate that I am further evolved. Born with one foot in the afterlife, connected to divinity. Your dad has bad sperm, and your mom was a shitty parent. That's not your fault. You were raised by some obscene village, so why would god believe in you yet? Your day will come. You just need to die first.

Closing Thoughts

Having read this preview, I am sure you are confused on "next steps" for you. Chant to yourself, *PS! You're so awesome. How can I even try to be like you?* In short, you can't. Don't try. It won't work. Like Dr. Manhattan from *Watchmen*, accept my benevolence and tolerance. Do what you can with my mythical mysticisms and carry on with your run-of-the-mill lives. Perhaps the next life will hold some higher purpose for you.

Consumerism:
Peace Instead of Another Television Set?

John Lennon once opined, "If everyone demanded peace instead of another television set, then there'd be peace." What a smartass. If money can't buy happiness, then it certainly can't buy peace. How do you purchase something intangible like peace on your credit card?

But money can buy televisions. Oh yes. Not just one television anymore. In our modern households, we *need* a television in every room, plus entertainment access from our computers, our smartphones, our tablets, our watches, our games.

In fact, that is the game: Need. Demand. Desire. Consumerism is alive and well. And suppliers are listening. As is the central government, our star-spangled politburo, too.

Consumerism: What is it?

Webster's Dictionary defines consumerism as "the preoccupation of society with the acquisition of consumer goods." Let's unpack that definition to understand the implication(s).

- **Preoccupation** – a fixation or obsession. Sounds healthy. Jeffrey Dahmer had a preoccupation with preserving severed heads and genitals in acetone, and he wasn't peculiar at all.
- **Society** – bogus term. As discussed earlier, society is an illusion created so the human animal doesn't resort to rampant cannibalism when the power grid fails.
- **Acquisition** – obtaining or buying something. According to the Central Government, the average American family is in credit card debt of $5,700. In other words, buying crap you don't need.
- **Consumer Goods** – speaking of crap we don't need?

So, for our purposes, I'll simplify the definition of consumerism as "a disordered, obsessive, covetous behavior, based in an imaginary reality that accrues further debt for shit we really don't need."

Consumerism: Why do we covet?

Now that we have refined our definition of consumerism, let's discuss why we covet in the first place.

Journey back with me six thousand years, when god created the earth and the incest chain started with our two Caucasian progenitors, Adam and Eve. Eve bit the damn apple when tempted by Lucifer, and the whole shit show of free will began. And menstruation. Most women will attest that "God's Curse" every month was a smidge heavy-handed for a little impudence.

God knew from that point forward that her inbred progeny needed some rails to contain their impetuous free will. Every generation was a little more genetically flawed that the prior one, and god needed to do some thinking for us little beasties. So, she gave Moses the Ten Commandments.

The Tenth Commandment proclaims: *Thou shalt not covet thy neighbor's house, thou shalt not covet thy neighbor's wife, nor his manservant, nor his maidservant, nor his ox, nor his ass, nor any thing that is thy neighbor's.*

Eclectic misogynistic tone aside, I occasionally covet my neighbor's ox. Her name is Oxana. A proud cow with nice teats. But god forgot to mention that thou shalt not covet thy neighbor's iPad nor his Beemer nor his terraced waterfall landscaping. I guess they fall under the "any thing that is thy neighbor's" catchall clause.

Fast forward six thousand years, and advertising (writ large) is our modern Satan in the digital Garden. God knew it was our nature to be covetous, yet she allowed the creation of the interwebs and commercials and credit cards. Given our nature, our rebellious spirit, and *sooooo* much temptation, what are we expected to do?

Spend. Spend. Spend. But to what end? What is the impact of buying all these unnecessary material things?

Consumerism: Pros & Cons

The impact of consumerism manifests economically, environmentally, medically, even spiritually. Let's consider the pros and cons.

- **PRO: Economic Growth** – the gaping, voracious maw of consumer demand drives production, creating more jobs, increasing wages, feeding more spending. Society embraces safety and security with a giant hug for Abraham Maslow.

- **PRO: Increased Innovation** – making the latest super-size licorice, mayonnaise, strawberry potato chip takes some knowhow and out of the box creativity. Factor in how to best use GMOs and a petri dish of unregulated preservatives, and you have a winner.
- **CON: Environmental Impact** – all that pre-packaged trans-fatty goodness must belch some noxious byproduct out of a smokestack in Guangdong. To the best of my knowledge, none of the millions and millions of tons of new trash are reducing our carbon footprint.
- **CON: Personal Debt** – who cares about consequences like bankruptcy or homelessness when you get the latest Frappa-Lappa-Strokie-Suckie-Latte at Starbucks today? Bonus points if you can be the first friend on Insta to *Like* it.
- **CON: Health Problems** – In the history of hunger, no one has ever needed a Big Mac. Never. But want one? Hell, I want seventeen. And I can sit my sedentary ass in my car, command their creation, and then drive myself to the ICU as the stroke starts to hurt real bad in the front of my face.
- **CON: Corrodes the Soul** – there is a potential cosmic impact in that god did warn us the Ten Commandments were no joke. That disobeying your heavenly mother carries punishment far worse than a slap from your mortal parent for defying your teen curfew. Guess we will find out when we go to our eternal dirt nap (while looking fine in the latest designer suit).

The facts seem to point to consumerism being bad. It has its good points, but the tone so far paints a less than rosy picture. And I don't want to go to hell. The underlying concern seems to be with necessity versus desire. Do we really need so much stuff? Let's explore a few examples to see if there's more to learn.

Consumerism: Tangible Examples

- **K-cups** - First, I love coffee. Second, I need coffee. Third, I *fiend* coffee. And my Keurig, with its limitless assortment of K-cups, saves me time every morning when I need that first succulent cup to feed my waking addiction. Yeah, it's more money. Yeah, it's probably not great for the environment. Meh. This is more akin to a prescription, a medical necessity, not wanton whimsy.
- **The Lottery** – Gambling is illegal in my state except for certain Indian reservations. And I love winning money. I am super lucky, so I buy $10 worth of Lottery tickets at the gas station every night after work. I win $100 and spend $4000 every year, but who cares? Is it magical thinking to believe I can win it big someday with *just a dollar and a dream?* I can stop anytime. Shut up.
- **Greeting cards** – Who has time to say "Happy Birthday" or "I'm Sorry for Your Loss" anymore? Nothing says you care more than using a stranger's trite words to tell the most important people in your life something super important. Bonus points if they use a sing-song cadence and can rhyme *true* and *you*. Plus, your dying parents can't keep up with housework like the old days, and a pile of recyclable paper cards on their coffee table requires far less dusting.

- **Designer Clothing** – When I was younger and poorer, a $35 pair of Husky blue jeans kept my legs warm and dry while preventing my penis from flopping out. Like all aspiring porn stars, I don't wear underwear. As I got older and more successful in black market porn, I discovered designer jeans. Sure, they cost $300 per pair, but my man bulge looks super obvious in them sans undies. The button fly eliminates any "franks and beans!" scrotal zipper moments. And the softer lining material helps reduce chafing.

Consumerism: Intangible Examples

- **Travel** – We Americans are renowned global travelers… and spenders! So why does the world hate us so much? Is it our boisterous voices overwhelming a 3-star Michelin dining experience? Could it be our loud complaints when the locals don't speak good English? And what German doesn't adore us constantly saying how different things are in America. We won the war. Show some damn respect.
- **Pets** – My dog, Hairy Kerry, costs us thousands of dollars per year. His life was valued at exactly $600 when we bought him from the puppy mill. From a pure return on investment perspective, that $600 mutt will cost us $45,000 over an estimated 15-year life. We could have owned nearly 80 dogs during that same period and let them roam into traffic. Who cares? Just buy a snuggly new one. Same love, different shell.
- **Children** – Speaking of bad investments. Children. Ouch. Dirty, smelly, expensive, not to mention the time wasted

rearing them. And the attitudes! Yikes, teenagers! Don't even get me started about the college years and the waste of money in continuing education. I have two daughters, each sinking me for around $200,000 in college-related expenses. Imagine what that combined $400,000 could have bought me in lottery tickets alone? Guaranteed I would be a millionaire by now with a lower likelihood of spending my retirement shivering in a wet cardboard box under some distant overpass.

- **God** – God is like the lottery. I'm willing to place a bet god is real. As my father always says, what's the risk in believing? But formal, institutional religion? Hell no. They are simply large corporations and bureaucracies with god as their pitchman. As a Catholic, although a 10 percent tithe is no longer mandatory, your canonical duty is to financially contribute into the Magisterium. For what? Bailing out, or—worse yet—hiding rapists and pedophiles from justice? Pass! I'll take hell if that is my only other option.

Closing Thoughts

Consumerism is a problem.

We go deeper in debt buying things we covet, can't afford and truly don't need. The negative impact of consumerism outweighs the positives up to and including risking our eternal souls. The more we examine both tangible and intangible consumption, the more the malevolent truth seems self-evident. But, since we now live in a post-truth reality, why let nettling little facts stand in the way of a good time?

Think about it. Doesn't it feel sexy to buy another set of $300 earpods? Those musical micro-penises making sweet love to your earholes as you crank up the massive bass of *Zeppelin II*? Feel it: You gotta whole lotta love.

Don't you relish the time you saved not going to the sink for free water and having that beautiful plastic bottle of water so chilly and willing? Never mind the habitats destroyed. You're busy... and thirsty now!

Don't you just purr when that fake soyball chocolate shake from McDonald's glides viscously down your gullet. Shit, they don't even bother to refer to them as *milk*shakes anymore. 'Cuz they aren't... and we don't care!

So, go on! Consume away! While you're at it, don't wear your masks during the next plague. If it doesn't feel good to you, don't do it. Facts are just science's opinions. And we all know their political agenda. How can we trust it?

Trust in the hard currency in your pocket and the currency of opinion. What could go wrong?

The Mandela Effect: Play It Again, Sam

"The Mandela Effect" describes a phenomenon where large groups of people have memories of something happening that supposedly never occurred.

The term "Mandela Effect" was first coined around 2009 by paranormal consultant, Fiona Broome. Ms. Broome observed that she and numerous others were certain that South African apartheid activist, Nelson Mandela, had died in prison during the 1980s. As this observation spread across the interwebs, many adherents also had vivid memories of a televised funeral. Some clearly recalled a eulogy by Mandela's widow on TV. Yet no evidence existed.

In this reality, Mandela was released from prison in 1990, served as South African President from 1994-1999, and lived until 2013. The peculiar thing is how vivid these false memories are for thousands of people and how adamantly they may debate their inaccurate correctness.

Mandela's demise aside, the term stuck, and investigations proliferated by the curious and even bi-curious. Movie quotes had changed. Brand logos had changed. History had changed!

In terms of movie quotes, wrap your flawed brain around some biggies:

Casablanca (1942)

- INCORRECT: "Play it again, Sam."
- CORRECT: "Play it once, Sam, for old times' sake."

The Empire Strikes Back (1980)

- INCORRECT: "Luke, I am your father."
- CORRECT: "No, I am your father."

Snow White and the Seven Dwarves (1937)

- INCORRECT: "Mirror, mirror on the wall, who is the fairest one of all?"
- CORRECT: "Magic mirror on the wall, who is the fairest one of all?"

Mind blown yet? A little bit pissed off at your own untrustworthy memory? And why do so many people think exactly the same wrong thing? Buckle up. This shit gets nuttier than a pistachio at a cashew convention.

Mandela Effect: The Man. Humor me. Nelson Mandela was amazing. He deserves a modicum of consideration before commingling his inspirational life with some half-baked conspiratorial thinking. In case you were born under a rock, Nelson Mandela was a South African civil rights leader who spent almost one-third of his 95-year life imprisoned for treason in his fight against apartheid.

Apartheid is an Afrikaans word for "apartness." It was a governmental policy of segregation as well as political and economic discrimination by the South African 20 percent white minority government against an 80 percent black majority population.

Under enormous international pressure captured in the cry of "Free Nelson Mandela," his life sentence was commuted in 1990 by then President FW de Klerk. Free at last, Mandela reinvigorated his anti-apartheid efforts. With Mandela, De Klerk helped actuate the orderly, peaceful dismantling of apartheid, earning them both the 1993 Nobel Peace Prize.

In 1994, Mandela was elected the first Black president of South Africa at a spry 75 years old. Retiring in 1999, Mandela founded the Nelson Mandela Foundation, a global organization that still promotes the tenets of equality, peace, and freedom. He died in 2013. What a life!

A few interesting tidbits about Nelson Mandela to wrap up our discussion...

- Mandela's Xhosa birth name was Rolihlahla, which means *troublemaker*. He was bequeathed the English name "Nelson" in elementary school for ease of pronunciation purposes. Not racist at all.
- Mandela's book *Long Walk to Freedom* recounts his notoriety as a master of disguise, evading arrest for several years. The media nicknamed him "The Black Pimpernel."
- Mandela was finally removed from the U.S. Terror Watch list in 2008—at the dangerously distinguished age of 85. WTF?!
- Mandela read the William Ernest Henley poem "Invictus" to inspire his fellow prisoners not to lose hope. Latin for "unconquered," *Invictus* was also a movie about Mandela, starring the transcendent Morgan Freeman.

Can the Mandela Effect be explained through parascience?

I believe there could be some truth in the paranormal. I have had personal experiences with what I believed to be ghosts. I am a believer in the possibility of the paranormal, despite the absence of evidence. As with my own stories, I have no pictures, recordings, videos, or other evidence of my encounters.

But for now, let's all just acknowledge that these beliefs are in no way mainstream thinking nor actual science. They are more akin to religion or misplaced faith.

Is there a possibility that parallel universes stack up, one upon the other, and maybe occasionally cross over each other? I join Thomas in the his gnostic (a.k.a. hidden) Scripture when he said, "Show me the holes." Me? I would be the first to step through them.

This is where we enter the event horizon of a metaphysical black hole we cannot escape. Some real *Twilight Zone* shit. The challenge is that all the evidence of alternate realities and parallel universes is only anecdotal. Ironically, it cannot be disproven either. If anything, Quantum String Theory supports the possibility. No wonder the Mandela Effect continues to fascinate—and frustrate!

Mandela Effect: The Psychology and Actual Science

Let's transition from science fiction to science fact. But really? The problem I have is that science is so damn boring. I write humor, and I am flagellating myself for having to tackle this almost-deleted section.

Keeping it simple and high-level, scientists and psychologists believe the following may explain the Mandela Effect:

- **We lie to ourselves.** It's called *confabulation*. It involves your brain filling in gaps in memory with fake memories that never happened to make the entire event make sense. Not malicious lying, more of an innocent fib. To yourself.
- **We are highly susceptible to post-event suggestion.** Fake News, anyone? Internet chat groups of post-Truth conspirators feeding us the cerebral sugar we crave. Chocoholics feeding fudgy imagination pudding to each other. This is also why eye-witness testimony so often unravels.
- **Schema-driven errors.** Schema are electrical packets of data that steer memory. In tests, subjects sorted out unfamiliar material and replaced it with alternate material to reduce distortion in the mind. For example, many formal clock faces display a more attractive non-Roman numeral IIII instead of IV. But on recall, most subjects said the clocks displayed the more familiar IV. Great googly moogly...yawn!

But why do many thousands of people recall the identical things? Is that level of group synchronicity explained away by confabulation, suggestibility, or familiarity? Consider some further examples that might bend your mind toward the IV on the fancy clock.

Mandela Effect: Examples

There is no question that the Mandela Effect is unsettling. As science indicates, are our memories so fragile and fallible? Am I the only person that felt, with 110 percent certainty, that the following errors were true:

- **KitKat was Kit-Kat.** There definitely was a hyphen at one time. Wasn't there? Even the Chinese social media espionage site is called Tik-Tok, right? Ah shit. It's TikTok?
- **Curious George had a tail.** What the paranormal hell happened to the little guy's tail? Monkeys have tails. Period. That is a fact of nature. Or is George like some simian version of a docked tail dog? Is he curious because he wonders where the hell his tail went?
- **Jiffy Peanut Butter lost some letters (Jif).** My childhood was a lie. I loved Jiffy peanut butter. Yeah, I know "Choosy moms choose Jif," but wouldn't it sound so much better with Jiffy. Choosy. Jiffy. Lines up so much more lyrically. Dammit all.
- **The Monopoly Man had a monocle.** If you asked me to wager $100 the Monopoly Man wore a monocle, I would have taken that bet and laughed at your naivete as I counted my hundo. Where did it go? Did he covertly lend it to Colonel Mustard in the drawing room of *Clue*? Was he hiding his Nazi heritage and gave it back to Colonel Wilhelm Klink of *Hogan's Heroes* fame? Shit. I will just "state my complaint and leave."
- **The Berenstein bears were Jewish.** Why, you ask? Well, turns out they were redneck Berenstain bears. Like a shit

stain. Maybe they had some secret religious conversion. Not sure when they found Jesus, but no one ever told me. L'chaim, bears. Either way, steer clear of the monocled Nazis. Just in case.

Mandela Effect: What The (Actual) F?

Certain of my own recollecting resplendence, and unsatisfied with the whole science thing, I researched some alternate conspiracy theories as to the cause for the Mandela Effect.

- **Alternate realities**. Quantum physics may be onto something. String Theory posits that a multiverse exists, infinite parallel universes stacked side by side with potential copies of us with some slight or extreme variations. If those realities somehow (which is the truly messed up unexplained part – how?) cross over each other, could certain original memories that Fruit Loops (false) was never Froot Loops (true) still be true even though the reality is altered?
- **Time travelers changing history**. Einstein proved that time travel is mathematically possible. But it takes a lot of energy. Hmm. Is the CERN Large Hadron Collider used to send people back in time? Is it possible that governments are sending sojourners back to screw with minor details in movies and packaged goods? I fail to understand the motivation, but with governments, you never know. Minimally, please change Rubik's Cube (true) back to the Rubix Cube (false) I loved as a kid.
- **Living in The Matrix**. Is reality just a computer program and our human existence a tiny subroutine

manipulated by some pock-faced nerd, gaming with our characters in his grandma's basement? Or as some postulate, is existence like the holodeck on *Star Trek's* USS Enterprise? Are we living in some sort of virtual reality where our memory errors are simply bugs or glitches in the software? Why mess with the *Looney Tunes* (true) logo when we all know it was once *Looney Toons* (false)?

The problem is these theories all have more holes than the souvenir Swiss cheese samples given after the God Particle ride in CERN.

Mandela Effect: Closing Thoughts

How are we supposed to understand our collective false memories? Maybe the right question is, #WWNMD, or "What would Nelson Mandela do?"

On one hand, it seems apparent he would listen to science. He would endure the boring science people explaining dull dorky concepts while he would smile and nod and never really understand what they meant. But it's science, so it must be true?

On the other hand, Mandela was a rascal and a troublemaker. And a notorious cheese lover. Given all the holes in these alternate conspiracy theories, perhaps he would gravitate toward them like a large piece of Gruyère.

Bottom line: I am personally overwhelmed by science versus parascience. It might be easier to offer a political answer instead. Something free of controversy.

The Mandela Effect explains a lot about the Cheeto's first presidency. For example, let's take the debate over corruption with mail-in ballots from 2020 and how it was pre-gamed for 2024. Even though the claims of voter fraud have been completely debunked, through the course of repetition and viral spread, Cheeto's Faithful believe it happened *en masse*. They are certain of it, and worse yet, certain it will likely happen again. And again. And again.

Cheetologists also believe the following phony "Top 10 Truths" with programmed certainty thanks to their scrupulous Savior:

1. Joe and Hunter Biden are treasonous criminals.
2. Joe Scarborough is a murderer.
3. Ted Cruz's father assassinated JFK. (Not to mention Cruz is the Zodiac Killer)
4. Barack Hussein Obama is Kenyan.
5. The Obama Administration practiced McCarthyism by wire-tapping the 2016 Trump campaign.
6. The noise from windmills causes cancer. And the ground beneath is a "bird graveyard."
7. Global warming was fabricated by China to make US manufacturing non-competitive.
8. Muslims celebrated the 911 attack by dancing in the streets of New Jersey.
9. The Clintons killed Jeffrey Epstein to save Bill from the inconvenient embarrassment of pedophilia.
10. Children are immune to coronavirus. Send the little bastards back to school.

It's all so difficult to prove. Worse yet, it's all equally challenging to disprove. Facts are simply not enough! We must now accept people's words, opinions, and anecdotes as proof.

For me, Occam's Razor may settle the score: When two or more theories predict the same result, the simplest solution is generally the right solution. Which would you choose – science, parascience, or politics?

DARK SHORTS 5: FATHER PAT MCGROIN

Father Pat McGroin greeted his parishioners after Mass. A young boy walked up and began tugging his cassock. "Father, Father. How can we see the face of god?" The greeting line paused, and a small circle of smiling charmed congregants nodded at the precocious boy, then looked to the priest for the lesson. Flushing and smiling, Father McGroin tousled the boy's brown hair and tried to shove him away by the face. "We will discuss this at Sunday school, Timmy," he said to the boy. "Run along now." But Timmy was undeterred. "Well, my daddy said you were going to see the face of god in person after touching my penis in the rectory." McGroin's last memory was a shadow approaching from the corner of his eye and the sound of a cocking shotgun.

PSILOCYBIN:
WHAT A LONG STRANGE TRIP IT'S BEEN

It's Sunday evening. I'm flipping channels as I luxuriate on my new leather sectional. Her name is Wanda. I love her. Our lockdown splurge. Wanda sighs as I settle deeper, sipping my umpteenth glass of a precociously tannic Cabernet Sauvignon.

Expectations are low. Buzz is high. Sunday TV generally blows. My wife reveals that her Chicago Cubs are playing. UGH! Kill me. Baseball. Three hours of watching pseudo athletes relentlessly spit makes my soul ache for an early death.

And then magic happens. A blessed alternative.

That sexy bastard, Anderson Cooper, is hosting a segment of *60 Minutes* about psilocybin. Isn't that the psychedelic compound found in magic mushrooms? Intrigued, the old retired Deadhead in me peeks out of his smoky back room in the attics of my mind.

He seems so real. His name is Jerry (yes, named after Jerry Garcia, the late lead singer for the Grateful Dead. Duh). Okay, so he resembles Jerry, too. Fine, it *is* Jerry. Screw you. My imagination, my rules.

Hey, PS. Long time. What's up, man? Jerry takes a long drag on his joint. It smells so wonderfully skunky.

Hey, Papa Bear. Yeah, I had to tuck you away after college. Sorry for that. Life. You know.

No worries, man. We had some good times, didn't we? I can taste the tendrils of spicy weed wafting across my face.

We sure did, Captain Trips. It reminded me of us when this TV show explored psychedelic drugs like psilocybin.

Whoa, yeah. Those shrooms would "steal the face right off your head" back in the day. Wisps of pungent smoke caress my cheeks with the sensuality of delicate fingers. So relaxed.

The smell transforms into a bear. A vivid blue Grateful Dead dancing bear with golden tufted neck fur. His name is Owsley, my long-lost totem. My college spirit animal. A solitary tear of joy rolls down my cheek at our reunion.

Jerry smiles. "Take good care of Owsley. He will help you remember. Better get truckin'."

I place my hand in Owsley's paw. And we're off, sliding down a shimmery rainbow into Time.

Psilocybin: "Purple Haze"

As Owsley and I traverse time through cosmic purple clouds, blaring with guitar feedback and fuzzbox effects, we are aquiver. The freedom, the music, the synchronicity—it's simply exhilarating.

Owsley nods, and we drop off the rainbow, freefalling through a hole in an azure sky, landing gently at the corner of Haight and Ashbury Streets in San Francisco. We have found ourselves in 1967, in the middle of the famous Summer of Love. Over 100,000 hippies converged on the Haight-Ashbury district that summer.

Beatnik bohemians are everywhere. Smiling. Laughing. Hugging. Humping. Oh shit, get a room. Tripping their balls off. The air smells of marijuana, patchouli, and body odor with a tinge of minge. As I watch a group of tie-dyed counter-culturists sharing a brown bag of magic mushrooms, they're quoting erstwhile Harvard professor Timothy Leary's famous "Turn on, tune in, drop out" mantra.

As the drugs kick in, there is no fear. Their receptivity to the impending mind-bending experience is sublime. As they slowly sip their beers the psilocybin works her magic and they talk about truly radical and subversive things. Shit the government should worry about. Connectivity with the universe. Expanding their self-awareness. Exploring a more profound spirituality. Promoting expressions of love. Dank, dangerous stuff.

It feels bittersweet. Sweet because of their authenticity. Bitter because of their naivete. Owsley always has a shit-eating grin on his face. No clue what he is thinking.

Little did our small brigade of trippy troopers know, the Nixon administration would sign into law the Controlled Substances Act (CSA) in 1970. With the massive concert event at Woodstock in 1969 as the final barometer of the flowerchildren's disinterest in authority or conformity, conservatives needed to reel in the rabble and ban their rebellious behavior.

Like we needed another reason to hate Richard Nixon. He killed love and served up the 1970s. Yuck. Owsley does not speak. He holds out his little blue paw, and away we go to kiss the sky.

Psilocybin: *Several Species of Small Furry Animals Gathered Together in a Cave and Grooving with a Pict*

Like a psychoactive ghost leading Ebenezer Scrooge, my blue bruin levitates us to the twinkling rainbow, and we once more permeate the veil of history. As we miraculously transcend relativity, Pink Floyd's trippy music is blaring from all the stars. Hauntingly experimental. Avant-garde sound collages. Ugly. Edgy.

We alight at the University of Rochester, Spring semester of my college Freshman year, 1988. I recognize it is Dandelion Day because I am sporting a daring Minnie Mouse costume and recently ate a fistful of magic mushrooms.

The school's flower is a dandelion as a joke. Dandelions are a prolific weed, so the school celebrated their botanical nihilism with a Friday holiday for the opening of Spring Fest weekend. Basically, it was a sanctioned reason to party. A few days to vent some steam amidst the intense academic rigor.

I am not in a good headspace.

- **My "Freshman Fifteen" was showing.** I feel fat. Some so-called friends reinforced that anxiety by telling me I looked fat in my Minnie Mouse skirt that was enjoying her magnificent April reprise from last Halloween's debut.
- **I am riddled with guilt.** My best friend had drowned just over a year earlier. I miss him terribly and feel enormous guilt for throwing him into a pool. Didn't matter I didn't know he couldn't swim. I blame myself.

- **I am failing out**. My grades are in the toilet. Fraternity life and rugby have completely overtaken my misaligned priorities for my lifelong dream of medical school. So unaccustomed to failure, I don't possess the coping skills to pull myself out of the academic ditch.

Sensing my looming depression, Owsley gives me a big fuzzy hug. I sneeze. Turns out, I'm allergic to his ethereal dander. Allergic even to magic? I am a hot mess.

As the psychotropics kick-in, my trip manifests my feelings of insecurity, shame, and inadequacy. Vivid visuals take over. Not the good kind. I am hanging by my feet, upside down on a meat hook, moving along some sort of eternal conveyance system. I stop in front of *Frankenberry* – yeah, the monster from the disgusting General Mills strawberry marshmallow cereal box. He repeatedly feeds me white and pink *Good & Plenty* licorice candy. He laughs deeply and mumbles some gibberish in old Scottish.

When the psychic torture ended, and it feels like forever, I spend several hours on the floor of our dorm bathroom, puking my mind out. All night as the trip continues for seemingly endless hours, I can only taste licorice choking in my throat every time I barf. I have never since ingested licorice.

Look. As Jerry and I concurred earlier, there were other times in college where I had positive experiences partying with close friends and taking psilocybin mushrooms. I was in a better headspace then. I was with experienced sojourners and the safety factor was high. Totally different experience.

I am in no way advocating extensive use of mind-altering drugs. But I think Owsley was showing me it was not always a bed of roses nor a mouthful of licorice. Please take heed. Everything in moderation.

Owsley tries another hug, and I shove him away by his perma-grin face. *No.* We join hand and paw, and our journey resumes.

Psilocybin: Tomorrow Never Knows

We glide along the glimmering prism of radiant energy, propelling us ... forward? The cosmic drums and sitar of The Beatles blare in Dolby surround sound. I am certain we are moving forward in time.

Colors fade, and I open my eyes, sitting on my leather sectional. Wanda has aged, her face creased and careworn with time. But still beautiful to me. Where I once held a glass of wine, I now hold a bottle of Ensure. I am old as dirt. *Ewww.*

On the TV, an elderly but still damn fine Anderson Cooper discusses all the miracles achieved using psilocybin. Turns out, identical to hydroxychloroquine and oleandrin, it's some sort of miracle substance.

Once a lonely experimental investigation site in 2020, the Johns Hopkins' Center for Psychedelic and Consciousness Research is a present-day global leader in the studied deployment of psilocybin therapeutics.

In addition to providing relief to people suffering from addiction, anxiety, and depression years ago, this wonder drug has also solved the following crises ...

- **Defeated COVID.** This is a bit of a misnomer. Psilocybin was administered to all Covidiots. Following the overthrow of the First Trump Regime, an armed CDC rounded up the Covidiots and fed them large (some say toxic) doses of the hallucinogen. They went crazy with self-loathing, dying from a rare ailment dubbed Douchitis. After they all died, the rational people stayed safely home until a tested vaccine emerged. Now the world is a happier, healthier, and more harmonious place.

- **Enabled First Contact.** Alien intelligence was too advanced for us to notice. It required a firm belief in the Mandela Effect to actualize into real parallel universes crossing over into our own. The Bobs (battery operated boyfriends) are a sentient species of dildos that have interdimensional cosmic pairings with humans. For every PS human, there is a replica PS Bob, similar in every prodigious detail of their essence except that PS Bob is a dildo. Our scientists are still hard at work deciphering their strange whirring and buzzing language.
- **Proved the existence of god.** Apparently to heavenly entities, psilocybin is a gateway drug to the Pearly Gates. Everyone on the other side uses it to attain a fuller, more personal connection to the *vibrations* of the Universe. The Bobs opened our eyes to this amazing vibrating reality. Also designated as "God's Dandruff" (G.D.), psilocybin is like dust in the *His Dark Materials* trilogy. The drug is a remnant of elemental consciousness, also once called the soul. By consuming G.D., consciousness joins across the cosmos to other States of Being (S.O.B.), creating one giant G.D. S.O.B.

Satisfied, I take Owlsey's mute paw one last time, as we return to our time and reality.

Psilocybin: The End

My middle-aged eyes flutter open. Wanda releases me from the warmth of our blue-leather cuddle as I sit up. Had I fallen asleep? Was this all a dream?

On the TV, a late-night homage, possibly an infomercial, blares music loudly. Something from The Doors. Jim Morrison screaming something about wanting to bone his mother. Disturbing, troubled times, the Sixties. Maybe Freud had it right after all.

Like a psilocybin trip, that dream was intense. So real.

I look around my living room, secretly wishing that Jerry or Owsley will jump out and startle me. Or maybe PS Bob will tickle my butthole with a quick hello. We would all have such a big belly laugh. But, alas, none of the above occurs. Sigh.

Tying (or perhaps tie-dying) it all together, what did I learn from this experience?

- Psychedelic drugs are neither good nor bad. People are. So, if you wish to take hallucinations for a test drive, do so wisely, cautiously, and safely. No judgment. You do you, friend. But if you are a Covidiot? Avoid.
- Therapy is on my agenda. Too many unresolved issues from the past, and if I want to meet god, I need to clear that up before some future psilocybin hallucination involves Count Chocula feeding me rat turds. Or, worse, getting the Violet Beauregarde treatment from Booberry. Brrr.
- I love my couch, Wanda, way too damn much. I am going to Lazy Boy tomorrow and getting an uncomfortable, overpriced chair. COVID has made me apathetic and

kind of weird. Need to work those kinks out before my wife gets her Bob to visit a lot more frequently.

For today, let's close with the unsettling lyrics of the Lizard King, *"This is the end / My only friend, the end."*

My Favorite Positions: PS Conway for President

Dear invisible reader friends (and potential voters), by the time this book has been published, the 2024 U.S. presidential election will be but a tiny twinkle in the tears that were shed by the 50 percent of voters in this great country whose useless candidate lost.

We need—nay, deserve—better options than the two morons (Tweedle Also-Ran and Tweedle Cheeto) who vied for the most powerful elected office in the world, one of whom should be President when you read this essay. Unless the next January sixth worked. In that case, you can find me camped out my cousin's heavily-armed MAGA compound in Texas. Although Texas may be its own country by then. So maybe Canada.

Enough screwing around. Let's get serious for a moment. I have ideas. Big, thick, swollen ideas. I acknowledge I have come too late and entered too far in arrears. But effective today, if or when Civil War II ends, consider me a legit goer for the office of P.O.T.U.S.

I further acknowledge I have no political experience, people skills, or perceptible intelligence. I smell bad. My feet are misshapen. I have a whistling septum. My penis is below average size. And i righteously abuse irony and satire.

But I have a vision. Visions, in fact. They come to me in dreams after crashing from binging too much psilocybin. I can vividly see a greater, more expansive, more satisfied America.

Similar to when you are size-testing dildos, you need to ensure the right fit. Let me know if we get snagged halfway there, or if we are rattling around like a stick in a coffee can, or if things glide in just right.

With that mental image firmly implanted, please allow me to share my ten favorite positions with you. Some will be uncomfortable and awkward. Others will make you shudder with happiness. All will make you reconsider the very nature of your own existence.

Abortion

Not only am I pro-choice, I am pro-murder. When I am your president, we will legalize murder once and for all. Stop all the controversy.

One thing we have learned from the COVID lockdown is that life matters less than we assumed. Christian conservatives lost their moral authority by refusing to wear masks at mass church gatherings. Well . . . when they next continued to overwhelmingly vote for a philandering godless predator. Then the mask thing.

With morality as the last ethical barrier, we can now embrace our most feral instincts with openness and integrity. Neighbor's dog shitting on your lawn? Stab it. Hell, shank the owner, too. Granny driving slow in the passing lane? Run her off the road. Watch for flames in your rearview. Douchebag talking too loud on his phone? Hit him with a hammer. Maybe a sledgehammer for good measure.

I know a satisfying head shot with a finishing double tap would feel great, but alas, no guns. More to come on that later.

Education Reform

Close all K-12 schools for a generation. Conscript all able-bodied children to manual labor camps. Let them hereafter be remembered as the Lost Generation. It's fine. American infrastructure is crumbling, and we need labor. This is a worthy sacrifice for many families and soon, the binding legal duty of all to give back.

Of course, teachers will need to join them if they want a paycheck. Plus, when K-12 education reopens for Generation AA or whatever pointless moniker we give them, teachers will have a newfound appreciation for what a full year of work looks and feels like. Maybe they'll bitch a little bit less.

Show your pride. When you speed past a seven-year-old with a jackhammer on the brand-new Interstate, give her a horn honk of patriotic support. That passing atta-girl is certain to soothe her sore muscles.

The Economy

Under my presidency, the State will seize all the money and assets from the top one percenters (TOPs) and march them into institutional slavery. Wealth and success are crimes against humanity. It's time the takers start to get their comeuppance against the producers who hired them.

Let's face it. It's just not fair. The TOP's success is really a combination of several factors: white privilege, institutional racism, and inheritance. Any hard work or good ol'-fashion gumption are by far the exceptions to those determinants.

At the end of the day, we are a capitalist nation that wants everyone to be economically equal, regardless of contribution or ability. Let's celebrate the fate of the TOPs as we tackle narrowing the racial divisions in our country.

Racial Inequality

My administration will take an even more punitively progressive approach to so-called reparations. There will be no money. Sorry, but the money is going to be spent on roads, bridges, and military bases. That said, each adult Black person in the USA will receive a white slave family from the conscripted pool of TOPs. You heard me: White slavery. Using rich white people! What better way to say Black Lives Matter?

Think of how clean Thad will keep your house! Or your satisfaction when Buffy is driving Ms. Ashanti? Consider how fulfilled you will feel when that karmic wheel of social justice has turned full circle. Some folks on my team are proposing the policy name as PIBB: Payback is a Bitch, bitch. Native Americans, sorry. Squeaky wheel gets the oil.

Immigration

You people have gotten spoiled with how good you have it in the United States. For you, my administration will reverse the policy of Immigration and implement our migration policy.

Codenamed GTFO, Get the Fuck Out, our policy will find any whiny ingrate or malcontent who is currently a U.S. citizen and relocate them to their country of origin. The military will pack your family, pack your shit, and drop you off at the nearest local refugee camp for assimilation training into your new culture. Let's see how life in Azerbaijan or Yemen match up. Should be an adventure! Maybe you could live in the same neighborhood as our *Friend*, Chandler Bing... "15 Yemen Road. Yemen." (R.I.P., Chandler Bing).

Insofar as actual Immigration to the U.S.A., the doors are back open to anyone who isn't a bitch. "Winners, Not Whiners," is our motto for you. Willing to work? Pay your taxes? Learn the American language? Comfy with being chipped through vaccinations, tracked, and surveilled? Welcome to the new 'Merica.

Climate Change

During Donald Trump's first administration, it was proven both orally and anecdotally that windmills cause cancer. I mean, if he said so it must be true. With that news, our last hopes for fixing or reversing climate change are crushed.

Humans are a virus that consume and destroy their host. Our dirty work is done, and Mother Earth has been eviscerated by our rapacious swarm of takers. Our smart science people calculate we have only three thousand years to move to Alpha Centauri before our continents are submerged forever under massive broiling tsunamis of briny death. While that is only half the time since god created the earth six thousand years ago, we need to start planning now. We will empower and fund Space Force to invent some important technology.

Firstly, Faster than Light (FTL) travel. Damn the math and physics, we are Americans, not American'ts. Secondly, space arks. Like Noah, but way bigger and less genetically treacherous. And thirdly, death rays. Something to *exterminate* a likely hostile indigenous population of Alpha Centaurians. Like a badass bunch of Doctor Who Daleks, we may need to *exterminate* the locals.

Gun Policy

We are taking your guns. There, I said it. All of them. Our STFU Policy will begin with rewriting the Second Amendment of the U.S. Constitution. This amended Amendment will contain the following strikethrough: "... the right of the people to keep and bear Arms, shall ~~not~~ be infringed."

Let the Infringement begin. Our forebears were rebels and terrorists, as are their progeny. My administration will not tolerate the risk of armed resistance from any Militia, or that fucked up looking Q-Anon Buffalo Man, especially given the breadth and depth of our aspirations for reshaping this great nation.

We all know the only reason you want guns is to overthrow the government. C'mon, duh. Now we are coming to overthrow you. There will be peace at all costs, and the nominal level of bloodshed from disarming a few tough guys should be well under the final coronavirus death count, which we all know, as a percentage of the overall population, was really no biggie anyway. Salute your flag while we achieve peace through all violent means necessary.

Healthcare

Social Security and Medicare were never intended to be around this long. The Federal Budget allocates nearly *three trillion dollars* in mandatory spending to support these obscene entitlements... per year!

That's it. We're done. Enough handouts. Someone must be the grown-up in the room and save our health system. In the first ninety days of my administration, we will implement a *national death* age of 65 years. If you are not already dead from hurricanes, labor conscription, contagion, Civil War II, or white slavery, you must call your local Board of Electors for a Summary Execution. Quick and simple, our new Death Force will show up at your home. Just show them your National ID card or let them scan your new Patriot Chip, and they will line you up against a wall and shoot you dead.

Your constant economic burden on society will end with a bullet to the frontal lobe, ensuring we keep the young and healthy even healthier while economically securing the Motherland for generations to come. Your Nation honors your sacrifice. Go gentle into that good night.

Military

Iran, nuked. Russia, nuked. North Korea, nuked. Problem solved. China better stop fucking around with creating hurricanes and deadly viruses, or they're next, too. After obliterating the Axis of Evil + One, all the world will love us even more. Our allies will thank us once they adapt to the vexing irritations following the radioactive fallout.

I will invest heavily in using our military to spread American values across the remainder of the world by creating massive military installations on every continent. Better said, expanding the bases we already have in place anyway. We have given so much for so long to policing the world, now we will nestle in as an occupying police force. It's time for our fair share of the apple pie. Like half. Maybe more.

You have your culture? That's nice. 'Merica. You have your language? That's nice. Speak American. Look, as many of you know when you see Americans traveling around the world, we know everything. It's simple: America. Or else.

In Summary: Why I Should Be Your Man (for President)

To recap, we can summarize my policy positions into these simple, digestible sound bites. Edible like the delicious fruit arrangement the government provides you after your grandmother's summary execution:

- Legalize murder.
- End education.
- Confiscate wealth.
- White slavery.
- Mass emigration.
- Leave earth.
- Disarm the public.
- Execute the elderly.
- America. Or else.

As you will clearly notice, the other political hacks do not orbit the same radiant, pulsating sun as me. My universe is uniquely suited for those with the balls and Icarian stamina to realize deep, penetrating change.

And get a load of this! When you come with me on this wet and wild adventure, you will receive a pair of signed assless chaps, knockoffs of the pubic pantaloons I will wear to all my public campaign events. Made of the finest, rich, Corinthian leather, these squeaky britches scream, *"Yeah, baby!"* to all my fetishist fashionistas.

Folks, I'm a straight shooter, cocked and loaded for action. But I need your help to finish. I can do it alone, but where is the fun in that? Join me today! Let's partner to ensure this effort reaches its climax, and we take the White House back for the future of the American race! Thank you. Stay safe, America.

LABOR DAY:
A REFLECTION ON LOVE, LABOR, & LOSS

Labor Day in the United States marks the end of summer. It is a national holiday intended to celebrate workers, specifically Labor Union workers. The meaning sometimes gets lost in all the rigamarole of parties, parades, and celebrations. Most Americans simply enjoy it as a long weekend with a Monday off from work.

Labor Day originated during the peak of the late 19th-century U.S. Industrial Revolution. Working conditions were horrific both for adults and children.

Of particular note was the Midget Uprising of 1886. Pejorative "olden days" nicknames aside, they worked in gold mines and were regularly mistaken for children, brutally beaten and paid a fraction of their taller counterparts. Under the leadership of Hank "Doc" Homunculus, the wee workers rebelled against their oppressive overlords by feeding them poisoned apples and summoning birds and squirrels to bite them.

The famous Labor chant of "Are you serious!? We're not kids!" became synonymous with Lilliputian rights in the American Labor lexicon.

Subsequently, labor union talks encouraged escalating strikes and rallies demanding higher wages and better working conditions. Following violent clashes with workers and police, resulting in dozens of deaths, some heavily industrialized states began recognizing workingmen's holidays on the first Monday of September.

Under enormous pressure, President Grover Cleveland signed Labor Day into federal law in 1894 to settle the mass unrest and bloodshed with workers. The national holiday has continued since.

As a pithy aside, Cleveland was a shitty president in his second term. The Veto President's biggest claim to fame after Labor Day was settling arbitration with Great Britain over Venezuelan boundaries. Wow. That's the stuff of American legend.

With Labor Day's historical backdrop so brilliantly revealed, let's explore other holidays impacted by organized labor and the cultural laziness we continue to perpetuate by federalizing more and more holidays.

Non-Labor Day(s)

Origins of American national holidays are fascinating to me. Part of the eclectic pastiche that makes me so damn interesting, eh? Among my other curiosities are the history of glues, 14th century grooming habits, and clown-hunting.

Organized Labor has impacted the federalization of many "Monday" holidays to include Martin Luther King, Jr, Day, President's Day, and Columbus Day. In fact, seven of the ten federal holidays currently recognized were the byproduct of labor union lobbying efforts in one fashion or another.

The remaining three federal holidays are not byproducts of Union handiwork. They cater to matters of historical unity and national pride and predate the Labor movement:

- **Christmas Day** – White Jesus's fake birthday. Thirty years ago, the USA identified as 85 percent Christian. Now it is 65 percent. How pissed is Jesus right now about the whole free will thing? Membership in the J Club continues to decline due to people truly sucking. Reasons cited range from greed and hypocrisy to politicization, Donald Trump, and child rape. Anyone bother to read the New Testament? Wow. Happy birthday, Jesus.
- **Thanksgiving** – a day to give thanks and appreciation for our boundless blessings through gluttony, family dysfunction, and shitty football matchups. Nothing says 'Merica more than your fat gut hanging over your unzipped pants, drooling down your man titties in a tryptophan coma. Too sleepy to hate yourself for joining the 70 percent of Americans who are overweight or obese. Several recent polls have shown steady declines since 2016 in the use of the statement "proud to be an American". Hmmm. Wonder why?
- **Independence Day** – the annual "suck it" message to the greatest Superpower of its Day from the upstart country that established justice through rebellion, terrorism, institutional slavery, and attempted genocide of the native population. I often wonder if there is a hidden collective guilt we Americans repress. For all the bravado and show of acting humble and thankful, we really can be so damn arrogant and entitled. Careful with your hubris, Ozymandias.

Which brings us to the longest non-Union holiday in American History: COVID Day.

It commemorates that charming vacation we enjoyed so much in the early 2020s. Instead of a refreshing long weekend, we were treated to months, *years*, of anxiety, fear, misinformation, malfeasance, and death unseen since the Spanish Flu a century ago. Eventually, most of us wanted to return to a normal work schedule.

Labor Day Traditions: Upsides and Downsides

So, let's start with this thought: COVID's psychological stranglehold intruded on beloved Labor Day traditions in 2020. Many may never be the same. Consider the following:

- **Parades.** My opinion? Who cares? How these events have ever passed for entertainment defies all logic. How bored must you be to stand sweating on the crowded sidewalk for hours to catch a fleeting glimpse of . . . Fire trucks? Go to your local Fire Department's fund-raising events. Clowns? *Brrrr*. What sociopathic dick nose ever let these makeup-wearing, soul-sucking, cannibalistic pedophiles out of Hell to chuck candy in your face? Marching bands? Suck. Sorry, I was in the marching band, too. I still have a smashed right testicle from my bass drum harness wailing on my nutsack for the endless dirges down Main Street USA. Good riddance. Thanks, COVID.
- **Barbecues.** The flip side of parades, for me. I unequivocally love barbecues. Eating zesty grilled food. Gathering for laughs with family and friends. Drinking

beer while throwing Frisbees. Plus, the whimsically quirky traditions growing up in rural America, too. Like conjuring nature demons from the cornfields and setting them loose on the city folk. Great fun. Also, dredging for dead foreigners in the local crick. If only they learned to keep their damn mouths shut and mind their own business. Once dry, however, they do make good kindling for the demon-summoning fires. And we cannot forget Bang a Quaker Night. This tradition harkens back to the original Quaker pilgrim's ritual molestation by the local Indian tribes to celebrate their need to loosen up and enjoy the end of summer. Today, it is slightly more voluntary.

- **Baseball Season Denouement.** September typically marks the final month of 162 unathletic games of professional spitting before the October playoffs. COVID did us a small favor for 2020 and cut the monotonous season to 60 dull-ass games. I'm still pissed about a few things. First, DirecTV. Should I not have received a 33 percent discount for a 33 percent season MLB Package? Shit is expensive. Second, piped-in fake fan sounds was like hearing a laugh track on a 1970s sitcom. Total cheese. We knew no one was there. Last, am I the only person who wanted to replace the cardboard fake fans in the outfield with bound and gagged clowns? Imagine their abject terror and our belly laughter when a Kyle Schwarber line drive nailed them in their painted-on faces? That would have been worth the price of non-admission.

- **Football Season Starts.** I love American football. It launches like a SCUD missile the weekend following Labor Day. Violence, aggression, testosterone. The apex of athleticism and manliness. I played tennis. I never took a hit from anything bigger than a bong until I played rugby in college. My body craved the teamwork, the comradery, the contact. Honestly, I needed to feel what it was like to get knocked on my ass and pummeled all the while sucking wind and pushing through it. Needed to feel tougher. Rugby scratched the itch perfectly. Having experienced the torn-out eye corners, the mystery bruises, and the undiagnosed concussions, I'm now more than satisfied to invest $150 each season and play Fantasy Football with my family. I have ample pain. I'm getting too old. Everything hurts in manopause. It hurts to fart sometimes. Let some other dumbasses get pounded.

So, Labor Day hasn't necessarily been the same for me after COVID. Roger that. Just give me football, god. A simple request. Don't make me abandon the last remaining strands of faith in your existence. Glad we are clear. Thanks.

Speaking of god, let's now transition into our Labor Day miracle.

Our Most Memorable Labor Day

Now for something Labor Day-related to truly celebrate.

My first daughter was born Labor Day weekend 1995. So, while my interest in examining collective bargaining and labor racketeering hovers around a 2 on a scale of 1,000, my daughter's dramatic – nay, traumatic – birth occupies my thoughts this weekend.

Freshly returned to the United States after an amazing honeymoon in Ireland, my wife and I had a robustly natural sexual appetite for each other as 25-year-old newlyweds. TMI?

We lived in the Capital Region of Upstate New York in November 1994. Staying with friends in Saratoga Springs for a party weekend, the night of my eldest's conception is, to this day, known as *One Drunken Night in Saratoga.*

Off to a stellar start, I never added my wife to my health insurance plan, and she was an uncovered grad student. In my defense, we were 25 years old and super healthy. Who thinks of such minor details as health insurance? Apparently not me. In speaking with our company Vice President of Human Resources, I discovered my wife's pregnancy fell under an exclusion I had never heard of prior: a "pre-existing condition."

A baby? What the what? What the heck would we do? We had no money. How would we pay for a pregnancy out of pocket?

As the Veep lectured me about personal responsibility and growing up, her voice faded away. An ocean's roaring tide filled my ears, drowning out all noise. I saw red. My heart raced. The anger pulsed in my head. Her voice surged back in, "Listen, you need to understand...."

"No, *you* need to understand me, you c*nt," puked forth from my mouth. The queen mother whore of all cuss words. The infamous C-word. I can taste the soap in my mouth from my mom as I type. Apparently suffering an insane fugue state, I had just called my VP of HR, a woman, the most dreaded word in all of misogyny.

"I'm sorry," was all I could muster as I hung up the phone to suffocate her enraged screaming on the other end.

Fast forward to March 1995. Is anyone a fan of the television series *ER*? As though a harbinger of things to come, I remember watching Season 1, Episode 19, with my wife. It was titled "Love's Labor Lost." Cool Shakespeare allusion without the pretentiously colourful British spelling of *labour*, of course.

Probably the most horrifyingly sad thing we have ever watched on TV. A pregnant woman dies due to a doctor's misdiagnosis of a bladder infection instead of preeclampsia. We were still in the first trimester. Could this be us? Rattled, I poured myself a few shots of bourbon. OK, I drank the bottle. Stop judging.

In May, my wife's blood pressure started getting scary high. As did the medical bills. By mid-July, she was diagnosed with preeclampsia. The ER-episode was indelibly seared into our retinas. We could not unsee it, and we were scared shitless. Why had we watched it? It's like watching *The Exorcist*, then getting possessed by the devil, knowing it's your fault because you watched the movie.

Sunday, September 2 dawned, one week before my baby girl's due date. As though by way of psychic premonition, my parents arrived out of the blue that morning. My mother-in-law called to say she was *en route* to visit soon thereafter.

Then the labor pains started. My wife's unforgettable Labor Day weekend.

As I circled looking for a parking spot, my wife suffered a placental abruption while my mom and dad walked her into the ER. When I entered the hospital, there was blood everywhere on the floor. Attendants had begun mopping it up. Nurses whisked me up to the Labor & Delivery ward.

The scene in the delivery room was worse. My wife's lovely vagina had turned into some sort of blood cannon. Crimson gore was sprayed across the floors, the walls, twinkly speckles across the ceiling tiles. Literally looked like a murder scene from a gruesome slasher flick.

It is moments like this when you realize you are *about as useful as a poopy-flavored lollipop*. Step aside, Patches O'Houlihan, and let the medical professionals save your wife and daughter's life. There was so much screaming. So much frenetic activity from the medical staff. So much blood. Then my daughter was out. But she swallowed meconium. (Baby shit. Swallowed her own shit.) A neonatologist was in the room. Suctioning her lungs with a ... wtf? Turkey baster?

All the while I had been holding my wife's sweaty hand. She was such an absolute rock star. No pain meds. So much happened so fast with such violence and chaos. But she was ok. And our baby girl would be ok. Et voilà, we were parents.

Labor Day Closing Thoughts

Let's recap. You've laughed a lot. Take a breath. Calm your pulse. I disclaim any liability if you have a stroke. If you peed yourself already, that's just funny.

Labor Day is one of ten federal holidays in the United States. We can always count on Organized Labor to continue working restlessly to help workers work less. Delicious irony. And Labor Unions may need to begin new collective bargaining efforts to save the other three non-Union holidays from obsolescence.

Labor Day 2020 spoiled a few traditions for me. It's my choice to continue with intelligent social distancing and allowing COVID to recede into memory. I know there are plenty of you Covidiot dickheads out there who don't care and would strangle your sickly grandmother with your bare hands for one more grilled hot dog. So be it. I hope you choke.

Labor Day for me is mostly about the birth of our amazing daughter. Life is tough. Shit happens. Our ability to overcome adversity, pain, and suffering makes us stronger. Forces us to grab fear by the haunches and hump it into submission. That's my wife. I will just sit quietly in my detached fugue state until called upon.

Meanwhile, I will need to contend with football-induced priapism and wear baggy pants to cover up my erection until the season begins and the excitement dissipates. Pray for me.

Afterword: The Labor of Love

I didn't want to make a big political statement in this story about the horror of *pre-existing conditions*. But our hospital bill was $35,000 for the birth of our daughter because of all the ichor and drama.

Wondering what happened? My wife is tough as nails. Or like the title to the porn movie I am working on, *Hard as Limes*.

She negotiated the bill with the hospital, claiming indigence, and got the costs reduced to $18,000. Still a ton of money for a grad student and a commissioned salesman in 1995.

We maxed out our credit cards to pay the hospital. And then the most amazing thing happened. Truly the reason I have remained in a sales career for the last 25 years: I sold shit. A lot of it. And we made good money. Within the next year, we had paid off the hospital debt in full.

Here's the thing. I worked my ass off. This was not a gimme or a free ride. I mastered my craft and harnessed every scintilla of charisma available to ensure the financial security of our new family.

And, as many of you have asked, it's why it has taken me 25 years to return to writing. I love writing deeply, but after this terrifying beginning, providing a high-quality of life for my girls has always come first. Easy choice.

Are You Ready for Some Football?

American football season starts every September. I get so excited I could soil myself. As you can tell, dear invisible reader friends, I love football. The action. The violence. The commercialization. The fun!

Picture my Sundays between September and January:

- **"Rise & Shine."** Mornings filled with ESPN and other TV sports shows prognosticating about the day's games to come. Player profiles, stat overloads, highlight reels, analysis of plays, touching vignettes. YES! Never too much.
- **Game time**! Turn on *The Red Zone*. I playfully term this add-on to my standard satellite *NFL Sunday Ticket* service as "ADHD Football" because it shows the scoring plays in real time for every game currently being played. I definitely have undiagnosed ADHD, so the ever-changing split screens make perfect sense to my easily distracted... look! A squirrel!
- **Technology.** I have my laptop, my iPad, and my iPhone strategically arranged around me for instant access to injury reports, Fantasy Football leagues, shit-talking group texts with family and friends, Twitter feeds,

to name a few. When the power grid finally fails, and you all resort to cannibalism, you can find me sitting despondent on my new leather sectional. My salty tears moistening my skin for easier chewing.

Aside from some other force majeure, the only thing that can go wrong is some godforsaken COVID redux. The NBA had their bubble. Baseball shortened their eternal season to adapt. Golf and tennis have...meh...who really cares? Will the safety changes the NFL stashed in the emergency file be sufficient? I hope so.

As with our everyday life, it will come down to how irresponsible the players behave away from the field and team. If they go clubbing, don't wear masks, don't attempt to socially distance, the season is at risk. That much physical contact and copious handling of balls (hehe, sorry) has infection written all over it.

For now, fingers (and toes) crossed. I remain cautiously optimistic...and super psyched for a full season with 32 healthy teams each playing 16 full games. Plus, the playoffs and Super Bowl!

How about we channel this athletic enthusiasm into some laughs and knowledge? Let's explore this love affair with football further and discuss the reasons why football is America's favorite sport. *Are you ready for some football?*

Football: Follow the Money

America's favorite sport, you ask? Yup. Revenue isn't even close with baseball, basketball, or hockey...

Cold hard cash fact, the NFL is the largest revenue producing sports league in the world, let alone the United States. The global question to debate is which is bigger, American football or World Football (Futbol)? For discussion's sake, let's call World Football its proper American name: soccer. But does revenue equate to popularity? If so, sorry soccer.

Many soccer-biased elitists will tell you that, as a worldwide sport, soccer is vastly more popular than American football. But viewership numbers are deceptively misleading. Soccer's World Cup Final draws 1-1.2B viewers every four years while the Super Bowl draws 100-120M viewers every year. Left on its own, that sounds impressive for soccer. But is it?

- U.S. Population is 330M, and 110M watch the Super Bowl. That is 33 percent of the available U.S. audience. The rest of the world is probably watching cricket, whatever the hell that is.
- If the rest of the world (7.8B people) would wise up and love American football, at a sustained 33 percent viewership rate, the Super Bowl might draw 2.5B viewers. Every year. No need to wait four years.
- Thus, on a per capita basis, American football is far more popular than World football. The rest of the world just needs to accept the sport. I rest my case. Suck it, soccer.

Like high school, the kid with the most money (and the BMW) is also the most popular. It's a combination of genetics and math. Who understands it? Not me. I would rather spend some time on another key reason football is so beloved: parity.

Football: Life Lesson in Parity

The NFL is considered to have the greatest parity of any professional sports league. This means that each team ideally has equal levels of talent. The net result of parity should deliver closer games, more ties, more overtimes. All of which we have seen in recent years. Most importantly, it should eliminate dynasties from occurring.

So how is it, with so many checks and balances in place – i.e., drafts that favor underperforming teams, salary caps, and free agency . . . the New England Patriots could have once claimed dynasty status for so long?

Outside of the elite temple of athleticism resides those of us who regularly trip over our own two feet when walking across level ground. In the workplace, our parity comes from allowing opportunity for anyone to compete for any job equally, irrespective of race, gender, sexual orientation, or religion. Given that equal "footing," the winner should receive equal pay and equal opportunity for advancement. Still a work in progress.

Yet there are better coaches. There are better companies. There are better cultures we could fit with. So, while we can agree to parity in opportunity, the real world has too many other unmanaged variables to impact parity in contribution.

That's capitalism in a nutshell. Warts and all, football is distinctly a byproduct of 'Merica. Big? Loud? Cocky? You bet.

Football: All Your Fantasies Come True

But 'Merica is also innovative. And we are good at making money. When those two attributes fornicate, their progeny is Fantasy Football.

Part of what makes American football so enormously popular is our ability to compete and gamble against each other while watching our favorite sport, drinking beer, and making chili. Pure unadulterated genius. And legal!

For those of you unfamiliar with Fantasy Football and how to play, I'm not consuming my wordcount with explanations. Check out a simple tutorial online. Meanwhile, each year, I gather with between eight and twelve guys; we collect $150 each and establish prize payouts. In a good year, that $150 could yield you $1,000 or more in good ol' USD greenbacks.

Then you draft a fantasy team comprised of 16 total players: 2 quarterbacks, 4 wide receivers, 4 running backs, 2 tight ends, 2 kickers, and 2 defenses. Each week, through your vast football knowledge of players, stats, weather, psychic premonition, wildfires, COVID outbreaks, and matchups, you start your best option(s) in each position against another team in your fantasy league.

Like AT&T phone plans, friends and family comprise our fantasy league. My team's name is Caligula's Napkin. Felt quite clever with that name. Just naughty and gross. Leaves you wondering what the napkin was for.

First year of our league, one of the younger, uneducated, inbred guys asked me if Caligula's Napkin once played as a cornerback for the Pittsburgh Steelers. I sighed, lied like Bill Belichick, and said yes. In the back of my mind I was licking my chops, thinking, *"A fool and his money are soon parted."*

That year, we developed a sensei/grasshopper relationship. He would ask me for fantasy football advice. I would give him the wrong advice. He would lose. I would take his money at the end of the season. My little gakusei learned many valuable lessons in trust. Sadly, he left me next season for another dojo.

Fantasy Football adds an insane layer of enjoyment to an already mirthful football season. Games with football teams you don't care about are suddenly interesting because you are starting their running back and defense that week. Your sports palate has expanded. You are now a football sommelier. A *footballier*. The only thing better is the Super Bowl.

Football: The Super Bowl

Jesus wept, but if the Super Bowl is not the most commercial, musical, recreational, and—oh yeah—metaphysical event of any year, I surely lack the mental capacity to divine the answer.

Labor Unions should be lobbying for the Monday following Super Bowl Sunday to be a national holiday. The hangovers are brutal.

The game itself is fine. But I have watched minimally all the red zone plays in close to 600 games over the last five months. I'm ready for the game, but the pageantry and events around the game? Feckin' brilliant.

- **Super Bowl Parties.** Adults gone wild. The amount of excess eating, screaming, laughing, and drinking that occurs during the Super Bowl is epic. Type 2 diabetes readings must spike in the weeks following the Super Bowl from all the gluttony-induced inflammation.
- **Puppy Bowl.** If you don't watch the Puppy Bowl on *Animal Planet*, you don't have a damn soul. It does not interfere with the Super Bowl, and I'm telling you, Team Ruff is ready to absolutely spay and neuter Team Fluff this year.
- **The Commercials.** Next to the Halftime Show, probably the biggest draw for non-football fans. Companies spend up to $5M for a 30-second ad. And they are genius. I can still remember the Wendy's fast-food commercial from 1984 with an old lady yelling, *"Where's the beef?"*

- **The Halftime Shows**. Music is so integral to the promotion and marketing of American football. Prince completely shredded the stage and his guitar on *Purple Rain* (in the rain) in Super Bowl XLI (2007). The Black-Eyed Peas, on the other hand, showed us what atonal steaming piles of shit look and sound like in Super Bowl XLV (2011). And Janet Jackson's boob? Pure teenage entertainment.

So many great memories with football. My only regret is that my youngest daughter's birthday falls the week after the Super Bowl every year, and every company I have worked for hosts their national sales meeting that week.

Missed a lot of my baby's birthdays to pay for her UW-Madison college education. Hopefully, her graduation gift to New Zealand with her Pops helps to fill the empty void my jobs created. Yeah, I'm going. Not going to miss all the cool *Lord of The Rings* shit awaiting us.

Football: The Final Seconds

I am exhausted when the Super Bowl finishes each year. So much energy and excitement has been invested. So much love. With football over, you look around and find yourself in the middle of winter. Cold, dark days mourn the passing of yet another incredible football season.

The TV still holds plenty of NBA basketball and NHL hockey action. I try. I swear I do.

Basketball is incomprehensibly alien to me. I played as a kid. Wrong choice of word. I embarrassed myself as a kid. I sucked. Is there a worse word than sucked? If so, that is me.

An old man once gave me a lollipop after a game because he thought I was special needs. True story.

Hockey is a sport I should have tried as a kid. Maybe they could have trained the suck out of me. I live in Upstate New York, which is basically iced over eleven months out of the year. Nine months now. Up yours, global warming. But, as with basketball, I have more concussions from falling and hitting my head on the ice recreationally skating than I ever had from the years I played rugby in college.

Maybe I will take up skiing this winter. Or just nap a lot.

REALITY TV:
I AM NOT WHAT I AM

Literary scholars, horticulturists, and astrologers widely consider Iago from *Othello* the most treacherous of villains in William Shakespeare's caboodle of tragedies. For those of you unfamiliar with *Othello*, first and foremost, please start reading something. Anything. Educate yourself.

Baby steps before Shakespeare. Perhaps I might suggest *The Berenstain Bears and Too Much TV*. Small words. Ironic foreshadowing. Bright Colors. And no, I'm not giving away the most dramatic ending in Berenstain history.

Then, when you possess the mental dexterity to navigate more than remembering Iago as Jafar's evil macaw from Disney's *Aladdin* . . . well, that is progress. And maybe the malevolent Disney character may just reveal something about Shakespeare's Iago.

Quick summary of *Othello*.

- Othello, the Moor (a Black man), is an honored general in the Venetian Army who has eloped with Desdemona, the white daughter of a Venetian senator. Scandalous! The Venetian Senate sends him to Cyprus to defend against

- From the opening scene, Iago plots to destroy Othello for mysteriously elusive reasons. Was Iago passed over by Othello for a promotion to lieutenant? Did Othello have an affair with Iago's wife Emilia? Is Iago motivated by misogyny and racism stating, *"an old black ram is tupping your white ewe?"* Is Iago in love with Othello?
- Through many deceptions (again, read the play for the juicy stuff), Iago plants a series of lies, stoking Othello's profound jealousy that Desdemona is an unfaithful whore. The resulting finale is murder, madness, and mayhem on a scale that only Shakespeare can provide.

Iago: Demand Me Nothing

Iago is manipulative, vindictive, and treacherous. A true Machiavellian antagonist to Othello's virtuous protagonist. Iago tells us, *"I am not what I am."* A religious Elizabethan audience would know that God told Moses, *"I am what I am."* This blasphemous oppositeness makes one question if Iago is the devil.

But Shakespeare turns that literary convention on its head. The viewer befriends the devil. Unlike our kinship for other great tragic heroes like Hamlet or Macbeth, who relate to us and tug our heart strings through their soliloquies, Othello is aloof. It is Iago who consistently addresses the audience with his magnetic asides, making us fully aware of his schemes.

Think Monty Python's *Nudge Nudge* sketch, *"A nod's as good as a wink to a blind bat."*

Iago hatches his subterfuges with such sociopathic charm and forthrightness, assuming our alignment with him, that we become complicit in his nefarious plans. As Othello is unmistakably trapped, so is the audience. Caught in an ill-placed admiration for the captivating justifications of a wicked man.

Ultimately, Iago personifies the misogyny and racism of Venice in those days. Like a mirror, Iago reflects the worst attributes of the day. And he epitomizes the worst qualities.

So when Othello succumbs to madness, and the killing begins, it leaves us horrified that we sat passively by as this malignancy metastasized through Iago. His final middle finger to us theatergoers, with no resolution for his actions, is captured in *"Demand me nothing; what you know, you know."*

Reality TV: Modern Day Iago?

Reality TV is our modern-day Iago.

It tempts us. Attracts us. Reflects us. But it is also deceptive. What we perceive to be reality is finely produced, sometimes engineered, reality sitcoms.

We know it is stale, moldy popcorn that was stored for years is a movie theatre basement. So why do we keep eating it?

- **Glamour** – if we didn't love it, why else would the *Real Housewives* series keep spreading like herpes to find yet another crotch in which to fester? These obscenely rich plastic princesses have spread this narcissistic plague to every major city in the country.
- **Fantasy** – ahh, the elusive search for the affirmation of love. Factor in some uber hot millennials with a side of cray cray, and you have invented *The Bachelor* series. Or the hope beyond hope that some defective adult incapable of finding naturalized, age-appropriate love finds imported, mail-order love on *90-Day Fiancé*.

- **Community** – shows now have apps. Are you kidding me? Not only can we watch five episodes a week of *Love Island* and interact on social media 24/7. We can also now feed our addiction and comment, vote, take quizzes, buy merch, and become a total loser with no life!
- **Train Wreck** – my personal fave, and why I like most Reality TV? The shit show of awful people's awful lives served up on a coprophilic hotplate of diarrhea in front of our hungry eyes. Like a drama vampire, I lap up their tears, their selfishness, their self-absorption. Absolutely succulent.

We leave Reality TV appreciating the safety and predictable dullness of our own lives and how much better we are than the people we have watched. We are not what we see on TV.

Yet this vortex pulls us into its gravity well. In orbit, we revisit these mind-numbing millennials, talentless de facto celebrities, creepy international wife shoppers, and disgruntled employees because, in part, we have been manipulated.

Producers edit most of the shows to shape our reactions (and interest). Character development gets distilled from hundreds of hours of actual footage into sound bites that create heroes and villains. Hell, scouts spend months profiling talent for the shows to ensure they meet a specific required psychological, emotional, or social profile.

We know this. And yet we watch. Mostly because the endings are relatively harmless. Some heartbreak. A little happiness. A few laughs. But no one dies. The action does not lead to any life-altering tragedies with moral or spiritual implications.

What would Iago do? These shows are manipulative, but do they take things far enough? I stand certain in the belief that

Iago would devise an entirely different reality entertainment. Things your eyes can never unsee.

Keeping Up with the Kardashians
Why do we watch it?

Like all good wholesome family fun, it starts with Kim's graphic sex tape leaked by her boyfriend. So, *E!* along with Kim's proud mother, Kris, said, "Let's make a less lascivious family show. One without happy endings!"

Then comes the multiple glamorous weddings, divorces, and surrogate births. Not reality enough? Throw in Olympian Bruce Jenner's transition to Caitlyn (notably without a Kardashian "K" Kaitlyn), cheating leading to surprise pregnancies, sleepovers with OJ Simpson, Khloe's real dad controversy, Kanye (notably with a Kardashian "K"), and a powerhouse social media maven mom micromanaging everything. Reminiscent of your real life, isn't it?

What would Iago do?

He would flip the story on its ear from the beginning. The new show's name: *Staying Woke with the Washingtons.*

The story begins with a fake woke white family who wears blackface and pretends to be African American in public, while hiding racist inclinations at home. All the kids marry white folks and force them to wear black makeup at home to be ironic.

The middle daughter Whitney is married to rapper Eminem. The story begins with Em murdering his Munchausen's mama in a fit of rage-rapping. *His daughter Hailie is beautiful, but she won't even show up at Ma's funeral.*

The matriarch Winona and father Wesley have marital troubles. Wes is questioning his sexuality. Winona doesn't put up with that shit and cuts his dick off, wearing it on a gold chain around her neck. Now he's her bitch.

The shocking series finale reveals Eminem is a Black posing in whiteface. Everyone knew no white guy could lay down those thick lines. He admits to hating white women and hires his Gangsta crew to kill all the Washingtons.

They spare Wes. He has suffered enough and lives to tell their story to the world. His new tell-all Reality, fantasy series: *The Bobbit*.

90-Day Fiancée

Why do we watch it?

After a Trump regime which stoked anti-immigration sentiment, isn't it exciting for *TLC* to profit on Americans marrying foreigners? Then put the couple on the K-1 visa deadline to be married within 90 days of arrival to the USA. All the while questioning the motives of the foreigner – is it genuine love, or are they conniving to become an American citizen? Piece of cake.

And while the show's ticking clock format is hard enough, especially these xenophobic days, producers' tight control makes the show even more challenging. There are so many things gloriously wrong with the show: weird-ass cast, staged or even scripted scenes, women forced to misogynistically pose in sexy positions... I could go on.

When the curtain falls, the show has successfully married a high percentage of the couples. That totally blows my mind. For every twenty-five couples, only three get divorced. That 12 percent divorce rate crushes the current U.S. divorce rate of 42 percent. Of course, to maintain the immigrant partner's green card, the couple needs to stay married for two years.

What Would Iago do?

Iago would recognize the opportunity to ratchet up the drama and tension with *90-Day Fiancée: Indoctrination*. Green cards are far tougher to obtain under the orthodoxy of Cheeto Christ. New immigration requirements could end in love ... or tragedy.

Each K-1 visa applicant will no longer sit bored and pensive at his fiancée's home. The government will house them in barracks on the southern U.S. Border under ICE command for indoctrination.

Authorities will return the contestants to their betrothed after completing a 90-day endurance course to prove how badly they love 'Merica. The frightened foreigners will first get sorted into teams.

- White immigrants are automatically naturalized. No questions asked.
- The smart immigrants, of course, referring to Orientals and Indians (duh), will spend 90-days as university teaching assistants. Audiences will laugh in delight as the TAs struggle to explain complex ideas to entitled white college kids. Also, the Central Government will retire the "broad brush stroke" and antiquated term *Asian*, favoring a return to more racially specific identifiers.
- Brown immigrants have two teams. The "Speak English" team will spend their first 90 days working in fields, picking crops. PhD in engineering? Peaches need

picking. The "No Speaka de English" team will sleep in cages until they can learn to speak patriotic American words like *bigly* and *covfefe*.

- Middle Eastern immigrants? If you are not ISIS, you have family who are ISIS. Shut up. You do. You get a special trip to Gitmo for the 90-day Advanced Interrogation seminar to ensure you or anyone you have ever met pose no risk to the U.S. Motherland.

Any resistance or griping will meet with a televised summary execution by firing squad with global camera crews at both families' homes capturing every dramatic moment. Donald Trump will reprise his famous "*You're fired*" tagline from *The Apprentice*, with the new tagline, "*Fire!*"

We have invested enough money trying to shape a proper American. Not wasting a dime on flights carting your American't ass and poor attitude home.

Love Island USA

Why do we watch it?

This one is my latest addictive regret in Reality TV. Much like the carnival that is *90-day Fiancée,* where the inbred bearded lady humps Bobo the Clown's arm all day for a green card, *Love Island* introduces us to a different tribe of miscreants: pretty millennials.

If you watch it, expect to get hooked on the quippy narration by Matthew Hoffman. The cast members are pretty. When I say these millennials are hot, I mean they are fit. Too much make-up, too much ink (for my untatted taste), too much shallow dialogue about nothing, and too much self-absorption. You know, the things that make this generation so undeniably special.

So we ask: Which couples will find love this season? Answer: Who cares? They will all cheat on each other the first time a voluptuous piece of ass walks by them in the real world. Much like their conversations, their intentions are drivel and lip service.

Is there a better way to spend five nights each week? I doubt it.

What would Iago do?

Iago would have a heyday with this reboot. The new show would be called *Love Island of Infirmity*.

Let's face it. We love young, attractive people. And we hate old, gross people. Part of the new top-secret Trump healthcare plan for his next run is the creation of the *Island of Infirmity*.

This uncharted and inescapable island will house all relocated seniors over sixty-five years old. This way, we can free up all the mandatory Medicare and Social Security money for making America an even greater, more perfect union. Think of all the money we can put into Space Force now!

Left to their own devices, these geriatrics will need to vie for resources with no social, medical, or physical support. They're literally abandoned to live or die, like some slow-motion, real-life version of the *Hunger Games*.

Introduce some sexy millennials to the scenario, looking for love in an exotic setting. What they find instead is some unbathed, starving Granny who has no qualms about cannibalism. Granny has gone full native. She doesn't have time for bitching about her aching back or what wig to wear to Bingo.

Hell no, this old bird is a killing machine of lean muscle, catlike dexterity, and a four-foot vertical leap.

So many conundrums. What will the millennials do without social media to share their every waking thought? How can they learn how to survive when they have literally had everything in their lives given to them? Once the strongest have formed a tribe, how will they endure the never-ending wave of weekly boats arriving full of determined senior citizens?

Tune in nightly for all the answers on the most horrific conflict in television history.

Closing Thoughts: That's a Wrap on Reality TV

Alas, while it's fun to imagine what Iago would do, we must live with what we have. I am guilty like the rest of you. No research necessary for this piece. I have watched all these shows. I will never have that time back in my life. I kinda hate myself for it.

In my defense, I became addicted during COVID quarantining. With everything closed for months, these ridiculous programs filled the void appropriately. They served as the mental bubblegum to help distract us from how shitty things were in the world.

Add to that the fact that my wife and I could polish down a guilt-free case of wine every few days to enhance the perception of escape and release. Now we are having a challenging time weaning ourselves off the wine and the Reality TV. Addiction is a powerful thing.

Back to Iago from *Othello*. Isn't that the beauty of Reality TV? We all know their creators are toying with us, trapping us in a manufactured quasi-reality. But we go along because life is so blasé. We crave bread and circuses to keep us tranquil and sedated. And producers have unlimited poison pabulum to serve.

They are making something we want to see. Where Iago's deceptions lead to mass destruction, TV producers desire mass consumption. Their ability to inveigle us to then ensnare advertisers and ratings is the master plan. We are their enablers.

So, pour yourself another glass of wine, my little lemmings. *Are you not entertained?*

DARK SHORTS 6:
BINGO AND GOMORRAH

Agnes loved Bingo. Since her husband died, she hitched a ride every Tuesday evening with Mert and Gert. Saint Barabbas of the Baptized Fire Immaculate Epiphany Catholic Church ran the best game in town. Seniors and suckers from all around the county would pack the bodacious Bingo Hall dreaming of striking it rich. But for Agnes, it was bigger than the money. It was the competition, and the sheer joy that came from rubbing a win in the face of her fellow seniors. Cheating bitches and lying whores. As they waited for the Caller to take his seat, Agnes kicked Gert's shin under the table, drawing blood, whispering, "I'm gonna finish you." Gert spit her half-sucked Werther's Original candy in Agnes's face, whispering, "Eat me." Mert sipped his coffee, excitedly eyeing the building hostility. Father Phil Mipocketz climbed athletically into the Caller chair. His lustrous brown locks and cherubim face stirred geriatric passions across the hall.

Agnes elbowed Gert and made an O-face. "Granny needs to change her panties," Agnes said. "What panties?" Gert replied. Mert stared intensely at the Bingo cards splayed out before him. I-22! Someone said shit from somewhere in the vast hall, and the game was on. Evening waned. Time passed. Losses accumulated. Agnes was despondent. Hands smeared with pink Dab-O-Ink, Agnes fixated on gouging Gert's over-painted eyes out of her hooker skull.

O-69! Mert exploded out of his chair and yelled BINGO! Murmurs of 'dirty bastard' and 'son of a bitch' filled the air. Looking at the battle-ready Agnes and Gert, Mert grinned. "$250 prize, ladies. Let's get some meth and go back to Agnes's house for a three-way." Overhearing him, Father Phil mouthed back over the silver heads of the crowd, "Be there in an hour."

What a Coincidence!

Life is full of amazing coincidences. I often wonder . . . are coincidences just a series of random events that happen in a vacuum? Or are they part of some fatalistic, grander design? Worse, maybe some perverse metaphysical joke?

My best friend, Bert, drowned my senior of high school. My youngest daughter was born on the same day he died, twelve years later. Now *that* is one crazy coincidence. The probability is shockingly unlikely.

Suffice to say, I have always viewed coincidence in the more supernatural sense. Bert was a committed jokester and prankster. I often wonder if his delightfully twisted humor from the Great Beyond has not helped shape some bizarre coincidences in my life.

For your esteemed consideration:

I Want to Ride My Bicycle

Meteorologists claim it was a warm Saturday midmorning in the summer of 2009. I wouldn't know.

Trapped in our downstairs half bath, this seventh trip of the day to *el baño* marked the return of yet another flare of ulcerative colitis. Green apple nasties painted my toilet bowl like some odious Jackson Pollock. The half bath is cramped.

Never intended for repeated, let alone extended visits. A claustrophobic coffin. Caught in the poop loop of this hellish soap opera called *As the Rectum Churns*.

"Dad, I'm going for a bike ride!" yelled my youngest daughter, slamming the front door. Screw my permission. She was off. "Okay, sweetie," I muttered uselessly. "Stay safe." Another wave of cramping anal morse code seized me in synchronized rhythm with each whispered word. S – O – S . . . .

Spastic colon aside, pun fully intended, my daughter was a shitty bike rider. I was physically close to empty, so I can only say I was scared shitless figuratively.

I recalled attempting to teach her to ride her bike a few years earlier. We trained in her elementary school parking lot on weekends. Vast space. Barren expanse. No teacher working overtime on a Saturday. Ever.

In hindsight, *trained* may be the wrong word choice. I yelled. She cried. She was so bad. Was I that much of an uncoordinated lout as a seven-year-old? No way. Confirmed as she smashed headlong into the side of my car for the twentieth time.

I think my wife took over the training after that day. She possesses this thing called patience. Still don't know what the hell that word means. Bottom line, despite all our efforts, now ten-years old, our baby could barely ride a bike. Up yours, Nurture. Nature always wins.

In Golden Pond

So, it was no great surprise to hear my wife's phone ringing in the other room after Baby had departed only ten minutes prior.

"What?! Oh my god, what? Are you okay?" her queries dulled beneath the baritone gravitas of another stressful, moist air biscuit.

Sounds like trouble: *"Oh, we got trouble. Right here in River City."* Lyrics from *Music Man* always invade my innermost thoughts in times of danger. A musical theatre fight instinct. But I still had business to attend to. Primal business that would not simply stop for curiosity's sake.

The door to my septic sarcophagus whipped open. My wife stood there. Tears in her eyes. Maternal worry painted all over her face.

As fresh cool air infiltrated, the rotten fetid air escaped. She gagged into her hand several times. Composing herself, she revealed, "Baby rode her bike into the pond."

I need to learn to laugh second and feign concern first. I didn't. Perturbed and/or nauseated, likely both, my wife replied, "The neighbor pulled her out of the pond and let her use his phone to call. And, yes, she is okay. But very upset. Finish up in here so we can go get her." She peaked through the crack in the doorway as she resealed my tomb. "And use some air freshener. For the love of god."

Colitis has a mind of its own. A piss poor attitude to boot. It doesn't give a crap about your plans or life's little dramas. When it visits, it owns you.

But parenting beckoned. I needed to put colitis in a chokehold and quiet the whistle belly thumps. It was time to don my Super Dad cape, grab Wonder Mom who was pacing by the front door, and fly in our magic Nissan to the rescue of Moron Baby.

Feels Like the First Time

"The Pond" is one of the many reasons we built our home in our residential community years ago. A small manmade lake, stocked with fish, surrounded by sylvan parks. It's lovely. Walking and biking paths circumnavigate it, as do some high-end homes.

This path caused the drowning of Baby's bicycle. Unclear if Bert felt intervening would ratchet up the dark irony, but Baby apparently was forced to swerve. Around pedestrians, around goose shit, who knows? In her uncoordinated maneuver, she left the path and rocketed down the hill into the pond.

The owner of one of those homes was Agassi. [*names changed to protect... me... from physical harm*]. Like a glabrous Gaston, having espied Baby's plunge into the lagoon, he heroically leapt into action and saved Baby from extending her waterlogged shame and humiliation.

Andre Agassi is a bald athletic man of Persian descent. This Agassi was like that, but on steroids. A giant, more muscular version of Mr. Clean. Maybe it was the lighting, but he seemed to glow with a slight tinge of Dr. Manhattan blue.

Even I got a little wood as we pulled into his driveway. But my wife gasped. At first, I thought it was the sight of our waterlogged ginger, her face redder with embarrassment than the color of her godforsaken bedraggled hair. But as Agassi waved, it dawned on me. My wife knows him.

My mind lunged to make a connection. We walked by this house on our daily exercise route. Had we said hello before? No, I don't think so. I had just cleaned the toilets from colitis damage. Was I recognizing him from the label on the bleach? This made me chuckle to myself.

"No way! I don't believe it. I slept with him. He was my first."

Gobsmacked. "Say whaaaaaaaat?" I had nothing more.

"Oh my god, I haven't seen him in twenty-five years. Impossible."

"What a coincidence!" I exclaimed with ironic titular panache.

As I put the car in Park, and Baby and Agassi wheeled her bike down his driveway to greet us, I shit my pants. *You are my bitch. Remember who calls the shots,* colitis hissed.

Hey Jealousy

As they neared the car, I froze. Embarrassment turned my joints to ice.

Anyone who has ever changed an infant can relate to the mystery of how bizarre it is when the spicy brown ass-mustard explodes up their back. The diaper could not contain the velocity. And thus, with me.

Shirt soaked up to mid-back, I looked at my wife. She was clearly lost in the moment's synchronicity. Rightly so. My mind tried to be in both places at once. Gathering herself, she said firmly, "Let's do this." And she exited the car.

What could I do? Only thought was to not turn my back and show my soiled shame to this studly dude who occupied such a quintessentially meaningful memory for my wife. Her first.

Dagnabbit. What in tarnation were the chances? I shook my head as I left the car, wondering why I was thinking with Dusty Dan's frustrated 19th-century gold prospector's voice.

Then my back-up musical theatre fight instinct took control. As I walked up the driveway, I leaned into it and started snapping my fingers to "Cool" from *West Side Story*. I had a *"rocket in my pocket,"* and I was keeping it *"cooly cool, boy."*

Agassi and my wife were total pros. Both knew who the other was, but any casual observer would have noticed nothing more. We spent a few minutes shaking hands and exchanging the required appreciative pleasantries. *Crazy cool.* All the while, my mind raced. *Her first!* The original guy who sullied her maidenhood.

I had heard the story. We had painstakingly shared all our previous sexual exploits with each other before we married. Mostly because I was such a man-whore in my early years. Wanting no surprises on the off chance that some sad bastard showed up at our front door looking for his daddy, like a soccer player named Peträc from Croatia who loved The Beatles. I told far too many lies when I was single.

I felt abashed and inadequate. Definitely recalled he was not only the first but also the biggest. And his family had money. Big money. And look at him now! Like some affluent, brawny, big dick Adonis. A new feeling beset me. Anger? No. Resentment? No. Jealousy? Yes.

A Dish Best Served Nude

My daughter cried the entire ride home. My empathy was at an all-time low.

I felt dirty. My back was now dry and tacky with ordure. But more brain-dirty because I was so angry. It's one thing to know a story and compartmentalize your feelings. It's another to meet that story in the hulking flesh and understand it is also your neighbor.

What was there to feel jealous about? I suck with feelings, so not sure I know. But that is how I felt. I think. Maybe thirsty, too? I was medically dehydrated, after all.

Now the proverbial finger in the eye was that, suddenly, I saw Agassi and his scrawny, Shelley-Duvall-looking wife everywhere. I kid you not. Everywhere. Hereafter we shall know her as Olive. Yes, for Olive Oyl. Shut your piehole. I'm petty. Sue me.

- Agassi and Olive at the gym. Who knew? Always when I'm there. Both so fit. Hate them.
- Agassi and Olive at the grocery store. Buying healthy yoga-weeds like kale. Barf.
- Agassi and Olive in their yard. Now we always had to wave and act appreciative when we were out walking our little pampered prince, Hairy Kerry. Barf.

I knew the only cure for my jealousy was to exact some sort of revenge. Marital vows aside, I couldn't schtup Olive with a homeless schlep's schvantz. Doesn't the *Shelley Duvall* reference say it all? She was rather uncomely.

Extending the metaphor, I fantasized about a Lorena Bobbitt moment with Agassi in the men's room of the gym. Claiming my titan trophy whilst hidden in a steamy sauna then skittering away into the dense, moist fog. Okay. *Focus, PS. You're a bit too preoccupied over that trophy.*

And then coincidence served up the dish for me. As we passed their house on our daily walk, Olive was heading into their open garage. Thinking the shadows obscured her from view, she took off her tank top and used it to wipe her exposed, bare breasts.

She looked up in time to see me staring. Apparently nonplussed, she sustained eye contact and made a "how you doin'?" head gesture toward me. She did not cover up. We sustained eye contact far too long for propriety. I responded with the flirt-appropriate, "*Sup,*" head nod in return.

A long, wet fart interrupted this precious moment of human connection and understanding, And I waved goodbye, scurrying home, knowing Agassi had never shit his pants while staring at a half-naked woman. NEVER. And that's why I suck.

Closing Thoughts: A Peaceful Easy Feeling

And that's all it took to end my bout of jealousy. A set of meh boobies. And another UC flare. But, like pizza, to any blue-blooded fella, even a pair of mediocre breasts are still better than none.

Plus, every drummer knows that come-hither look she gave me. *I'm game if you are*. Name any gig you have ever played, and there are always one or two girls with those bedroom eyes in the crowd. And while I never would act on it, it was enough of a minor ego boost to pull me out of my moody, bitchy little ditch.

None of my feelings were rational anyway. They began in a very fragile, insecure state induced by the ulcerative colitis attack. I felt bad about me, and the jealousy was a manifestation of those emotions. But these coincidences! Seriously. What are the chances!?

Good job, Bert. You got me. Cheers, brother. Rest in peace.

STOP TELLING ME WHAT I SHOULD THINK!

Is anybody besides me sick and tired of being told what to think? Worse yet, being told what we *should* think?

Today, invisible interwebs friends, we shall discuss the word "should." Terrible word. Maybe the worst word in the English language. First, it implies judgment and criticism. Second, it suggests superiority in ethos by the speaker. Third, intended or not, it exacerbates anxiety and stress.

Think of the impact.

- **Self-Sabotage.** How many times have you asked yourself, *"Why did I stick my penis in that light socket?"* I know! Beating yourself up today over events in the past that may or may not have permanently disfigured your tallywhacker is as useless as your present-day pecker. Bury that shame with the other skeletons in your psychological walk-in closet.
- **Self-Loathing.** How does it feel when Slim Kim tells you, *"You should lose some weight,"* while you're shoving a Triple McHeart Attack into your slavering maw? Meanwhile, she sits across from you batting her

doe eyes in faux concern as she tentatively nibbles the edges of some braised carb-free quinoa chips. Hot gorge swells.
- **Self-Doubt.** You are super-psyched for the Dead Baby Seals concert in a few weeks (imagine we are in some fantasy post-COVID world). It mortifies PETA Paul. "*Do you know that their name implies brutality to animals? You should boycott that concert and join our protest.*" What do you do? PETA Paul is so cool. He wears hemp.

But that's the trick with the word "should." It creates a power dynamic of superiority by the speaker and inferiority by the listener.

Consider the nuanced changes in receptivity it would create if we stopped saying "should." Case in point: wearing masks during a pandemic.

You should wear a mask

Without a doubt, we *should* all have worn masks to slow and control the spread of COVID. But for Covidiots, the admonition was a trigger. Did your condescension motivate them to wear a mask? Or were they more likely to join another militia to plot the overthrow of the government?

Q'Anon had instructed them that a Satanic cabal of elite liberal pedophiles was raping and eating your children. We were not working from a balanced frame of reference as it pertains to wearing masks. They believed that shit. *Should* they? Irrelevant! They had the guns.

The better way to handle a Covidiot is to communicate in terms they understand. While visiting for Sunday dinner on the Compound, stand up as though you're about to make a toast. Carefully withdraw your hidden flask of lamp oil, spray it all over their grandmother, light a match, and throw it on her.

As Granny explodes in searing flame, screaming and wailing, you yell, *"See how it feels?! Wear a mask, you redneck inbreds!"* As the bullets fly, and your body buckles with repeated bloody impacts, you can meet your celestial discharge from this world with dignity and pride.

Who knows? Maybe they will start wearing masks after burying the charred remains of their barbequed kinfolk. Worth a try. It's certainly less judgy and more courageous than preaching they *should* wear a mask. Don't be such a passive-aggressive simp.

Let's pull back the sarcasm shade to reveal some more greasy, satirical windows into the word "should." Tell me. What else *should* I think or do?

You should meditate

Me? I'm the most relaxed damned person on the planet. Ask anyone.

What is meditation anyway? Answer: a nap to spa music. Should I also braid my ass hair, stop bathing, and mask my intensifying stink with Patchouli? Thank you, no. "Live and let live" has always been my mantra. If you derive value from dredging up old, well-buried feelings and re-opening a bible-length catalogue of unresolved issues, then have at it. I'm busy dealing with today's current list of crises.

Furthermore, meditation requires a modicum of focus. You clearly don't know me at all if you're telling me I *should* meditate. Can't stop giggling at the notion. I have literally checked Twitter (now so stupidly called "X") thirteen times while writing this sentence.

Last thought: how do I choose what meditation to try? Mindfulness, mantra, movement . . . . "Calgon, take me away!" Too many options. Transcendental meditation seems cool, but I'm scared I might confuse it with astral projection. That would be bad.

I wonder how many cosmic tchotchkes might capture my defocused attention span. Oh, look a nebula! Next thing I know, my ADHD soul is adrift in time and space, never to return to my body. Pass.

You shouldn't eat meat

Oooh. Tricky. A sleight of hand telling me what I should *not* do. Still, piss off and mind your own business. I am, at this moment, craving a bowl of boiling dolphin blood served in a California condor skull while wearing a snow leopard fur coat.

Humans did not reach apex predator status on this planet by planting and harvesting crops, only to not serve that buttery corn with a hemic hunk of fawn meat. Come on! Every edible creature on this planet fears us. We tamed this planet and bowed it to our will with wheels, fire, and thumbs. Evolution favored us. But that conquest comes with a fragile stability. Animals are waiting for their revenge. Biding time for the human cattle to go full herbivore.

When lambs realize how brittle our bones have become from lack of vitamin D3 and calcium, they will exact their revenge. We *should* be terrified when the lambs go quiet. In the immortal words of Hannibal Lecter from *The Silence of the Lambs*, "Tell me, Clarice. Have the lambs stopped screaming?"

Speaking of which, consider yourself duly warned, vegetarians. Tell me one more time I should stop eating meat. Our susceptible civilization teeters on the edge of total collapse into cannibalism when the power grid finally fails. Guess who is my main course when that happens? I see you, little lambs.

You should believe in god

Why? My soul? My liability, isn't it? Like politics, humanity cannot even accept a universal divinity. Isn't there one creator? One god to rule them all. I'm so confused. Here is the most recent breakdown I found:

Religion	Worldwide %
Christianity	28.2
Islam	24.4
Hinduism	15.4
Agnostic/Atheist	14.1
Chinese, Ethnic, African Traditional	10.3
Buddhism	6.4
All Other (e.g. Judaism 14M)	1.3

Folks, someone is wrong here. Every god can't be God, can they? What happens to most of our global community who have made a major existential mistake? Roll the dice? According to science, even atheists have a reasonable statistical chance of being correct about non-god.

That said, if I should believe in god, what you're really saying is I should believe in *your* god. Your religion. It is the essence of the word "should." Implied superiority and correctness.

The arrogance is terrifying. And consequential. If we can't agree on the same god, why can't we at least worship similarly when we believe in the same god?

Christians comprise 28.2 percent of the world's population. But there is so much disagreement, contention, and name-calling across their many denominations. Did you know Lutheran doctrine teaches the Catholic Pope is the antichrist? Shit, and here I thought that was Donald Trump.

Some lucky Christians are instantly "saved" by accepting Jesus Christ into their heart. But not very many. The rest must go to hell. Except Catholics, they fabricated a place called Purgatory where they can chillax until heaven weighs in on their entrance eligibility.

My head hurts. Just as the *should-isms* create a right-wrong dynamic, seeking to control the narrative, so do religions seek to control you. They are manmade poker games where your soul is the ante. Until it all gets figured out, I think I'll worry about being a good person. No thieving, raping, or murdering. Do my best to treat others fairly and be the best me I can be. And when I do screw up, have the decency and humility to apologize and forgive myself. As religious role model and icon of substance, Melania Trump, tells us, "*Be best.*"

You shouldn't be so crass

Me? Crass? Fuck you. Okay, fine. Maybe I'm slightly crass at times. But I'm crass for a plethora of good reasons.

First, efficiency. One finger trumps two words. Second, impact. I learned a long time ago to follow your brain because your heart is daft as shit. Shock-and-awe works. Ask Baghdad. Third, irony. Is it crass for me to write crudely, *intentionally*, if I'm highlighting the behavior of a certain Orange pussy-grabbing vulgarian?

The fourth reason divulges something revelatory about me. I have a lot of Hate in my heart. Sometimes I'm crass because it serves as a release valve, pushing the Hate out for a moment. A karmic sigh of relief from my heart until my soul fills it back in with more Hate. I hated so many things during lockdown. Here are the Top 10, with extra added crassness:

1. **COVID.** Made me want to scream, poke my eyes out with the pins from my dead wife's golden brooches, and run through the streets of town searching for answers from Tiresias. Masked, of course. I'm not an animal.
2. **Covidiots.** COVID killed more than one million Americans. But Covidiots still deny science; they reject public health policy; they favor religion and conspiracy theories. I truly wish they would die off. I'm super comfortable with helping.
3. **Donald Trump.** Callous, narcissistic, orange, lying, bullying, old, conspiracist, megalomania aside, great guy. Total Commander-in-Chief material. Glad the nukes may once again rest in his very stable hands.
4. **Joe Biden.** Nice wasn't a qualification for President. What, in all things 'Merica, happened to our country? I read his Top 100 policies and agreed with 6 of them. He barely didn't suck the last 50 years of public service. Jesus, take the wheel.
5. **Nancy Pelosi.** Her plastic surgeon was a demented bastard. Those insane dead eyes like some blinkier

version of *Coraline*'s evil Other Mother. Retirement and inconsequential silence has never suited someone better.

6. **The news.** I am so damned done with the editorialization and interpretation of facts by the news. We should force anchors to wear shock collars to retrain their negative opining behavior. Every time they use an overly nonfactual adjective or adverb? ZAP!!

7. **Buffets.** Worse yet, the sneeze shields. While the underpaid buffet workers sit mindlessly in the corner huffing the cleaning fluid instead of using it to create a germfree line of sight over the slop, Wayne-Doug is poking in the baskets underneath trying to figure out how to work a pair of salad tongs.

8. **Slow Drivers.** If you cannot drive the speed limit, call an Uber. It's not merely for old people. That is far too lenient. A special "screw you" shout-out goes to truckers in the passing lane, Canadians in the passing lane, and Prius drivers in general. Assholes.

9. **Like.** Overuse of the word "like" when speaking is like nails on a chalkboard to me. Been around since the '80s. But every vapid twenty-something in America now uses "like" more times than a poorly applied simile in a stuttering contest.

10. **Spitting.** This is so unhygienic and unnecessary on every conceivable level. Unless you are a conscientious porn star, I struggle to conceive where spitting is remotely acceptable. Basic rule of etiquette: if you cannot swallow something in your mouth, don't put it there in the first place.

Damn. What a mind-blowing *hategasm*! I need a cigarette and a sandwich.

This Should End

It's cray. The word "should" is everywhere today. Poisoning our minds and hearts. I want to offer a challenge to all of you, dear invisible friends. For the next thirty days, stop using the word "should" in your conversations. Force yourself to describe things exactly as they are versus your interpretation or opinion of them. Mayhaps even take time to notice how many of your trusted news sources use this judgment word. Constantly.

Here is my guarantee:

- You will feel less stressed. Anxiety will diminish.
- You will become more skeptical of what others are telling you. You'll ask better, more inciteful questions and challenge them intelligently.
- You will seek to verify your media outlets against other sources. Fact-check the fact checkers.

As for me, if you don't like what I say or how I say it, there's the door. No one forced you to read my writing. Why spike your blood pressure if it bothers you? Godspeed. Piss off.

For the rest of you, I love you. Thanks for having the intelligence and wit to understand the method to my madness. I present nothing in my writing without intention. There is always a purpose. Even if to simply offend or shock. You're welcome.

THE OCEAN:
VELVET PAW. REMORSELESS FANG.

These are the times of dreamy quietude, when beholding the tranquil beauty and brilliancy of the ocean's skin, one forgets the tiger heart that pants beneath it; and would not willingly remember, that this velvet paw but conceals a remorseless fang.

– Herman Melville, Moby Dick

The ocean. Melville successfully captures the essence of my love-hate relationship with it.

In terms of love, I have concluded it is mostly aesthetic and at arm's length. Standing on a bluff, staring out to the world's edge. The assuaging cadence of a pounding surf. The beauty of the sun settling like a decapitated, burning clown's head melting across a vast, gray cage floor. Euphoria.

I love the notion of the ocean. Also, the motion of the ocean. Because it determines the size of your rise. Thank you, I'll see myself out with the other ten-year-old boys.

The ocean inspires me to write. There is something purifying and liberating in a salty sea breeze. Natural beauty holds hallowed court. The grandness of it all. The relentless ebb and flow of the tide amplifies my imagination. The tantric resonance echoes into my essence with each crashing wave. Feckin' brilliant.

I love it because I am not touching it. Floating helpless over its unseen depths. I am not second-guessing what type of hidden death will drag me down to Davy Jones' Locker. But I am certain there is some cutesy sea Monkee waiting down there to drown me in annoying backtracks of *Daydream Believer*.

In terms of hate, let's start with any song by the Monkees. And Davy's idiotic dance moves. The entire act was staged, made-for-television tripe. Yet somehow, those fools sold more albums in 1967 than the Beatles and Rolling Stones, combined. Yeah. Let that sink in.

So, I hate the ocean because I am terrified of it. I have a visceral fear of immersion in the ocean. The clinical term is thalassophobia, an intense and persistent fear of the sea.

The caveat is standing in shallow surf. Doesn't bother me. However, once I pass thigh height, anxiety overwhelms me like a tsunami of diarrhea after eating spoilt fish. First wave that grazes my nutsack? Flight instinct kicks into overdrive, and I flee for the safety of my fluffy beach towel. And so, I have wrestled my entire life with this paradox.

Jaws

I have not a shred of doubt that Spielberg's aquatic slasher flick psychologically scarred me. It captures the essence of the fear of the unknown and then transforms it into a prehistoric-sized great white shark hell-bent on human revenge.

Scared the absolute bejesus out of me as a kid and is front of mind whenever I enter the water today. But why is this movie so indelibly burned into the minds of so many people?

- **Irrational Fear.** We all know you have a better chance of getting hit by lightning (twice) before a shark attacks you in the water. Doesn't matter. You can rationalize your fear of sharks all you want, but you watched the morgue scene in *Jaws*. Torsos. Partially denuded bones. It could happen.
- **The monster is real.** We all know that Freddie Kruger killing you in your dreams is not real. We can rationalize the scare away after watching it because there is no tangible "What if?" moment when the movie ends. Sharks? These alpha predators of the sea are as intelligent as a doorknob. But they are very real. Programmed by evolution to kill, kill, kill.
- **That damn music.** Oh, John Williams, you gorgeous, rotten bastard. You got us good with that simple, foreboding, driving score. Like the movie, can you ever forget the music? It's forever synonymous with impending danger. And it plays in my head every time I stand on the shore, skittishly looking out to sea.

And while the movie embedded the fear, I experienced a real shark moment on a day off from work at my summer job in Montauk. Let's explore my psychosis further, shall we?

Montauk

I spent some of the best college summers of my life with my friends in Montauk. Barbacking, waitering, bussing tables, all on the ocean. Big money. Big party.

Montauk feels like the end of the world. East of the Hamptons' glitz, this small fishing town is a welcome respite for New York urbanites. After all the grime, noise, and chaos of New York City, the four-hour drive in bumper-to-bumper traffic, at thirty miles per hour, defines the apex of relaxation and decompression.

The denizens of New York, oft celebrated for their relaxed personalities and polite dispositions, typically require an extra week of vacation to shake it off.

All that joy. Then on a day off, my buddy and I go ocean-fishing in a small rubber raft, chumming the water to draw our prey. Perhaps smoking a little too much doobie, it went unnoticed that we had been pulled out to sea in a rip current.

By the time we noticed, the twenty-foot-high sand dunes along the Montauk shoreline looked like the raised eczema on the forearm of the Irish summer worker who wanked me outside the bar the night before. Barely noticeable. Just wished I hadn't touched it.

The water gets deep quick off the Montauk coast. And then I heard the *Jaws* music. Too stoned. WTF? Senses heightened; I scanned all around. A gray fin broke the surface. A shark began circling our thin rubber vessel, a vessel barely worthy of floating in a still pond. Let alone above the abyss. We were so screwed.

My friend, who grew up along the shore, said it was an eight-foot Mako. I didn't give a flying flip if it was a four-inch Beta fish. I froze in abject terror. The music was so damn loud in my ears. He started yelling while swatting at the monster with our oar. I covered my ears and curled up in the fetal position, gestating in the raft's bottom.

As I lost consciousness, the massive fish leapt from the brine, grabbing my friend by the arm, dragging him into a turbulent, thrashing wake of blood and froth and foam. His screams were horrific. Then silence. Everything faded to black . . . .

Wrightsville Beach

Montauk's close encounter with a shark solidified my seafaring fears. But for some perverse reason, its siren's song still summoned me.

Fast forward fifteen years, and the Conways have rented a beach house with another family in Wrightsville Beach, North Carolina. Built on the sand, this gorgeous home had a giant wrap-around shaded porch that yielded an endless view of the crashing surf. All the senses piqued except touch. Fine with me.

So predictable. By day two, those selfish bastards all wanted to go down to the beach for a day. The nerve! Honestly, the day passed uneventfully. A not unpleasant mix of activity, beers, and shady umbrellas created an easy elixir. The tide never reached our sandy encampment, but we were close enough for my eight-year-old and four-year-old daughters to frolic safely in the shallows.

Then, on cue, my oldest daughter ran toward my wife and me, howling in pain. Damn you, ocean. You betrayed me yet again!

Now, to set the picture properly, you must know my wife and two daughters have a skin pigment one shade above albino. Literally, the two things you can see from outer space are the Great Wall of China and the sun reflecting off their alabaster flesh.

As she neared, the searing red tentacle marks across my eldest daughter's exposed bikini abdomen told us all we needed to know. An octopus had attacked her. I reached for my trident, as I knew battle was nigh.

My internal monologues never stay in my head like they should. "Octopus?" My wife slapped my arm. "She got stung by a jellyfish!" I lowered my trident to the sand. One of our friends yelled, "Maybe it was a Portuguese Man of War!" Oh my, I'm no marine biologist, but that sounded bad.

Ever the problem solver, I bellowed, "What do we do?" Espying the chaos and clamor, a lifeguard ran up to our boisterous group. My daughter had asthma and was wheezing through her tears as the angry stings radiated pain.

"You need to pee on her!" he yelled over the group and reached into his shorts to extricate his Russell the One-Eyed Muscle. My daughter and wife looked at me in horror. "No, you don't!" I replied, shoving him to the sand. I'm the hero of this family. "If anyone is pissing on my daughter, it's me!"

Cancun

Please join me in July 2005. Cancun, Mexico. Category 4 Hurricane Emily had recently decimated the Yucatan and Tulum. Luck on our side, we stayed at the JW Marriott, the local hurricane and nuclear fallout shelter. This sturdy and beautiful resort barely had a scratch. But the hurricane had left a hell of a savage surf in her wake.

Stinger, now ten years old, was an ocean-hardened mofo. She had survived the coelenterate's venom two summers before. She was a total badass now. And she wanted to bodysurf in the eight-foot waves with her fearless father. How could I say no?

The joy we experienced that day was immeasurable. I crossed the Rubicon. And we took a beating from the massive waves – scratches, scrapes, and bruises all over our bodies. Oh, and my undiagnosed concussion. You see, friends, that's the only way I can explain my senseless, stupid behavior that night at dinner.

The resort had a lovely Italian restaurant on prem. The maître d' sat us by a wall of windows, capturing the surging ocean, the twilight sky mottled purple and orange—like our bruises. My wife and girls looked regal, dressed to the nines. I have never felt so much love or pride.

Feeling randy, I surveilled the wine list for a good value. This is where the concussion surfaces. The establishment priced their menu in pesos. *No hay problema.* Currency conversion is simple math. In 2005, ten pesos was roughly equivalent to one dollar. So, when I saw this fabulous 1997 Barolo for 14,000 pesos, I figured I'd treat us to a $140 bottle of wine.

The waiter's *ojos* went wide with delight. Best dining experience ever. Hands down. The staff treated us like royalty. Crystal decanter. Roses for the girls. A violin playing tableside. Michelin posh. All this for a $140 bottle of wine? Maybe they were having a slow night. Yes, I know, mathletes. The damn bottle of wine was $1,400 USD.

Dry Tortugas

Cancun taught me not only to further respect the sheer power of the ocean but also the importance of math in personal finance. Lesson learned.

And now it's ten years later. Our senior leadership team from my company is having a strategy retreat in Key West. Oh, boohoo! I know, poor white privilege. So many First World problems. STFU. Trying to tell a story here.

If the meeting locale bothered you, you'll love this: We took a "team-building" day to snorkel in the Dry Tortugas. Discovered and named by Juan Ponce de León in 1513, this archipelago of tiny islands (keys) is a seventy-mile boat ride west of Key West in the Gulf of Mexico.

We docked at Garden Key where the ruins of the massive Fort Jefferson occupy eighty percent of the island. After Spain sold Florida to the USA in the early 19th century, the US military discarded this unfinished Spanish garrison due to the absence of potable water and a disgusting amount of sea birds shitting everywhere.

Suffice to say, this was not remotely my pick for our team-building event. But the proponents vastly outnumbered me. All my work friends tried to soften the blow for me. They bought me a nice pair of surfer shorts, some flip-flops, and a rash guard to inspire my courage. The original joke was the rash guard was to prevent the blistering Florida sun from instantly inducing skin cancer on my pink Irish skin.

The bigger joke occurred when I tried it on. I needed to drop some pounds anyway, but this skintight outer-derm made me feel like Buffalo Bob from *Silence of the Lambs* after a good skinning. *I'd fuck me.* Not!

It was painfully tight. I resembled a stretched sausage casing when the butcher realizes he doesn't want the excess sausage to go to waste. And he stuffs that banger as densely as physics allows.

Insecurity and fat-shaming aside, we snorkeled. If you had to pick between rubbing shit in my eye or penile crucifixion, I would take both with a side of anal fisting. Every time above snorkeling.

Standing on the small beach on Garden Key, all my fears surfaced as I donned my rental mask, rental snorkel, and rental flippers. All my coworkers jumped in the water yelling, "Meet you at the buoy!" It looked to be five miles offshore.

I swam out maybe one hundred yards. My heart was pounding. What if a school of barracuda mutilated me? What if a shark ate me? A jellyfish stung me? A sea turtle raped me?

Never considered the stingrays that now swam directly underneath me. Didn't Steve Irwin get stabbed through the heart by one of them a few years before? Is this how I'm going to die? Panic set in.

Deep Thoughts About the Deep

Sorry for screwing with you by having so many cliffhangers in these stories from my fake life, my beloved invisible reader friends.

Let's wrap this discussion with what really occurred to conclude each of these pelagic vignettes.

- **Montauk.** I passed out. My friend scared off the shark, jumped out of the raft, paddled us out of the riptide, and rowed us safely into shore. He carried me like a medieval maiden in his arms and lay me gently upon the shore. As my eyes batted open, I saw my Lancelot standing over me. He said something unintelligible and dumped the remaining bucket of chum all over me. As he walked away, his derisive laughter echoed off the sandy cliffs and up the coast for all to hear. Flies began swarming.
- **Wrightsville Beach.** My wife grabbed my arm and warned me if I pulled my penis out in front on my daughter, let alone pissed on her, she would tear my member off and wear it around her neck as some sort of below-average, consolation trophy. With a huff, she carried my wounded, crying angel into the house for some Benadryl and a nap. Too much stress. A nap

sounded great, so I headed back to the porch, climbed in the hammock, and drifted into a dream-filled bliss with the sound of the lulling ocean telling me all was right in the world. You are a hero. Your girls are lucky to have you.

- **Cancun.** We spent nearly all our discretionary money on that damnable $1,400 bottle of wine. I had to lie to my daughters that our "Swim with the Dolphins Day" was canceled because all the dolphins died in the hurricane. How could I admit I blew all our money on a bottle of wine? My dignity was already trampled under the heel of my wife's justified disdain. The truth was too vexing. I still hate myself for this one. The girls cried all day. I sat on our balcony on the twenty-fifth floor in grown-up time out, marveling at how my girls looked like little grains of white rice floating in the pool below
- **Dry Tortugas.** Too scared to swim further, I walked back into shore, smashing all the coral under my flippers. Probably ruined an entire ecosystem. My coworkers were laughing and diving for lobsters by that distant buoy, so I sat on the shore. The lapping waves grew stronger and knocked me over. I would sit back up and then get knocked over again. This was fun, and I laughed and splashed like an idiot. Parents became aware of the crazy guy, tumbling, splashing, and laughing like a demented fat bastard Weeble Wobble in a rash guard. The beach cleared as concerned parents scurried their children away to safer ground.

All these terrible moments of titular, remorseless fangs aside, I keep coming back to the sea for that soft, velvet tiger paw. This dangerous and tempestuous relationship will always be best served at arm's length. We need a platonic truce. No touching. Putting us in the friend zone. And in those rare, loving moments when I succumb and enter her, I will do so with slow control. Stay shallow. Ease in. Just the tip.

Halloween:
Ghosts of Long-Dead Cookies

> *"The house smelled musty and damp, and a little sweet, as if it were haunted by the ghosts of long-dead cookies."*
> – Neil Gaiman, American Gods

Oh, Neil Gaiman. My heart. Invisible friends, if you like fantasy and horror as genres, and you have not read his work, shame on you. Gaiman is like Stephen King, but different. Better. Far more literate and intelligent. You get all the chills but maintain, if not grow, some brain cells when you read his books.

If you love language, as I do, read that sample quote. Gorgeous. The imagery from his simile makes me drool, wanting to taste that stanky-ass ghost cookie.

That said, first:

Happy Halloween and Samhain to all! In celebration of these holidays, Christian or pagan, the topic here is ghosts. Specifically recounting some supernatural events that occurred in my life.

I do not seek to convert anyone into believing in ghosts. And you are well within your rights to call bullshit on any of these depictions I claim as real. Because I lie all the time. Aren't all writers simply practitioners of deception? After all, stories are all just a bunch of *navacancha*.

Ghosts

And so it is with ghosts. I think most folks either believe or do not. Atheists are probably the biggest skeptics since they do not believe in anything after this life. One and done.

Best as I can tell, for those somewhere on the spectral belief spectrum, there are four theories about what a ghost might be.

- **Fantasy.** Given that Q-Anon has convinced some arguably gullible people that a Satanic cabal of liberal pedophiles is molesting and eating children, is it really a stretch that people might imagine a ghost? Especially when far more worldly explanations would suffice. I know when I inadvertently leave my wife chained to the bed after Naughty Night, those rattling chains and gagged screams of rage could pass for a furious spirit. However, the subsequent, sharp kick to the jimmy is 100 percent human.
- **Soul of human deceased.** Ah, the soul. What a topic! Faith defies proof, and I am not here to convince anyone of anything. For argument's sake, let's assume that smooth bluesy music and human beings both have some soul. Is a ghost a divine mistake? Did god's staff somehow mess up? Left a soul behind because of what? A rounding error? Essence trapped earthbound forever, watching their family grow old, die, move on to heaven (or hell). What a cruel notion. God needs to replace the person running her supply chain, I think.

- **Supernatural beings.** Angels, demons, et al. If you believe in a soul, then you believe in heaven and hell. If you believe in these places, you must believe in angels and demons. Elemental creatures from the dawn of time in a supernatural power struggle of good vs evil. It just seems imbalanced that most ghostly diabolical hauntings are always demons. Where are the angelic possessions? Have you ever seen a little girl levitating above her bed, singing *Barney* songs, and blowing butterflies from her mouth and rainbows out her ass? Maybe I missed that movie.
- **Interdimensional traveler.** Something akin to the Mandela effect. It's so frustratingly annoying, but that pesky "Science" cannot disprove it either. Damnable quantum theory. Can a ghost be another entity seen through a temporary rift in the multiverse? Can parallel dimensions sometimes twist together like a hernia and bleed into each other's realities? But what kind of interdimensional perv dresses up like Granny, smiling at the end of my bed, asking if they can explore my latest scars while I'm sleeping? Nasty. *Ewww*.

Whatever they are, ghosts are scary. An encounter with a ghost can change you forever. I will now share with you some personal preternatural stories that still haunt my nightmares to this day. You decide if they are vivid imagination, soul remnants, malevolent demons, or traveling perverts.

The Blood-Stained Ceiling

We moved a lot when I was young. As an adult, I know my dad wanted more space for our growing family. As his career advanced, and we had more money, he moved us to bigger homes. Closer to family.

But kids develop theories. I know we once thought he was a master criminal, on the run from the Federales. We also thought we were gypsies, living a life of unrestrained freedom with our dog named Boo.

By the time I was eight years old, we were in our fourth (and final) house. Oddly, all within a twenty-mile radius of each other. Thus, our little hypotheses. Right away, the house creeped us out.

Anyone who is Catholic, particularly of Irish or Italian descent, had a Jesus room in their house. For us, that was our formal living room off the foyer on your left when you walked in the front door.

For those not in the know, a Jesus room is a creepy-ass room with formal furniture, lace curtains, an open bible on a table resembling an altar, and pictures of Jesus judging you from every wall.

Hey, sing along: "Jesus is Just Alright With Me." But the effect of this room was like being watched by god. Constantly. The sole purpose of mentioning it for the story is setup for future tales from my life involving this scary room.

But the true omen of things to come was the bloodstain on the second-floor ceiling at the top of the stairs. We all noticed it the moment we set foot in the house. My dad seemed surprised. He searched the attic and found no animal carcasses or satanic sacrifices. But kids know. Someone had been murdered in this house.

The Holly Hobbie Sewing Machine

After the initial shock of the blood-stained ceiling, time passed normally for a few years. While my parents became more deeply involved with our church, we evolved as kids. You know, normal kid stuff. Wounded bird vivisection. Kitten basketball. Run for Your Life. Death in the Dark.

Death in the Dark matters most because it took place in our unfinished basement. A windowless, dank, dark, horrific place. My four-year-old brother (a.k.a. the "booger baby") hunted us in the pitch dark with a piece of plastic Mattel racetrack. When found, he would whip us and laugh sadistically at our cries of agony. As explained, totally normal childhood events.

Imagine our surprise when the first paranormal event occurred one dark, windy night . . . in the basement closet. Had our violence activated something evil?

I awoke at 3:33 a.m. to a strange noise that sounded like CHUGGA-CHUGGA-CHUGGA. It echoed through the house. I opened my bedroom door at the same time my dad opened their bedroom door. Hot damn. He had a shotgun in his hand. Shit was going to get real.

We both stood at the top of the stairs on the second floor, below where the bloodstain had once resided. The sound was getting louder as we tiptoed down the stairs. CHUGGA-CHUGGA-CHUGGA.

Reaching the foyer, we realized the sound was coming from the basement. We were like a badass Navy Seal team. My dad nodded at me. Two fingers to his eyes then motioning forward. We manned up and headed to the basement door. Ready for anything.

Dad dragged the creaky cellar door open. CHUGGA-CHUGGA-CHUGGA. So loud. He turned the basement light on, and it flickered ominously. I think I had an erection. We were going to kill an intruder tonight.

We glided like assassins down the basement stairs and lit on the concrete floor. No one was there, but the noise was bombastic. Disorienting. CHUGGA-CHUGGA-CHUGGA. Coming from the toy closet. We floated like ninjas across the floor. My dad leveled his shotgun, and I flung the closet door open. Darkness and the source of the loud hammering sound. My sister's Holly Hobbie sewing machine!

"The hell?" my dad queried. He picked up the active sewing machine, shook it, and it kept chugging in his hands. The lights flickered again. He opened the battery compartment... NO BATTERIES! CHUGGA-CHUGGA-CHUGGA.

In one adroit motion, he smashed the sewing machine on the floor and bashed it to pieces with the butt of his shotgun until it stopped running. Or so I was told. My ninja-warrior-seal ass was halfway up the stairs *en route* to my bedroom, my blanket, and my bed. If this island of protection could keep me safe when the floor turned to lava, it could keep me safe from possessed sewing machines.

The Law of Partial Pressures?

Priests frequented our house more often following the Holly Hobbie event. These weren't the rape-y kind, so we mostly ignored them. Fighting ghosts and demons was grown-up work. We had a project that summer: the 1980 Roadkill Calendar.

My friends and I "borrowed" my dad's prized 35mm Pentax LX camera. The Pentax captured pristine pictures, which was essential for our calendar. For weeks, we would ride our bikes for hundreds of miles throughout the boonies in search of roadkill:

- Ms. June was a pretty possum whose guts had barfed out her mouth following a gory abdominal trauma
- Ms. July was a fresh-killed squirrel, its legs and tail still winsomely dancing around its crushed skull
- Ms. August was quite the fox. Literally. We found her and her pristine kit, both dead but intact, on the side of the road. Cause of death a delightful mystery.

Summer 1980 was winding to an end. The August doldrums that preceded the impending return to school burned within us as the humid, hot summer sun burned our pasty skin outside. One sweltering Saturday, my friends and I were reviewing our stack of calendar photos from the camera, fresh from the Fotomat. My family room was the only air-conditioned room on the first floor, and we all welcomed the relief from sweat-induced tit dirt, especially Fat Randy.

But the air was freezing. No way that old window air conditioning unit worked that well. Swear to this day, I could see my breath. Now all I think of is the scene from *The Sixth Sense*: "I see dead people."

We all looked up from our work. The glass door into the garage was making a weird creaking, vibrating sound on its own. Through a mouthful of Cheese Puffs, Randy said, "I think your door is open."

As I stood to close the door, a loud rumbling occurred for a few seconds. The glass in the garage door bowed outward as though responding to some unseen pressure. As the rumbling sustained its low timbre, my ears popped. Like when you shake your head free of clogged liquid after emerging from your weekly baptisms in the Jordan. Similar effect followed by a *WHOOSH* that seemed to pull all the air toward the door.

The glass violently exploded into the garage. Not a shard remained seated in the sill. It had all burst into the garage. No large pieces whatsoever. Only tiny, crystalline fragments scattered everywhere. After checking on our safety, my mom yelled out the window for my dad to call the priests back.

We heard one more brief cracking sound. The lens of my dad's Pentax LX, resting innocently unmolested on the couch, had fractured similarly. Utterly destroyed. We all sucked in our breath in horror as the summer heat repatriated the room. Well, most of us did. Fat Randy sucked on his inhaler. Fucking ghosts.

Sorting It All Out

Whatever caused the strange, ghostly experiences at my house eventually subsided.

Maybe the priests eventually scared off some demonic force. Perhaps some restless spirit moved on to another house or another plane of existence. Mayhaps some distortion in the space-time continuum corrected itself, and our interdimensional seamstress astrally projected elsewhere.

Or maybe it was all readily explainable with science. Who knows? It's funny, upon reflection. These events terrified us as kids.

The fact that my grandmother would converse with the ghost of my deceased grandfather in her third-floor attic never struck me as odd. It was sweet. Plus, she might have been crazy. Nor did Aunt Hattie's rocking chair that spontaneously rocked without a mortal soul sitting in it. Harmless ghost relaxing after a hard day's haunting. No biggie.

Hell, my oldest daughter and I think we saw a ghost right before COVID hit. We were talking at a coffee shop and a person was staring at us, unmoving from the top floor of a house across the street. As we stared back, the image disappeared without a trace. Meh, old house. Why not? Unlike me, the jury is hung.

My logical brain knows there is no such thing as ghosts . . . or aliens. Don't even get me going about the time in college where I overindulged for twelve sleepless days on recreational, possibly illegal num-nums and saw a squadron of UFOs flying in formation over Lake Ontario.

I am not religious. Not a firm believer in most things mystical except maybe exorcism and reincarnation or Samhain fairies. Otherwise, total science-head. There is a reason none of these ghost hunter TV shows ever capture a ghost. Tons of circumstantial evidence. No ghost pics. Yet I watch every episode, secretly hoping.

Could it be some sort of Mandela Effect? Could it be hallucinations from that pint of residual psilocybin still coursing through your spinal fluid? Could it be you ate a lot of paint chips when you were a kid, Tommy Boy?

My demi-divine instinct tells me the emotive power of stories can trigger our brain to believe things that never really happened. But I am open to being wrong. Kinda.

Dark Shorts 7: Above the Clouds

Mrs. Coyneslot ran a tight ship. Her fifth-grade class knew better than to rock the boat, as their Captain had a fickle temper that could blow like a North Sea gale in December. Suggestions unwelcome. Input admonished. Coyneslot's meticulous daily plans governed the actions of the day. Back turned to the room, she scrawled and scratched her history lesson across the chalkboard, white dust flying in the wake of her data maelstrom. Kids being kids, the room devolved into silent chaos when Coyneslot faced the board. Wriggling eels gestured, waved, made funny faces, stuck out tongues and mouthed expletives all in mutinous silence. That is, except for Windy. Windy was poor with stormy eyes. She wore paper bags for clothing. The unfortunate byproduct of her environmentally-woke but dismally drab brown attire was that her smallest movements made loud, scratchy, irritating sounds. The one and only time Windy ever waved back at that nasty little jackanapes, Jimmy O'Brien, Coyneslot immediately heard the crunching and scraping from Windy's arm bags. Coyneslot's head whipped toward the offending sound, a tempest of rage flaring across her face. In a fit of panic, Windy soared from her chair and blew toward the hallway door like a pile of dry crunchy autumn leaves. The friction from the sudden movement created a spark. The spark created an ember. The ember erupted into a conflagration that disintegrated Windy midway toward her escape. As the horror settled into the hushed room, and order was hers for the taking, Coyneslot turned back to the chalkboard whistling, "Everyone knows it's Windy."

Counting Troubles, Counting Joys

Before the 2020 election, I had never contemplated the concept of counting. It seemed the only televised events in the USA were media updates from volunteers counting the presidential election votes. Watching Nevada add 53 votes? Better than sex.

Since my earliest days of counting, plunked down in front of my television babysitter, I watched *Sesame Street*. Aside from socialization, why did we ever go to school?

In the early years, those shabby-looking Muppets looked like hands covered in the scree you would drag out of some hippie drug dealer's shag carpet in Times Square. Complete with glued-on eyes and arms taped to a stick.

And still we loved them! We learned we are okay just the way we are. And that everyone is different, giving us reason to celebrate. Feelings are complicated and a little scary. And learning is frickin' fun.

All before they threw us into "society." The education system. Playground culture. Then we learned the truth.

- You are not okay. You are fat or poor or ugly or dumb. Kids are such dickheads. Always pulling at the string tethered to a ball of yarn that is your self-confidence.

- Differences need to be concealed if you don't want to be teased relentlessly. Unless your skin color is different, then god help you. Judgment rules the playground.
- Feelings make you weak. Life is competition and dominance. Crying is for babies (or when listening to Bette Midler's "The Rose" – sorry; not sorry).
- Learning is fun in secret circles of trusted nerds and chess club only. Outwardly, "We don't need no education." Popularity trumps intelligence.

But in the sacrosanct space of my living room, watching *Sesame Street* in the early 1970s, I was still me. Nurtured with good, wholesome, liberal, maudlin idealism. Reality could wait.

The Count

One of my favorite Muppets was the Count. Truth be told, I was a bit of a child prodigy. Learning came easily, and I had a voracious appetite. I was also raised Catholic, so the Count, an unapologetic vampire, initially scared me. He was evil. BAD. Big time.

But the repetition of *Sesame Street's* life lessons on tolerance finally sunk in, overruling orthodoxy and church doctrine. I could accept mastering math from an evil, bloodsucking demon because... we're all okay.

That toothy S.O.B. had everything. Bats. Lightning. Creepy Castle. Insane laughter. And music! The combination created an indelible mark on my brain. Numbers were awesome. Counting was ecstasy. "Ah. Ah. Ah. Ah!" (I miss that maniacal laughter). And my undernourished parietal lobe lit up.

I took seven years of Latin classes in school. My vocabulary was always more . . . good . . . than most, but Latin unlocked something in my gray matter when contending with English. A neural pathway that solved the challenge in understanding the root of big words. And a passion to figure them out.

As a four-year-old mathlete, the Count's impact on me was similar. After enough singing, laughter, repetition, and blasphemy, numbers made sense. More than that. Counting made sense. Math made sense. And the accompanying ardor to excel at it consumed me. Remember your first bump of cocaine? Like that, but as a kid after a tall glass of *Tang*.

The only entertainment more impactful from my childhood was *Schoolhouse Rock*. If you cannot sing the preamble to the U.S. Constitution, you either grew up on a compound without electricity or hate 'Merica.

If you could not sing the "Ready or Not, Here I Come" song, part of *Multiplication Rock*, your parents failed you. Counting by fives led to understanding simple multiplication. Which opened the universe to algebra, then trigonometry, then calculus, then differential equations.

Yeah. My neural pathways shutdown at calculus. Took Advanced Placement calculus in high school. The AP exam scored you 1 through 5. You received a 1 if you put your name on the test. I answered every question . . . and got a 1. Back to the basics.

Counting

The gerund (*a verb acting as a noun – sorry, non-Latin lovers!*) "counting" implies more than merely math. Let's ensure we define it thoroughly to set the table for the rest of this discussion.

Counting Definitions:

- **To Add** – e.g. "I'm counting my mother-in-law's number of husbands." Currently seeking number five. Hey, we all need a little sexy time, and COVID was lonely. Cut her some slack as she trolls the bingo halls for a fellow octogenarian.
- **To Rely** – e.g. "I'm counting on you to lower the toilet seat." Pain is an effective teacher. Living in a houseful of women has taught me not only to lower the seat but also to leave it down. I sit when I pee now. My grandmother said, "Men who wear bowties sit when they pee." Sigh.
- **To Include** – e.g. "Thanks for counting me in on your shenanigans." Who remembers shenanigans? Whacky capers and hijinks we would pull as kids to exert control over our worlds. A personal fave was stuffing kittens into a piñata and laughing when Fat Randy wailed on it, expecting candy to spill out. Oh, the fun!
- **To Matter** – e.g. "My vote counting in the 2020 and 2024 elections were very important." We want our actions to mean something, don't we? I mean, imagine how impossibly surreal it would feel if someone powerful leveled false claims, lies, and conspiracy theories about our elections being rigged and stolen from them with no evidence whatsoever? Crazy.

Counting Your Blessings

Fyodor Dostoyevsky once told us, "Man is fond of counting his troubles, but he does not count his joys. If he counted them up as he ought to, he would see that every lot has enough happiness provided for it."

I know every night when I finish manifesting in my bedazzled Gratitude Journal, I think of Fyodor and his audacity to hint at expressions of dark humor or even joy in Russian literature.

While on the topic, why did Vladimir Nabokov hate him so much? He once referred to Dostoyevsky's magnum opus *Crime and Punishment* with a "who cares?" Of course, Nabokov hated jazz and William Faulkner, too. That said, what kind of despicable imbecile hates William Faulkner?

I take it personally. Faulkner is one of my literary heroes. A writing deity. *The Sound and the Fury*? *Light in August*? *As I Lay Dying*? Jesus wept, what was wrong with Nabokov?

I know a certain pretentious, pedophilic Russian immigrant who should count his blessings that his scandalous masterwork *Lolita* didn't land him back in a Soviet gulag praying for a pedophile to kill him. Sting and The Police should have never made him so famous in their 1980 hit, "Don't Stand So Close to Me."

Counting Your Chickens Before They Hatch

My grandpa was a great guy. And a character. He developed late onset Type II diabetes, probably in part due to his Depression Era penchant for eating anything at his disposal in case some unseen economic downturn created scarcity of food again. And I mean *anything*. His puke-worthy favorite sandwich was canned sardines, liverwurst, and Limburger cheese. Dry-heaving whilst typing.

His breakfasts were renowned. Poached eggs, waffles, home fries, slathered in margarine, butter, syrup, lard, or any lube-like substance made from pure trans fats.

His practical jokes were epic, too. As a bartender, he once smeared chocolate pie on his shoe and pretended he stepped in dog crap just to elicit a laugh when he ate it. And I hope you recall what he did to Ass Ache McGee? Legendary.

Then again, what he did at breakfast one Sleepover Saturday, after a hard night of Friday Bingo at St. Daniel's Church, may be no surprise.

He loved to tell us the yolk in eggs was liquefied baby chicken that never hatched. Anything to get you to say, *Ewww*. This Saturday in question, he ratcheted things up another level.

Before poaching the eggs, he added fresh fingernail clippings into one of the poaching cups. Ensuring he had served me the offending egg, grandpa grinned at me wide-eyed as I chewed upon the breakfast feast.

When I crunched down on the altered ovum, and spit the brittle bit onto my plate, he burst out laughing from his toes. "Well, I'll be goddamned," he said. Grandpa had zero inhibitions with cursing around kids. "The little bastard melted trying to form a beak." I ran away from the table in horror and nausea. My tears flowed in time to the rhythm of his cruel cachinnation.

Counting Sheep

Sancho tells Don Quixote in the knight's eponymous novel, "Let your worship keep count of the goats the fisherman is taking across, for if one escapes the memory there will be an end of the story, and it will be impossible to tell another word of it."

Counting goats (or sheep) may have first appeared in 1605 with Miguel de Cervantes' *Don Quixote*. Some scholars believe the myth of counting sheep to fall asleep pre-dates this literary work by many centuries. Super. Another non-sequitur.

First, the concept of counting sheep is gross. They are filthy creatures, incapable of properly cleaning themselves without assistance. So, as I'm mindlessly counting those bleating sheep leaping over a white picket fence, I will mainly perseverate on the smears of fecal matter caked in their ass wool. Like Seinfeld with the soft talker. Utterly fixated.

Second, I will then imagine the poop smell of animal farms. Not Orwell's delicious dystopian denizens. Oh, heck no. Something far more real ... and nasty. The stink will infest every molecule of my existence. Always in my nose. Impossible to wash away.

As I'm snuggled down in my warm, freshly washed linens, the relaxing scent of dryer sheets filling my mind with lilac and lavender, I hear the nasty honk of some unfortunate mutton snagged on the fence, defecating in terror. The smell is overwhelming. I cover my head, wishing I would die.

Third, this image leads to insomnia worse than if I hadn't counted the grimy jumbucks in the first place. That massive disruption in my relaxation fuels delusional, eye-vibrating hate which, in turn, nourishes my compulsion to write decent, albeit dark, poetry.

... and counting ...

There are myriad things in our lives requiring counting. Perchance a few more brief examples?

- **Counting cards** – pack your favorite Rain Man and head to Vegas, baby. The casinos are desperate for more know-it-all suckers to visit. Count those cards, and win big. And remember, as Tom Cruise said to Dustin Hoffman: Kmart sucks.

- **Counting on one hand** – unless you lost your hand in an ironically tragic wood-chipping incident while disposing of a dead body on a cold winter night in North Dakota. Or if you have "grandma's nubs." A tragic story for another day
- **Counting down the moments** – until we meet again? Barf. Cliché, anyone? Even greeting card writers want to stick an ice pick in their temples when they hear this tripe.

Most importantly, dear invisible friends, keep counting on me to provide you with thought-filled laughter. Perhaps with a side dose of cringe on occasion. You can handle it.

GRATITUDE:
A QUALITY SIMILAR TO ELECTRICITY

"Gratitude is a quality similar to electricity; it must be produced and discharged and used up in order to exist at all."

– William Faulkner

In case this caught you unaware, I love William Faulkner. Not sure if he is my favorite author. Toni Morrison may occupy that vaunted aerie. But he is among the elite.

As Faulkner indicates, we sometimes need to dig deep to find our gratitude; to *produce* it. Equally important is *discharging* it. Using it. Showing it.

Whatever it takes – a text, a FaceTime, a nice message online? Perhaps an oft-maligned dick pic? We need to (perhaps should?) always find more reasons to express gratitude after the Machiavellian lockdown of 2020. Cuz it sucked.

With Thanksgiving now on the doorstep in 2024, what could be more relevant than releasing all that pent-up electricity? Minimally to burn some extra calories. I mean, hasn't Thanksgiving always been yet another calorie in a lifelong string of fattening meals. A choice opportunity to nap away our existence in a combined carb coma and tryptophan buzz.

But this year? I am feeling a massive charge of thankfulness welling within me. In fact, I am going to take it so far as to emulate Jesus's Sermon on the Mount, where he delivered the Eight Beatitudes with Reg. I know! Thanksgiving is a secular holiday, but c'mon, man. I'm a sinner. Any little shoutout to the J-man might bridge the distance between Limbo and Perdition when I croak.

Therefore, hence and forsooth, I will deliver unto you, my faithful invisible reader friends, my "Four Gratitudes." The very thought of writing eight of them after a busy work week makes my butt pucker with dread and exhaustion. Be happy there are even four of them. I'm tired. Cue smallest violin in the world.

Gratitude 1: Blessed be My Daughters

I am so grateful my daughters weren't born with hooves, tails, or scales after my prolific drug binging in my younger years. In fact, they look remarkably human.

But who else believed this urban legend? Seriously, I had an inherent fear that I may have literally altered my DNA from the magic mushrooms and psylocibin I consumed during my great college experiment. I believed this because my friends heard it from some guy who knew a guy.

Word of mouth, much like social media, is truly the worst way to communicate information for several reasons.

First, most of us are gullible as hell. I remember college friends telling me that your body stored hallucinogenic compounds in your spinal fluid. Those substances stayed there until you ejaculated. Totally believed it. Couldn't have worked harder to clear those naughty compounds.

Second, facts get morphed, even lost, in translation. Put ten people in a line and whisper "Turkey tastes like an unsalted chicken's taint" in the first person's ear. An unimpeachable, scientific fact. Have each person whisper what they heard in the next person's ear. By the time the tenth person repeats the phrase, it sounds something like "Turkeys are a cabal of Satanic pedophiles eating the salty taints of chicken babies." Think about it. At least they got taint correct.

Third, stories turn into rumors, and rumors spread like a Napa wildfire. The *Timex Social Club* song, offered us some sage advice about how rumors get started in their eponymous song. That they're started by jealous people, mad people, who had something that "somebody else is holding."

Word. I don't want my knowledge coming from people with that big of a chip on their shoulders! . . . and I also don't want no scrubs.

Gratitude 2: Blessed be My Wife

I am so thankful for my wife. But not in the misogynistically traditional or kinky sexual ways you might instinctively assume.

To begin, I'm grateful for her being a germaphobe. It only took a 2020 plague for her obsessive handwashing, bathing in Purell, and hating eating perfectly good food out of the garbage to resonate with me. Never realized what a filthy animal I was.

Also, I'm grateful for her resourcefulness in securing life-saving equipment (perhaps hoarding it,) continuing to keep us safe and sterile long after the pandemic. During lockdown, she cleverly posted as a dentist and acquired gallons of medical grade wipes from an online dentistry supplier in one of the Koreas. Nice job, baby. Way to think outside of the box. I canceled my root canal last week because I now question if our dentist's office is sufficiently clean.

We also (still) have enough toilet paper to build a sleeping barracks for Trump's fascist youth club if we're ever forced to quarter them in our home. Don't be naïve, friends. You know Civil War II is coming. I don't own any guns. The fascists own most of them. Simple risk-reward equation.

And finally, Christmas. My second favorite holiday. My wife now puts up our Christmas decorations for four consecutive months: two months before and two months after Christmas. Maybe longer lately. It's her attempt to inject joy, yule, and merriness into a life that once knew very little of it. I do sometimes worry one of those overused light strings might spark and burn us to death in our sleep. That would still be better than reliving lockdown.

Gratitude 3: Blessed be My Dog

I am so appreciative for Hairy Kerry. Best dog ever.

First, he has perspective. Sleeping. Excreting. Eating. Snuggling. Pretty simple mantra for happiness in life, isn't it? The problem occasionally arises when he merges those activities. Because he is a pampered Prince, we always have a pee-pad laid out for him. Sometimes it's a poop-pad. The other day it was apparently his dining room table as I caught him delightedly munching on a turd like a tootsie roll. So gross. But is it even worse when I see him later that day giving lots of sloppy "kisses" to my wife's face . . . and I say nothing about the subsequent rash on her erstwhile alabaster skin?

Second, his one true emotion is love. And not from necessity. He can't help himself. He appreciates every small kindness and returns it with an adoration that borders on obsession. He is my furry shadow. Well, I guess fear is an emotion for him, too. Running the vacuum sends him into abject terror. As do thunderstorms. The printer, too. Can't forget fireworks (although I am convinced it's our dickhead neighbor, Gary, shooting at his wife again). As do low frequency delivery truck engines, cats half his size, and the ghost of our dead dog, Keely.

Third, he has no guile. There is no hidden agenda, except for sneaking into the kitchen after I prepare a meal to graze my abundant food droppings off the floor. More because I am a slob, and he is a servant to his nose. An animated Roomba. Sometimes I drop some medicine merely to see what will happen. Is that bad?

Gratitude 4: Blessed be Electricity

I am especially grateful for electricity. Not the electricity metaphor that Faulkner referenced. No. The real energy coursing through our highly flammable homes. Why?

Here are my particulars:

First, it powers the floodlights in my backyard. This way I can catch that jackass, Gary, sneaking around at night when he crosses over my newly installed fence. And it potently electrifies that new fence so I can teach that asshat a near-fatal life lesson: stay the hell off my property. Give me back the damn tools you borrowed years ago, Gary!

Second, it powers my interwebs so I can watch all the right-wing fun happening on the darkest of dark MAGA webs. Have you checked them out? Oh boy. Buckle up. Figured if nearly 74 million Americans voted for Trump in 2020, I ought to see what it looks like when the mainstream 'freedom fighters' mingle with the extreme conspiracists. Free speech never looked so anti-Semitic!

Third, it powers the Christmas trees(s)—yes, we have multiple—and all the twinkling decorations my wife has decked throughout our halls. I have curmudgeonly tendencies since I turned fifty years old. And though difficult to admit, there is a corner of my black Grinch heart that warms to their gentle glow, and, moreover, the loving intentions they represent. For at least four fucking months each year.

Time for Dessert

Those are my Gratitudes. Trying to make lemonade from life's inevitable lemons.

Since 2020, we celebrate an extended family gathering at my brother's house. One of my favorite events of the year. A lot of laughs. An abundance of food and drink. Most of all, a *whole lotta love*.

But the crowd is not as big as it once might have been. A few of our parents have died since lockdown, and they are missed. Our daughters are older and live far from upstate New York now with their boyfriends. Their young, burgeoning lives and loves are their priority now. But this year, they are all coming home for Thanksgiving!! And I am more grateful than ever, he says as he puts away his Harry Chapin record.

But is it horribly selfish to acknowledge that less people at Thanksgiving means more kick-ass quantities of leftovers for me (and Hairy, too)? Turkey sandwiches. Reheated stuffing. Plus, my wife's specialty: Brussels sprouts baked in olive oil with parmesan and pancetta. My heaven!

But I am most looking forward to her homemade apple cake with cream cheese frosting. Which she's intentionally leaving at home, just for us. After the kids fly back to their homes. If the best sex of your life could be converted into a dessert, you would select this dessert 100 percent of the time.

Our plan is to divide the cake in half, then eat it until we sleep, barf, or die. Sure, my blood sugar will top 500. But if COVID didn't kill me in 2020? I'll take my chances.

Happy Thanksgiving, everybody, this year and every year! Gobble, Gobble.

Epilogue

WOW. My dearest invisible friends, I've finished my book. I hope that this reminiscent little excursion into my introspections during the Time of Plague accomplished several things for you:

1. **It made you laugh.** The title says it all. Life sucks. It especially sucked during COVID lockdown. So, it is essential that we retain the ability to laugh at it, or at least about it. Otherwise, maybe you can find your release in other ways? Perhaps hire a private anesthesiologist to snow you to sleep, *perchance to dream*. That worked out better for Shakespeare than it did for Prince or Michael Jackson.
2. **It offended you.** At least once, or I failed with my most acerbic satire. When I was editing the book, a few parts definitely made me flinch . . . hard. Harder than the plastic Q-tip up my schmeckle at the free STD clinic toward the end of college at SUNY Oswego. Proud to say, I was the only one of us without chlamydia.
3. **It made you think.** Maybe learn a little bit? NAH! I hope you voted for Trump again; everything was perfect when he was President in 2020. History never repeats itself. And you can make history in 2024 by electing

the first felon to the Oval Office. Personally, I could use another four years of narcissistic Shakespearean revenge plays, bloated tariffs on the world, trains overflowing with deportees, and more guns. For sure, more guns.
4. **It inspired you** to read my poetry book, *Echoes Lost in Stars*. Available now globally in all Amazon markets. After reading this book? After this? What a *long, strange trip* it would be to read my poetry! Grab Owsley's hand, drop some psylocibin, and enjoy the ride. You won't regret it.

Remember Literary Comedic Nihilism?

My closing thoughts? Forget about it. Forget about this book. Forget about me. Forget about the lessons of COVID. Forget about the insanity that was the Reign of Cheeto Christ I. All of it.

Just like my sage colonoscopy advice. Feel assuaged by your lack of empathy. Caring hurts. Introspection? Who the hell even knows what self-actualization means? Maslow was a hack.

Keep on keepin' on, my peeps. Safe and secure within your tribe of Sames. Keep the Others away by talking louder than them. Scream, if necessary. USE CAPS on social media. You need to be heard. You matter to your tribe. Those pesky Others will eventually go away.

To borrow from Queen's *Bohemian Rhapsody*, "Nothing really matters." It was all just an elaborate distraction anyway. Wasn't it?

Namaste, my sheeple.

Wait! There's More!

I would be sorely remiss if I did not say a special thanks to all the talented individuals who contributed to turning an obscure, defunct blog into this likely Pulitzer-winning book.

It all begins and ends with Jack Rochester: friend, editor, sparring mate, publisher, therapist, and sensei. His experience and guidance have been instrumental and utterly invaluable.

And how could I not offer my deep appreciation to Kourtney Jason and her brilliant PR firm, Pacific & Court, for all the publicity and promotion they will generate for this book, likely making me millions of dollars.

Also, huge thanks to Yucen Yao for her extraordinary cover art and original fleuron, designed especially for my book. What a fun process! Both truly capture the essence of the book. Heck, *The New Yorker* should call her for a staff job!

Last, but most certainly not least, thank you to Mary Driscoll for her laser-precise copyediting work; Abigail Monti at P & C for her copyright documentation guidance, and Sophie Hanks for her handsome design and layout for this challenging book you now hold in your hands.

It took a village. And I was the village idiot, screaming into the night, waiting for someone to listen.

About the Author

PS Conway has published more than 50 poems across four online journals and 16 poetry anthologies. Two anthologies have been Amazon Best Sellers (so far). He released his first poetry collection *Echoes Lost in Stars* [Literary Revelations Publishing House] in March 2024. To date, it has garnered significant critical acclaim. In April 2025, PS will release *Life Sucks: Memories and Introspections During the Great COVID Lockdown* [Fictional Café Press], a compilation of satirical essays from COVID lockdown. A two-time Pushcart Nominee, PS also serves as the 2024-25 Poet-in-Residence for the online literary journal, The Fictional Café. He finds fascination in words birthed from dark, literate, and emotive places. Find him online at psconway.com and poetrybyps.com, and follow him on social media (Facebook; Instagram; and Twitter/X).

ABOUT THE PUBLISHER

Fictional Café Press is the book publishing arm of The Fictional Café, an online literary arts 'zine where the author is currently serving as Poet-in-Residence. The Fictional Café began publishing innovative and extraordinary poetry, short stories, novel excerpts, creative nonfiction, fine arts and podcasts in 2013 and continues to do so in books. Its 2,000 Coffee Club members create in 75 countries worldwide.

www.ingramcontent.com/pod-product-compliance
Lightning Source LLC
LaVergne TN
LVHW010707160325
805845LV00005BA/17